FIGHTING
INDIAN
WARRIORS

Artist's conception of the celebrated "Wagon Box Fight" near Fort Phil Kearny, Wyoming, August 2, 1867. Thirty-two soldiers against several thousand Sioux under Chief Red Cloud. From painting by Otto Selzer.

FIGHTING INDIAN WARRIORS

True Tales of
The Wild Frontiers

By

E. A. BRININSTOOL

INDIAN HEAD BOOKS
New York

This edition published by Indian Head Books,
a division of Barnes & Noble, Inc.,
by arrangement with Stackpole Books.

1995 Indian Head Books

ISBN 1-56619-854-2

Printed and bound in the United States of America

M 9 8 7 6 5 4 3 2 1

DEDICATION

To the fighting Indians of the Plains, of many different tribes; and to the Frontiersmen, the Soldiers, Scouts, Trappers and Hunters who fought them, between 1866 and 1890.

PREFACE

The winning of the old West was no child's play It was WAR—war of the most brutal and inhuman type, on the part of both Indians and whites. The Indian was fighting for his home, his commissary, his lands—lands ceded to him through solemn treaty with the United States government—and what man, of any nation, (if he is any sort of a man) will not fight "for home and native land?"

The white man fought to advance the cause of Civilization, irrespective (in most instances) of the rights of the Indian, and without regard to his future. "Civilization" won—and to Civilization's shame, it was at the cost of unnumbered thousands of lives, and the shedding of much human blood of both whites and Indians.

I am not a believer in the old saying (said to have originated with Gen. Phil Sheridan) that "the only good Indian is a dead Indian." My sympathy is with the Red Man. The early white traders who trafficked with the Indians, were, as a rule, a class of men of little conscience and few scruples, who would stoop to any deceit or trickery to rob the Indian of his furs and pelts. It was the early trader who introduced whiskey among the Indian tribes; who, through fraud and knavery, turned the red man against the whites of whatever class. This was the beginning of the hatred and contempt which made all white men, good or bad, look alike to such warring Indians as Red Cloud, Crazy Horse and Sitting Bull.

Unscrupulous Indian agents, tricky post traders, unprincipled government officials at Washington, and a few—a very few—inhuman army officers fed fuel to the flame of contempt which quickly spread through the Indian tribes of the far West, especially among the Sioux and Northern Cheyennes.

Briefly, the whole miserable situation can be summed up in just five words: *"THE WHITE MAN WANTED IT!"*

In this volume I have written of a few of the most noted battles and skirmishes between the red man and the white man. No fiction is employed in these pages. Every incident related actually occurred, and is a part of the history of the old West. Some biographical sketches of noted frontier characters are included.

Acknowledgments are due many friends for valuable information and photographs, which are noted on a separate page.

E. A. BRININSTOOL

1953.

CONTENTS

TABLE OF ILLUSTRATIONS

ACKNOWLEDGMENTS

The author hereby expresses grateful appreciation to the many persons, both living and dead, who rendered valuable information in the construction of this volume:

General Chas. King
Col. W. A. Graham
Sergt. Samuel S. Gibson
Frederic Claus
Sigmund Shlesinger
Mrs. Olive K. Dixon
Jeff C. Riddle
Major George Ingalls
George Geier
Jacob Geier
Max Littman
Jesse Brown
Capt. James H. Cook
Mrs. Mary E. Graham

Prof. Gilbert E. Bailey
Col. Homer W. Wheeler
Gen. H. W. Wessells
George E. Bartlett
Capt. A. R. Chapin
Charles R. Foley
Walter H. Martin
Joe E. Milner
Robert Lynam
Major A. B. Ostrander
C. A. Patton
Howard Morton
Oscar O. Mueller
Maynard Dixon
Dr. Grace Raymond Hebard

Supt. W. C. Randolph, Acting Supt. Tongue River Agency, Montana, 1935

CHAPTER I

~

"FETTERMAN'S FOLLY"

The True Story of the Tragic Fort Phil Kearny Disaster

~

B UT, Colonel, those Indians should be punished for depredations they've been committing, and we'll never give
them the sound thrashing they deserve as long as we remain
cooped up behind these stockaded walls. If you'll just give
me eighty men, I'll guarantee to ride through the Sioux
nation."

The speaker was Capt. Wm. J. Fetterman; the place, Fort
Phil Kearny, Wyoming; the year, 1866.

Col. Henry B. Carrington, post commander and builder of
Fort Phil Kearny, wheeled in his chair, looked up at Fetterman and smiled sarcastically.

"Captain Fetterman," he said, speaking slowly and with
great emphasis, "such talk is all folly. You have had no experience in fighting these Indians, or you would have a more
wholesome respect for them. Red Cloud is nobody's fool. If I
were to allow you to take eighty men, and start out to 'ride
through the Sioux nation, as you express it, it would be nothing short of suicide on your part, and the needless sacrifice
of that many men. You simply don't know what you are
talking about," and Col. Carrington grew stern.

"But I don't believe that the Indians would bother us, or
dare attack an armed force of that proportion, Colonel,"
Fetterman exclaimed incredulously.

1

"Neither do I," chimed in Captain Frederick Brown, who was standing at Fetterman's side during the conversation. "I've got to join my command in the east very shortly, and I haven't had one single crack at the Indians yet. I want old Red Cloud's scalp, and if I have to leave here without it, I am going to be most awfully disappointed."

"Be, eh?" broke in a tall, gaunt, grizzled old plainsman who had just entered the room. "Wal, all I hev got to say is that you young bloods are a passel of fools. Lemme tell you sum'thin' right hyar—an' see that you remember it—whar' thar ain't no Injins, thar you'll find 'em thickest. Don't furgit that it's ol' Jim Bridger that's a-tellin' ye."

"You hear what Major Bridger says, gentlemen," quietly observed Colonel Carrington, "and what he tells you, you may absolutely rely upon. I reiterate—it is foolishness to discredit the fighting capacity of Red Cloud and his Sioux warriois."

"Right you are, Colonel," nodded Bridger, knocking the ashes from his pipe. "Red Cloud knows what he's about, an' my opinion is, he's a-gittin' things in shape to give us a dose hyar we ain't a-goin' to furgit. You mark my words."

"But, Colonel—"

"Captain Fetterman," sharply exclaimed Colonel Carrington, "there need be no further discussion about this matter. I positively forbid the carrying out of any such plans as you and Captain Brown have in mind. We have no men here to sacrifice."

Disappointment showed itself on the faces of both Fetterman and Brown as they left the room. Jim Bridger, post scout, looked after them with an amused smile on his grizzled countenance.

"I reck'n they mean all right, Colonel," he said, "but they jest don't know what they're talkin' about. Ride through the Sioux nation with eighty men? Huh! They're plumb crazy!"

"Well, crazy or not, I shall not allow my judgment and

common sense to be led into any such schemes. I may be cautious—possibly over-cautious—but we've no men here to be sacrificed needlessly," declared Col. Carrington.

Carrington and Bridger were right. Bridger saw the wisdom of the commander's words. His entire life had been spent on the frontier, fighting Indians and matching wits with the savage tribes.

"They may yit git a dose of Injin fightin' they'll remember for many a long day," observed Bridger.

Colonel Carrington smiled, and thus the conversation ended.

Fort Phil Kearny had been under almost constant siege since its erection, but five short months before, and already many of Carrington's force had fallen victims to Indian subtlety and cunning.

Red Cloud, the great Sioux fighting chieftain, had warned the government officials at the Laramie peace council in June, that any attempt to build forts or maintain soldiers north of Fort Reno and along the Bozeman Trail, would be followed by immediate war.

"I'll kill every white man who goes beyond Crazy Woman's Fork of the Powder river!" the wrathful chieftain had shouted, as he stalked haughtily out of the council, refusing any of the presents which the commissioners had brought for him.

And Red Cloud was attempting to keep his word, and was succeeding even beyond his own most sanguine expectations. Not a day passed without its skirmishing in the vicinity of Fort Phil Kearny, while every wagon train bound for the upper country felt the weight of Red Cloud's merciless hand.

But at the Laramie peace council, the government representatives had treated his war declarations with contempt. What! Allow this insolent redskin to dictate what should be done about travel up the Bozeman Trail? Was he to prescribe the policy for Uncle Sam to follow? Suppose it did mean the invasion of the last and best hunting grounds of

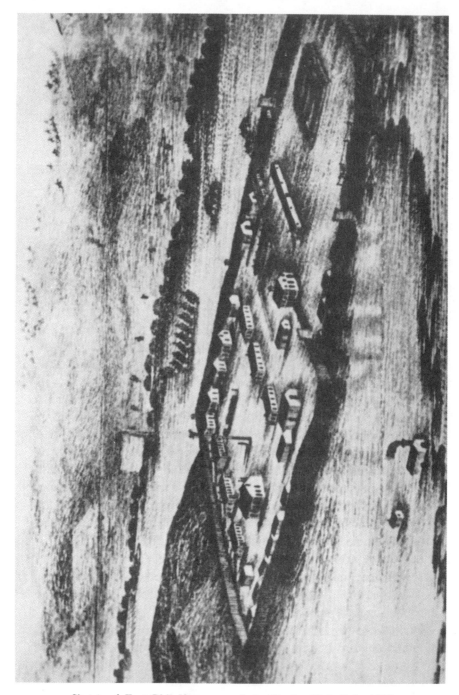

Sketch of Fort Phil Kearny made by Bugler Nicholi in 1867.

the Sioux nation? What if the game was frightened out and driven away, and the entire Sioux tribe cut off from its commissary? Who cared, anyhow?

Red Cloud cared. Keen and sagacious in war, wise in council, and with an eye for the future good of his people, this mighty warrior intuitively recognized that if the country were opened up for white settlement the hated pale-faces would come streaming up in hordes, and the Sioux—well, the Sioux might starve so far as the government cared, or else learn the white man's way of living—and the Sioux were not prepared for any such sudden change and further, Red Cloud declared it could not and should not be.

But the white man wanted the country, and that was enough. And so, Colonel Henry B. Carrington, of the 18th United States Infantry, had been sent into the forbidden territory, with an armed force, under instructions to build at least two more forts along the Bozeman Trail. His orders were to re-stock and better equip old Fort Reno, and then erect the two other posts about one hundred miles apart, further to the northwest, up the trail.

It was thus calculated by the government that with this array of soldiery, Red Cloud's warriors could offer but little resistance to the long train of white-topped wagons which would shortly begin rumbling in from the east, with "pilgrims" bound for the Montana gold fields and the further agricultural sections of Oregon and California. Surely the soldiers at these proposed forts could easily protect the passage of the emigrants through the Indian country.

But it was no ordinary Indian with whom Uncle Sam was reckoning. Red Cloud gathered together a mighty army of the flower of the fighting strength of the Sioux nation, and hardly had the ringing axes and buzzing saws of Carrington's command begun transforming the pine logs from the adjacent timber into lumber for the necessary buildings at Fort Phil Kearny, before Red Cloud's warriors began taking their toll of death, and making good the threat to "kill every white man in the country."

Scarcely a day passed without its depredations by the Sioux. None of the logging parties sent from the post into the timber were safe one foot of the seven miles of Indian infested country without a heavy escort of armed troops. Often these logging trains would be attacked and forced to go into corral when within a mile of the fort. Relief parties would then have to be sent out from the post to drive the savages away, and the result would inevitably be "Private Haggerty dangerously wounded," or "Sergeant Bowers killed in action." Generally, however, a mountain howitzer (of which the savages were mortally afraid) would stampede them.

But at that, there were many casualties. Depredations and raids became more frequent, and it was plain to be seen that Red Cloud was being heavily reinforced. The Indians made heavy inroads upon Colonel Carrington's little force. Guards were picked off; men out hunting were waylaid and killed. It was taking one's life in one's hands to venture alone a hundred yards from the stockaded walls of Fort Phil Kearny.

Colonel Carrington's prudent policy of refusing to go out and attack the savages, meeting them in open battle, was scoffed at by many of the younger officers at the post, who were loud in their declarations that "something ought to be done."

"Glover's killed!" shouted Jack Stead, one of Carrington's scouts, as he dashed into the post one afternoon in mid-September. Glover was an artist for Frank Leslie's Illustrated Weekly, who had come up the trail a short time before, with an escort for the purpose of making sketches of the Indian country for the magazine.

"I tol' that 'ere artist feller he'd lose his ha'r some day," exclaimed old Jim Bridger. "I warned him time an' agin to stay in clus' to the post. Whar' was he, Jack?"

Colonel Henry B. Carrington, 18th U. S. Infantry, builder of
Fort Phil Kearny.

"I found his body over there by the edge of that ravine, not
three minutes' walk from here. He'd been tomahawked,
scalped and stripped. I'll tell the Colonel. He'll want to send
out a detachment to bring in the body."

Not two hours later, heavy firing was heard out toward
Piney creek, where several pickets were stationed. Soon the
news was passed around that a band of Sioux had crept up

and fired several volleys, but fortunately no damage had been inflicted.

Early in November a new face had appeared among the officers at the post. This was Captain William J. Fetterman, an officer unused to Indian warfare, but possessed of a most pleasing personality, and who at once became a general favorite.

With great interest, but contempt, Fetterman listened to the accounts of the activities of Red Cloud's warriors.

"Why, it's all foolishness to let those Indians run things as you say they're doing," he declared to several of the officers at mess, shortly after his arrival. "I'll guarantee I could take a detachment and run old Red Cloud and his painted devils out of the country. It seems to me that Colonel Carrington is altogether too cautious. He needs some young blood here to stir things up. You just wait till I get a chance to go out and show old Red Cloud a thing or two "

His brother officers had smiled knowingly, but they kept their own counsel. It would be better to let Captain Fetterman learn by experience what he refused to believe in story.

And then, a few weeks later, came Captain Frederick Brown, who had been ordered from the east to join his company at Fort Phil Kearny. He had but a short time longer to serve. Both Brown and Fetterman took a great liking to each other, and both freely expressed their opinions regarding Colonel Carrington's cautious Indian fighting policy. Like Fetterman, Brown was anxious to demonstrate his fighting capacity.

"Fetterman, we've got to do something to wake up this bunch of sleepyheads," he declared. "I believe you and I are just the ones to start something. I don't want to go back to civilization and say I lived in the Indian country and never had a brush with the redskins. If I can only get the sights of my rifle lined up on old Red Cloud's topknot, he's my meat!

I want his scalp to take back east as a souvenir How can we arrange it?"

And so these two officers had gotten their heads together and concocted a scheme to "drive all the Sioux out of the country." If Colonel Carrington would give them eighty men, Fetterman declared, he and Brown would ride through the Sioux nation.

But Colonel Carrington, after listening to their suggestions, had sternly forbidden any such operations.

Meantime, logging trains were bringing in timber from the pineries, both for lumber and the winter's fuel supply. On December 21 it was estimated by Colonel Carrington that only one more trainlöad of logs would be necessary. There was yet a little work to be done on the post hospital, after which the fort would be officially declared completed.

The morning of December 21 dawned bright and beautiful, although Jim Bridger, after a careful glance at the sky, predicted "Sum'thin' in the air sort o' feels like a blizzard wuz due."

With Christmas but four days away, everybody at the post was looking forward with joyous expectancy to the happy holiday season. Although the lower country about the post was bare of snow, the hillsides were covered, and the air was keenly sharp and crisp.

An unusually long wood train had left the post early, for what was expected to be the last trip for the winter. An extra force of armed guards had accompanied it.

"Picket on Pilot Hill reports the wood train attacked " came the not-unexpected announcement to Colonel Carrington, just as the latter had the hospital plans and specifications before him to lay out the unfinished work.

As the colonel hastened outside, he observed Captain James Powell running forward. Powell saluted and exclaimed, "The wood train has been attacked, sir."

"Take command of a detachment, Captain Powell," ordered

the colonel, "and drive those Indians away. You will only relieve the wood train; but do not follow the Indians and invite any unnecessary engagement."

"Yes, sir," replied Powell, saluting and starting toward the stables.

Sputtering shots could be heard in the direction of Sullivant Hills, and through his field glasses Colonel Carrington could see many of the Indians gathering to obstruct the advance of the logging train.

Captain Fetterman had been walking up and down in front of his quarters in close conversation with Captain Brown, who seemed to be urging him about some matter. At length Fetterman exclaimed, "All right, I'll ask him," and, followed closely by Brown, he hurried toward Colonel Carrington, who was still watching the Indians through his glasses.

"Colonel," he said excitedly, as he hurriedly saluted, "my seniority allows me the right to command this relief party. Have you any objections to my going?"

Colonel Carrington hesitated. The captain's request was in proper form, as he was the ranking captain of the post; but he was not an experienced Indian fighter, and the colonel had not forgotten his request of a few days previously. Would Fetterman use tact and caution if sent out?

Finally Colonel Carrington said, "Very well, captain. You may take command of the infantry, and Lieutenant Grummond will have charge of the cavalry. I do not like this idea of you, Grummond, leaving your young wife on this dangerous work. Have you forgotten that you barely escaped with your life on the 6th of this month in that encounter not two miles away from the post?"

"But I'm here for duty, colonel," retorted Lieutenant Grummond. "There's no especial danger; we'll fire a few volleys and the Indians will scatter—they always do."

"Well, if you insist——" and Colonel Carrington reluctantly gave his consent.

The detachment was now ready. Just then two civilians who had been doing messenger duty at the post, carrying dispatches from Fort Phil Kearny to Fort C. F. Smith, the new post further north, came running up.

"Here, Colonel, we want to go out with 'em," exclaimed Isaac Fisher. "Me and Wheatley want to try out these new sixteen-shot Henry repeaters of ours."

"Very well, but remember, you go out at your own risk. You should be a formidable addition to the party with those repeating rifles, but don't run any unnecessary chances."

"Say, Fetterman, don't tell the colonel," remarked Captain Brown, his eyes snapping with the excitement of the moment, "but I'm going along with your command. Here's my last chance to bring in old Red Cloud's scalp. Hist! Here comes the colonel now to inspect the party. Remember—mum's the word." And Brown slid toward the rear just as Colonel Carrington hurried up.

Strange, indeed, that it should have been seemingly ordained, but when the relief party was formed, it consisted of exactly eighty-one men—the number Captain Fetterman had declared necessary to "drive all the Sioux out of the country "

"Now, captain," ordered Colonel Carrington, "I want you to remember my instructions. Support the wood train; relieve it and report to me. *Do not engage or pursue the Indians at its expense, and under no circumstances pursue the Indians beyond Lodge Trail Ridge yonder.* You understand these instructions, do you?"

Captain Fetterman nodded in reply. The stockade gates swung open, and with the jingle of accoutrements, the relief party trotted outside.

Colonel Carrington paused a moment as the gates clanged

shut. "I wonder," he muttered to himself, "if Fetterman understood me thoroughly?"

He ran hurriedly across the parade ground and sprang upon the sentry platform.

Captain Fetterman, who led the troops in the disastrous fight of December 21, 1866.

"Captain Fetterman—oh, Fetterman!" he shouted.

Captain Fetterman, at the head of the command, turned in his saddle as the party came to a halt.

"Remember, sir," called the colonel, in ringing tones which were distinctly overheard by every member of the party, "that *under no circumstances whatsoever are you to cross Lodge Trail Ridge.* Do you understand?"

Fetterman nodded, but made no audible reply, and immediately ordered the command off at a trot.

Old Jim Bridger witnessed the departure of Fetterman's party with many misgivings. "That reckless feller ain't no sort to go out after Injins," he declared to his associate, Jack Stead. "I'm affeared the colonel is a-goin' to regret it. Sum'thin' tells me that feller is out on his fust an' last Injin hunt."

"Well, Wheatley 'n' Fisher, with them new-fangled shootin' irons, is a mighty comfortin' addition to that bunch, anyhow," commented Stead.

"Yes," nodded Bridger, "but if them fellers run into an ambush, a derned sight of good them new-fangled smokepoles 'll do 'em, even if they do shoot sixteen times 'thout loadin'."

Colonel Carrington had remained on the sentry platform after warning Fetterman. Now he was observed scanning the ground with his field glasses. He finally noted that the wood train had proceeded on its way toward the pinery. Plainly the Indians had ceased to harrass it. But what of Fetterman's command? Where were they?

Feverishly the colonel paced back and forth for twenty minutes, pausing every few seconds to look over the country in the direction Fetterman's command had disappeared.

"Bridger," he finally called out, as the old scout sauntered past on his way to his quarters, "I'm awfully afraid of an ambush out there. I can see a good many Indians in the brush, and my glasses plainly show others in the thickets. What do you think of the situation?"

Bridger scratched his head, somewhat perplexed as to what to say.

"Wal, colonel," he finally observed, "I wuz dead sot agin yer lettin' Cap'n Fetterman command that 'ere party, but it war'n't fer me to butt in, o' course. He don't know nothin' 'bout Injin fightin', an' 'twixt him an' thet other reckless cuss, Brown, with him—"

"Brown!" exclaimed Colonel Carrington in astonishment. "Did he go along? I gave him no permission to accompany the command. He is out there without any authority from me."

"Yas, colonel, an' that's the wust on't," replied Bridger, with a shake of the head. "Between the two of 'em, I'm powerful 'feared they'll git into trouble—the reckless cusses."

Hardly had the old scout ceased speaking than scattering shots were heard out toward Peno creek, *beyond Lodge Trail Ridge;* then came the sound of rapid firing, followed by what appear to be several volleys! What could it mean?

To Colonel Carrington it could mean but one thing— Fetterman had disobeyed orders, gone over Lodge Trail Ridge, and was hotly engaged in battle. That he was in extreme peril could not be doubted.

"Have the general alarm sounded at once!" he shouted to the officer of the guard.

Instantly the warning bugle note—sounded only in cases of dire necessity—blared forth. Soldiers came tumbling from their quarters, guns in hand; officers dashed from their cabins, buckling on swords and accoutrements. All was excitement in an instant.

Colonel Carrington surveyed the officers keenly, quickly and critically. Who should lead this detachment? It would re‑ quire an officer of unquestioned bravery, coolness, caution and skill.

"Captain Ten Eyck," he called.

Captain Tenodore Ten Eyck, an officer of known courage, whose heroism and fearlessness had been tried in many an encounter with the savages, stepped forward and saluted.

"Captain," spoke Colonel Carrington, with just a trace of excitement in his voice, "I want you to take a detachment of

Captain Ten Eyck, who was sent to the relief of Captain Fetterman.

well-armed men and hasten at once to the relief of Captain Fetterman. I fear he has gone over Lodge Trail Ridge, against my positive orders, and is in great danger. I forgot to order out a surgeon with Fetterman, and Dr. Hines started later, but was unable to join him because of the Indians. You will take Dr. Hines and Dr. Oulds with you. Don't lose a second."

Quickly Captain Ten Eyck gave his orders. Within twelve minutes his command started on the run to the relief of Fetterman. Would they arrive in time to save him?

As Ten Eyck's men galloped forward, the roar of guns boomed out from the direction of Peno Valley across Lodge Trail Ridge with increased fury. But shortly before his command reached the hillside which led down into the valley below, all firing suddenly ceased. Perhaps Fetterman had succeeded in driving the enemy before him.

"God grant we may not be too late," muttered more than one of the troopers, scanning eagerly the country ahead.

But when the command, after a toilsome climb, reached the hilltop, they paused, appalled by the scene spread out before them in the valley below. Indians by the hundreds were swarming about in every direction, whooping and yelling, and upon catching sight of this new enemy, they darted back and forth on their nimble ponies, uttering shrill war-cries, challenging and shouting in broken English for Ten Eyck's command to come down and fight them. Nothing whatever could be seen of Fetterman's command.

Turning hastily to Orderly Sample, Captain Ten Eyck exclaimed:

"Orderly, I want you to take this note to Colonel Carrington as fast as that horse of yours can cover the ground!"

He had taken a note book from his pocket while speaking. Now he scribbled a hasty message to the effect that he was confronted by Indians in countless numbers, who were daring him to come down and fight them, but that nothing whatever could be seen of Fetterman's command.

"Send out a howitzer so I can clean the valley of Indians and go down and investigate," concluded the message.

Tucking the note in his pocket, Orderly Sample dug the spurs into his horse and dashed down the hill for the fort, while Captain Ten Eyck and his subordinates sat on their horses, watching in consternation the barbaric hordes down in the valley, stunned by the overwhelming numbers of the savages, who made no attempt to advance against them. Dozens of the Indians were dismounted and congregated near several large rock-piles, walking back and forth, occasionally pausing to stoop over, as if examining objects on the ground.

"Where in God's name can Fetterman be, do you suppose?" Ten Eyck finally exclaimed in an awed tone to Dr. Hines.

But the surgeon, with blanched face, shook his head. "Maybe he has had to retreat," he finally hazarded.

"Well, it would be suicide for us to make a forward movement in the face of such overwhelming numbers, unless the colonel can send out that howitzer I asked for. That is the largest body of Indians I ever saw. Why, there must be a thousand or two of them!"

"All of that, captain. Heavens! hear them yell! I wonder what that means?"

Sample, meantime, on a panting and lathered horse, reached the post and delivered Captain Ten Eyck's note to Colonel Carrington, who read the contents with dismay and consternation. Then he hurriedly wrote a reply as follows:

"Captain: Forty well-armed men, with three thousand rounds of ammunition, left just before your courier arrived. You must unite with Fetterman; fire slowly and keep your men well in hand. I ordered the wood train in, which will give fifty more men to spare."

"Rush this right back to Captain Ten Eyck," he ordered, thrusting the note into Sample's outstretched hand.

No howitzer could be sent to assist Ten Eyck, because in the first place, no horses could be spared to haul it, and further, no man of Ten Eyck's command was familiar with the gun, and it might be needed at the post.

Then Colonel Carrington gave further orders.

"Release all prisoners at once from the guardhouse; arm them and place them on duty; dispatch couriers to the pinery to order in all the guards and the wood train. Every man, civilian and soldier, will hold himself in readiness for immediate action."

At this perilous crisis, there remained but one hundred and nineteen men at the post to protect the women and children! Oh, well for Red Cloud that he knew not of this puny force behind the stockaded walls of old Fort Phil Kearny!

"Now, Mis' Carrington," calmly observed old Jim Bridger, in an effort to calm and soothe the terrified women and children, "don't you fret none. We ain't licked by a long shot, an' old Jim Bridger is right yere to tell you that he'll pull trigger fer the hull kit an' b'ilin' on ye as along as they's a cartridge left. We're a-comin' out all right," and he patted the rosy cheek of little Jimmie Carrington, the colonel's six-year-old son, affectionately, as the little chap clung in affright to the skirt of Bridger's well-worn buckskin coat.

Meanwhile, Orderly Sample had arrived at Ten Eyck's position and delivered his message. The forty additional infantrymen arrived from the post shortly thereafter, which made a formidable addition to Ten Eyck's command. Soon, the Indians, observing that an officer of caution was in command of the troops on the hill, and that they could not be induced to accept their leering challenges to come down into the valley, began to withdraw, and shortly had all disappeared.

"Now, then, we'll go down there and see if we can locate Fetterman," ordered Captain Ten Eyck. "Keep well together, men," he cautioned. "Let there be no straggling, and every man be ready for any emergency!"

With a few of the best shots in advance as scouts, Ten Eyck marched warily down the hill, every man, every gun ready for instant action, momentarily expecting to run across the Fetterman command entrenched behind the large rocks which were strewn about, and which would have formed an excellent defensive position.

And then—then a most appalling discovery was made!

Loud shouts from two of the advance scouts, who were

excitedly beckoning from several of the largest of the rock formations, drew the rest of the command thither.

What they there discovered is a matter of history—the history of the most bloody encounter between United States soldiers and hostile Indians on record up to that time. It chilled the blood of Ten Eyck's command and brought gasps of horror from every man.

Behind that pile of rocks lay the bodies of forty-seven members of Fetterman's command—all dead, stripped naked, scalped and mangled beyond recognition. Not a living thing —horse or rider—was to be seen. Not far away the bodies of Captain Fetterman and Captain Brown lay side by side, each with bullet holes in the head. Foolish, imprudent, indiscreet officers! What folly to think that with their puny force they could "ride through the Sioux nation!"

"Where are the others?" went up the cry.

"Where, indeed? Could it be possible that they might have escaped the savage avalanche of death which had been hurled upon and annihilated these? It was possible, but not at all probable. Where was Lieutenant Grummond, whose young wife, with weeping eyes, was at that moment awaiting, with breaking heart, his return? What of Jim Wheatley and Isaac Fisher, armed with the new magazine rifles with which they had expected to do such deadly execution?

Dusk was not far distant now. "It's too late to make further search," huskily remarked Captain Ten Eyck. "Men," he commanded, "load those bodies into the wagons at once. We must get back to the post before dark, or they'll think we have all been wiped out. Merciful heavens, what a slaughter! Handle them tenderly. Remember they were your comrades."

With loving hands the soldiers loaded the poor, mangled remains into the wagons. Eyes that had seldom known tears, were moist, as the men recognized in their butchered comrades some particular identification mark which stamped that body as one with whom they had fought, marched and bivouacked. And vengeful were the muttered imprecations against Red Cloud and his blood-thirsty warriors, as the command sadly wended its way back to the post.

The crunching of wagon wheels over the frozen ground indicated to the anxious watchers at the post the return of Ten Eyck's command.

"Jest as I expected," sadly commented old Jim Bridger

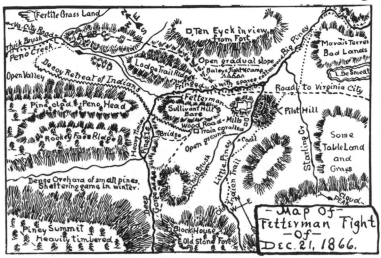

Map of Fetterman fight of December 21, 1866.

with a shake of his head, as the wagons, with their precious dead, were driven to the hospital, and the news of the appalling disaster was flashed through the quarters.

Consternation and dismay, tears and sobs were everywhere—even among the enlisted men, while the bereaved women could only cling to one another and weep in their grief and agony of soul. Nearly one-fourth of the entire command at the post had been wiped out in less than a brief half hour!

"You saw nothing, then, of the balance of Fetterman's command?" queried Colonel Carrington of Captain Ten Eyck, after listening silently to that officer's report.

"Not a thing, colonel, but it's pretty certain they must have all been killed. Any survivors, unless so badly wounded as to be unable to travel, would of course have come in to the post. And of course all who fell into the hands of the Indians would be killed. Fetterman must have been led into an ambush."

"It's the worst disaster in the history of Indian warfare on the plains," soberly commented Colonel Carrington. "If Fetterman had only obeyed my orders, this terrible calamity never would have happened. It seems unbelievable that such a catastrophe could have occurred."

All night long, lights flashed through the quarters. Guards were doubled. An attack upon the post was looked upon as a surety. Would Red Cloud follow up his bloody victory of the day and attempt a night attack?

"It'll be God's mercy if we don't have to fight the hull Sioux nation afore mornin'," remarked Jack Stead to Bridger. And Bridger agreed with him.

But there was no night attack. Doubtless the Sioux were satisfied with their first tremendous victory, and were content to spend the night in celebrating and scalp-dancing.

Early the following morning Colonel Carrington ordered "officers' call" sounded, and soon all the company commanders were at headquarters. It was a sober, grave gathering.

"Gentlemen," said the colonel, "I would like an expression from you as to the advisability of sending out a searching party for the balance of Fetterman's command. Personally, I am in favor of it. What say you?"

Dead silence followed these words. At length Lieutenant Matson arose.

"Colonel," he said earnestly, "I am absolutely opposed to such a move. It will require a considerable command to make a formidable party—and suppose the post is attacked in force during our absence? Why, the Indians could clean it out in no time! It's taking too much chance. The men are dead—God rest their souls—and are beyond all aid from us, and it doesn't seem to me just right to jeopardize the lives of our women and children by leaving the post with only a handful to defend it during our absence."

"That's right," voiced others in chorus. "It's too risky."

"Gentlemen," quietly spoke Colonel Carrington, "I have a wife and children here myself. Nevertheless, I shall not let the Indians entertain the conviction that the dead cannot and will not be rescued. If we cannot rescue our dead (as the Indians always do at whatever risk) how can you send details out for any purpose? That single fact would give them an idea of weakness here, and it would only stimulate them to risk an assault."

He paused and surveyed his officers keenly.

"I shall take personal command of the detachment," he continued. "Orderly, have 'assembly' sounded at once."

There was no lack of volunteers for the dangerous mission. Every able-bodied man at the post begged permission to accompany the detail.

To Mrs. Grummond, the heartbroken young wife of the missing lieutenant, Colonel Carrington said in earnest tones:

"Mrs. Grummond, I shall go in person and bring back to you the remains of your husband, even if it costs me my own life."

And then, to the officer of the day, he gave an order which showed the perilous conditions of those early frontier days, and the possible consequences following an Indian attack:

"*Fire the usual sunset gun, running a white lamp to masthead on the flagstaff. If the Indians appear, fire three guns from the twelve-pounder at minute intervals, and later substitute a red lantern for the white. If, in my absence, Indians in overwhelming numbers attack, put the women and children in the magazine. with supplies of water, bread, crackers and other supplies that seem best, and in the event of a last*

Capt. Frederick Brown, killed in the Fetterman disaster.

desperate struggle, destroy all together, rather than have any captured alive!"

Accompanying Colonel Carrington on his sad mission, were Captain Ten Eyck, Lieutenant Matson, Dr. Ould and eighty men. Jack Stead, observing this, remarked to Jim Bridger, "The colonel ain't superstitious none, is he? D'ye notice he's got jest about the same number o' men Fetterman had?"

"Wal," replied the old scout, "but ye wants to remember, son, that no hot-headed fool is a-leadin' 'em. The Colonel ain't goin' to ram his head agin a stun' wall, er run into no hornet's nest, ye kin depend on that!"

With several wagons and ambulances, and doubly supplied with ammunition, the command started on what many confidently expected was a fatal errand. Many were the sad farewells and wishes of God-speed given them, as the heavy gates were shut and barred, and many were the predictions that the colonel's party would never return alive.

"Yes they will," positively asserted old Jim Bridger. "The colonel knows what he's about, an' he'll bring in the rest o' Fetterman's men either alive or dead. You wimmen folks needn't worry none a mite. Ol' Jim's a-tellin' ye what he knows, so cheer up."

Thus, in his rough but kindly way, the noted old frontiersman was a source of real comfort and kindliness to the aching hearts behind the stockaded walls.

Straight over Lodge Trail Ridge marched Carrington's party, every moment expecting to sight the enemy, but not an Indian was to be seen. Down into Peno Valley they cautiously advanced, to the spot where the first forty-nine bodies had been recovered. Only a short march from that ghastly field was necessary to solve the mystery of the other missing thirty-two of Fetterman's command.

"Look at the arrows and spear shafts scattered about here!" exclaimed Dr. Ould. "And—look—there's a body—and there's another and another! They were trying to make a break for the post and must have been surrounded right here."

Such indeed appeared to be the facts. Bodies were strung along the road toward the fort, and doubtless they had fought desperately as long as their ammunition held out, when the savages must have rushed in and dispatched them with spears, arrows and tomahawks. *Only four bodies were found bearing bullet marks.* The carcasses of many horses, all headed in the direction of the fort, lay scattered about. It appeared to have been a most desperate hand-to-hand struggle. Most of the bodies fairly bristled with arrows. All were stripped, scalped and shockingly mutilated in a manner similar to the other forty-nine.

"Isn't this Lieutenant Grummond's body, Colonel?" called a gray-haired old sergeant, as he turned a badly disfigured corpse over for identification.

Only one glance was necessary from the colonel. "Yes, that's Grummond, poor chap! How can I ever tell his heart-broken wife?" and Colonel Carrington broke down and bowed his head to hide his grief.

Strong men, unused to tears, wept freely as body after body —comrades who had fought at their side in many a desperate encounter—was tenderly laid out in the wagons.

"Here's Wheatley and Fisher, over here behind these rocks," called Lieutenant Matson. "Their guns are gone of course, but look at the empty shells—at least fifty close to each body. I'll guarantee that old Red Cloud had to pay dearly for their scalps!"

"No doubt about that," observed Colonel Carrington shaking his head. "Look at those great blood clots on the snow directly ahead of their position. Every one means either an Indian or a pony. They must have taken a heavy toll of life with those repeating rifles. It's a pity the whole command weren't armed with them."

"A lot o' good their guns 'll do Red Cloud's redskins," growled a grizzled corporal. "They took a special make of shell, an' the Injuns can't buy 'em this side of Omaha."

Hour after hour had passed in covering the ground over which the battle had progressed. Not an Indian was seen during the entire day. Doubtless they were rejoicing in their tepees and had no time for battle. They could kill off the balance of the soldiers at their leisure in the "hated fort on the Little Piney," as the savages styled Fort Phil Kearny.

It was growing dusk before the last mutilated, stiffened

corpse was placed in the wagons and the return to the fort began. Advance scouts and flanking parties maintained constant watch against attack, and great was the rejoicing in

John ("Portugee") Phillips, the Courier who carried the news of the Fetterman disaster to the outside world.

the command when the white light at the top of the flagstaff was seen, indicating that all was well with the garrison.

That night a frightful blizzard broke loose, the thermometer dropped to more than 25 degrees below zero and the snow piled so rapidly against the stockade that forces of men worked in fifteen-minute shifts shoveling it away, lest the drifts attain a height whereby the Indians could climb over the stockade. But the severity of the weather kept the Indians within their own shelters. Guards and snow-shovelers were changed every fifteen minutes, and even at that many of them were badly frost-bitten. Lights burned in all the quarters, and everybody fully expected an attack to be made upon the post after this first great bloody victory by Red Cloud's warriors.

It was imperative that help be summoned at once from Fort Laramie, and the news of the frightful disaster given to the Washington authorities. This could only be done by courier. Carrington called for a man with the required nerve. Nobody would volunteer from among the troops. Finally a frontiersman known as "Portugee" Phillips, well trained to Indian fighting and with accurate knowledge of the country, stepped forward and said that as long as no one else would volunteer, he would go himself.

It meant a ride of 236 miles through a country swarming with hostile Indians, where constant watchfulness was necessary, with snowdrifts that had completely obliterated the trails, and in zero weather. All Phillips asked for was the swiftest horse at the post. This was a blooded animal owned by Col. Carrington himself. This request was instantly granted by the colonel, and at midnight, with only a few crackers for himself, and a hatful of feed for his horse, Phillips rode out through a little side-gate of the stockade and slipped away into the howling storm. Everyone at the post expected that he would be apprehended before he had gone a hundred yards, but there was no demonstration. Apparently the Indians were flushed with their first victory and felt that they could take their time to finish the balance of the command.

I have always looked upon this ride of John ("Portugee") Phillips as the *greatest and most daring in all the annals of American history*. The ride of Paul Revere, to give notice of

Christmas eve arrival of "Portugee" Phillips at Fort Laramie, after 236 mile horseback ride from Fort Phil Kearny with first news of the Fetterman disaster. The temperature was 40° below zero. From painting by Otto Selzer.

the approach of the British, was a summer's day canter in comparison. To leave out all the thrilling details—the cold, hunger, fatigue—which Phillips and his faithful horse endured, as well as the constant watchfulness to avoid capture, he arrived at Fort Laramie on Christmas eve, while a great ball was in progress at "Bedlam," the building where all the post activities and social functions were held. The daring rider reeled from his saddle on the parade ground as his gallant horse dropped dead under him, staggered into the midst of the festivities—a gigantic, swaying figure, swathed from head to foot in buffalo overcoat, leggings and cap, and gasping incoherently the news of the catastrophe at Fort Phil Kearny, he dropped in a dead faint from over-exposure and exhaustion.

There was a wire east from Fort Laramie, and the news of the appalling disaster was immediately spread broadcast. It caused a gasp of horror to sweep over the country. In spite of the fact that Col. Carrington had conducted himself in every way as a brave, prudent, cautious, skillful, capable soldier, it was, of course, necessary that someone be "made the goat." He was immediately relieved of the command of Fort Phil Kearny by Gen. Philip St. George Cooke, department commander at Omaha—whom, by the way, Carrington had constantly importuned for improved arms, more men and more ammunition, *all requests being promptly turned down.*

Col. Carrington was notified that he must report at Fort Casper, several days' journey to the south, at a certain date. He was obliged to leave Fort Phil Kearny early in January, 1867, when the thermometer stood at forty degrees below zero, with his wife, two small children and a guard. So frightful was the weather that some of the teamsters were so badly frozen by the time Fort Reno was reached, that amputation of the lower limbs of one or two was necessary; one of the teamsters died, and several days elapsed before Carrington's party was able to proceed to Fort Casper.

Col. Carrington at once demanded a full and complete investigation of his conduct as commander of Fort Phil Kearny. It was *20 years* before the Washington authorities listened to his appeal and granted him a hearing, at which he was completely exonerated from all charges of incompetency, and it was proved beyond question that he at all times had acted wisely, cautiously, prudently and ably in all his engagements with the Indians, and that the entire blame for the Fetterman disaster was through that officer's flat disobedience of orders and his own rashness and desire to "show" Carrington his ability as an Indian fighter, thus sacrificing his entire command.

Two years later the government arrived at the conclusion that Chief Red Cloud was too strategic and able a warrior to fight. Another conference was called at which Red Cloud reiterated his demands that the entire country be abandoned by the government, all the troops withdrawn and the forts dismantled. He would listen to no other sort of a compromise. The government wisely concluded that "discretion was the better part of valor" and came to Red Cloud's terms.

In August, 1868, Fort Phil Kearny was abandoned. Before the troops had marched a mile from the post, the Indians swarmed out of the ravines and applied the torch, and from the distant hills the soldiers watched the great structure go up in smoke.

The site of this noted frontier fort is on land now owned by George Geier, the land being originally homesteaded in 1878 by the late Judge Thomas J. Foster of Sheridan, Wyoming. In 1913 I made a visit to the spot accompanied by Judge Foster. Where had been the parade ground of the old post I found a fine alfalfa field. Scattered about were yet the remnants of some of the old stoves and baking ovens used by the troops, and the east line of the old stockade was yet discernible. A three-foot section of one of the original logs was sticking out of the ground, and I asked and was given permission to cut this off and bring it home, and today this blackened, well-worn bit of tough pine stands in a case in my den, a grim reminder of one of the greatest tragedies on the western frontier.

In 1908, Col. Carrington, then in his 86th year, made a trip from his distant Massachusetts home to the site of Fort Phil Kearny for the purpose of dedicating the cobblestone monument on "Massacre Hill." Chief Red Cloud, then aged, blind and infirm, at Pine Ridge reservation, was also most earnestly invited to attend the ceremonies, but owing to his advanced age and poor health, said that while he would have been glad to be present and shake the hand of the great White Chief, his former foe, his health would not permit.

Col. Carrington died in 1912, and Chief Red Cloud in 1909. The state of Wyoming has placed a suitable marker on the site of the old fort, and today automobiles spin along the highway where in 1866 Red Cloud's warriors laid in wait for scalps.

OFFICIAL REPORT OF COLONEL HENRY B. CARRINGTON ON THE FETTERMAN DISASTER

The following report came into the possession of the author in 1940 through the courtesy of Colonel W. A. Graham, USA Retired, author of The Story of the Little Big Horn and other books on Custeriana.

> Fort Philip Kearny, Dak.
> Headquarters Post
> January 3, 1867.

Asst. Adt. General, Dept. of the Platte.

Omaha, Nebr.

SIR:

I respectfully state the facts of the fight with Indians on the 21st ultimo. This disaster had the effect to confirm my judgment as to the hostility of Indians, and solemnly declares, by its roll of dead and the number engaged, that my declaration from my arrival at Laramie, in June, was not idle conjecture, but true.

It also declares that in Indian warfare there must be perfect coolness, steadiness and judgment. This contest is in their best, and almost last, hunting grounds. They cannot be whipped or punished by some little dash after a handful, nor by mere resistance of offensive movements. They must be subjected, and made to respect and fear the whites.

It also declares, with equal plainness, that my letter from Fort Laramie as to the absolute failure of the treaty, so far as relates to my command, was true.

It also vindicates every report from my pen, and every measure I have taken to secure defensive and tenable posts on this line.

It vindicates my administration of the Mountain District, Department of the Platte, and asserts that the confidence reposed in me by Lieut.-General Sherman has been fully met.

It vindicates my application so often made for reinforcements, and demonstrates the fact that if I had received those assured to me by telegraph and letter, I could have kept up communications, and opened a safe route for emigrants next spring.

It proves correct my report of 1,500 lodges of hostile Indians on Tongue River, not many hours' ride from the post.

It no less declares that while there has been partial success in impromptu dashes, the Indians, now desperate and bitter, look upon the rash white man as a sure victim, no less than he does a coward, and that the United States must come to the deliberate resolve to send an army equal to a fight with the Indians of the Northwest.

Better to have the expense at once than to have a lingering, provoking war for years. It must be met, and the time is just now. I respectfully refer to my official reports and correspondence from Department Headquarters for verification of the foregoing propositions, and proceed to the details of Fetterman's massacre.*

On the morning of the 21st ultimo, at about 11 o'clock a.m., my picket on Pilot Hill reported the wood train corraled

---

*Gen. Carrington is in error in reporting this as a "massacre." You cannot call a disaster a "massacre" when men go to their deaths with guns in their hands, fighting desperately to the last.—*The Author.*

and threatened by Indians on Sullivant Hills, a mile and a half from the fort. A few shots were heard; Indians also appeared in the brush at the crossing of Pinery by the Virginia City Road. Upon tendering to Brevet Major Powell the command of Co. C, 2d U. S. Cavalry (then without an officer, but which he had been drilling), Brevet Lieut.-Col. Fetterman claimed by rank to go out. I acquiesced, giving him the men of his own company that were for duty, and a portion of Co. C, 2d Battalion, 18th U. S. Infantry.

Lieut. G. W. Grummond, who had commanded the mounted infantry, requested to take out the cavalry. He did so. In the previous skirmish (on Dec. 6) Lieut. Grummond was barely saved from the disaster that befell Lieut. Bingham, by timely aid.

Brevet Lieut.-Col. Fetterman also was admonished, as well by myself, that we were fighting brave and desperate enemies, who sought to make up, by cunning and deceit, all the advantage which the white man gains by intelligence and better arms.

My instructions were, therefore, peremptory and explicit. I knew the ambition of each to win honor, but being unprepared for large aggressive action through want of force (now fully demonstrated), I looked to continuance of timber supplies to prepare for more troops as the one practicable duty. Hence, two days before, Major Powell, sent out to cover the train under similar circumstances, simply did that duty when he could have had a fight to any extent.

The day before, viz., the 20th ultimo, I went myself to the Pinery and built a bridge of 45 feet span to expedite the passage of wagons from the woods to open ground.

Hence my instruction to Brevet Lieut.-Col. Fetterman, viz: *"Support the wood train; relieve it, and report to me. Do not engage or pursue Indians at its expense. Under no circumstances pursue over the ridge, viz. Lodge Trail Ridge, as per map in your possession."*

To Lieut. Grummond I gave orders to report to Brevet Lieut.-Col. Fetterman, *implicitly obey orders, and not leave him.*

Before the command left, I instructed Lieut. A. H. Wands, my regimental quartermaster and acting adjutant, *to repeat these orders.* He did so. Fearing still that the spirit of ambition might override prudence (as my refusal to permit 60 mounted men and 40 citizens to go for several days down Tongue River valley after villages, had been unfavorably regarded by Brevet Lieut.-Col. Fetterman and Capt. Brown), I crossed the parade, and from a sentry platform, halted the cavalry *and again repeated my precise orders.*

I knew that the Indians had for several days returned, each time with increased numbers, to feel our strength and decoy detachments to their sacrifice, and believed that to foil their purpose was actual victory, until reinforcements should arrive and my preparations were complete.

I was right. Just as the command left, five Indians reappeared at the crossing. The glass revealed others in the thicket, having the apparent object of determining the watchfulness of the garrison, or cutting off any small party that should move out. A case-shot dismounted one, and developed nearly 30 more, who broke for the hills and ravines to the north.

In half an hour the picket reported that the wood train had broken corral and moved on to the Pinery. No report came from the detachment. It was composed of 81 officers and men, including two citizens (Wheatley and Fisher), all well armed, the cavalry having new carbines, while the detachment of infantry was of choice men, the pride of their companies.

At 12 o'clock firing was heard toward Peno Creek, beyond Lodge Trail Ridge. A few shots were followed by constant shots, not to be counted. Capt. Ten Eyck was immediately dispatched with infantry and the remaining cavalry, and two wagons, and with orders to join Col. Fetterman at all hazards.

The men moved promptly, and on the run; but within little more than half an hour from the first shot, and just as the supporting party reached the hill overlooking the scene of action, all firing ceased.

Capt. Ten Eyck sent a mounted orderly back with the report that he could see and hear nothing of Fetterman, but that a body of Indians on the road below him were challenging him to come down, while larger bodies were in all the valleys for several miles around. Moving cautiously forward with the wagons—evidently supposed by the enemy to be guns, as mounted men were in advance—he rescued from the spot where the enemy had been nearest, 49 bodies, including those of Brevet Lieut.-Col. Fetterman and Capt. F. H. Brown. *The latter went out without my consent or knowledge,* fearless to fight Indians with any adverse odds, and determined to kill one at least before joining his company.

Capt. Ten Eyck fell back slowly, but not pressed by the enemy, reaching the fort without loss. The following morning, finding general doubt as to the success of an attempt to rescue other bodies, but believing that failure to rescue them would dishearten the command, and encourage the Indians, who are so particular in this regard, I took 80 men and went to the scene of action, leaving a picket to advise me of any movement in the rear and to keep signal communications with the garrison.

The scene of action told its story. The road on the little ridge where the final stand took place, was strewn with arrowheads, scalp poles and broken shafts of spears. The arrows that were spent harmlessly from all directions, show that the command was suddenly overwhelmed, surrounded, and cut off while in retreat. *Not an officer or man survived.* A few bodies were found at the north end of the divide, over which the road runs, just below Lodge Trail Ridge.

Nearly all were heaped near four rocks at the point nearest the fort, these rocks inclosing a space about six feet square, having been the last refuge for defense. Here were also a few unexpended rounds of Spencer cartridges.

Fetterman and Brown had each a revolver shot in the left temple. As Brown always declared he would reserve a shot for himself, as a last resort, so I am convinced that these two brave men each fell by the other's hand rather than undergo the slow torture inflicted upon others.

Lieut. Grummond's body was upon the road between the two extremes, with a few others. This was not far from five miles from the fort, and nearly as far from the wood train. Neither its own guard nor the detachment could by any possibility have helped each other, and the train was incidentally saved by the fierceness of the fight in the brave but rash impulse of pursuit.

The officers who fell believed that no Indian force could overwhelm that number of troops well held in hand.

Their terrible massacre bore marks of great valor, and has

demonstrated the force and character of the foe; but no valor could have saved them.

Pools of blood on the road and sloping sides of the narrow divide showed where Indians bled fatally; but their bodies were carried off. I counted 65 such pools in the space of an acre, and three within 10 feet of Lieut. Grummond's body.

Eleven American horses and nine Indian ponies were on the road or near the line of bodies; others, crippled, were in the valleys. At the northwest or farthest point, between two rocks, and apparently where the command first fell back from the valley, realizing their danger, I found Citizens James S. Wheatley and Isaac Fisher, of Blue Springs, Nebraska, who, with Henry rifles, felt invincible, but fell, one having 105 arrows in his naked body. The widow and family of Wheatley are here. The cartridge shells about him told how well they fought.

Before closing this report, I wish to say that every man— officer, soldier or citizen—received burials with such record as to identify each. Fetterman, Brown and Grummond lie in one grave. The remainder also shared one tomb, buried as they fought, together, but the cases in which they were laid are duly placed and numbered.

I asked the general commanding to give my report, in absence of division commander, an access to the eye and ear of the general-in-chief. The department commander must have more troops, and I declare this my judgment solemnly, and for the general public good, without one spark of personal ambition, other than to do my duty daily as it comes, and whether I seem to speak too plainly or not, ever with the purpose to declare the whole truth, and with proper respect to my superior officers, who are entitled to the facts as to scenes remote from their immediate notice.

I was asked to send all the bad news. I do so as far as I can. I give some of the facts as to my men, whose bodies I found just at dark, resolved to bring all in, viz.: mutilations: eyes torn out and laid on the rocks; noses cut off; ears cut off; chins cut off; teeth chopped out; joints of fingers; brains taken out and placed on rocks with other members of the body; entrails taken out and exposed; hands cut off; feet cut off; arms taken out from sockets; private parts severed and indecently placed on the person; eyes, ears, mouth and arms penetrated with spear-heads, sticks and arrows; ribs slashed to separation with knives; skulls severed in every form from chin to crown; muscles of calves, thighs, stomach, back, breast, arms and cheek taken out. Punctures upon every sensitive part of the body even to the soles of the feet and palms of the hand.

All this only approximates the whole truth.

Every medical officer was faithfully aided by a large force of men, but all were not buried until Wednesday after the fight.

The great real fact is that these Indians take alive when possible, and slowly torture. It is the opinion of Dr. S. M. Horton, post surgeon, *that not more than six were killed by balls*. Of course the whole arrows—hundreds of which were removed from naked bodies, were all used after removal of the clothing.

I have said enough. It is a hard but absolute duty. In the establishment of this post I designed to put it where it fell the heaviest upon the Indian, and, therefore, the better for the emigrant. My duty will be done when I leave, as ordered, to my new regiment headquarters, Fort Casper.

I submit herewith a list of casualties, marked "A." I shall also as soon as practicable, make full report for the year 1866 of operations in the establishment of this new line.

I am, very respectfully your obedient servant,

HENRY B. CARRINGTON,
Colonel 18th Infantry
Commanding.

NOTE by E. A. Brininstool:—

In a second report written the day after the above report was sent, Col. Carrington sent additional information of the fight of December 21, 1866, as follows:

Relative to the tragedy of December 21, and to make more definite than set forth in my official report the exact movement of Brevet Lieut.-Col. Fetterman, I add these facts:

The picket on Pilot Hill, having reported the wood train as having broken corral, and moved forward on its daily duty, I entertained no apprehension of further danger.

Fetterman's command had been joined by Grummond's

just west of the ordinary ferry crossing. It moved in good order.

I remarked the fact that he had deployed his men as skirmishers, and was evidently moving wisely up the creek, and along the southern slope of Lodge Trail Ridge, with good promise of cutting off the Indians as they should withdraw, repulsed at the train, and his position, giving him perfect vantage ground, to save the train if the Indians pressed the attack. It is true that the usual course was to follow the road directly to the train, but the course adopted was not an error, unless there was taken a purpose to disobey orders.

Upon inquiry, I found he had no surgeon, and sent Dr. C. H. Hines, with two orderlies, to the wood trains, instructing him, if not needed there, to join Fetterman and return with him.

There was no danger of casualties except at the train, and in Fetterman's movement toward cutting off retreat of the enemy, and the Indian force south of Piney could not oppose his connection with the train, which had already repulsed attack.

Dr. Hines came back quickly, reporting the train to have passed safely on; that Brevet Lieut.-Col. Fetterman had crossed Lodge Trail Ridge toward Peno Creek, and that Indians were on the western slope, and between him and Fetterman, so that he could not join him. Brevet Lieut.-Col. Fetterman evidently disregarded those that were on that slope (if he saw them) and was led off into Peno Valley, perhaps after the party who had been at the ferry crossing had attempted precisely the same decoy practiced December 6, 1866. When Brevet Lieut.-Col. Fetterman was lost in sight from the post, his command was moving westward along the slope of Lodge Trail Ridge, and apparently in good order, with no indications that it would pass over it.

My office orderly soon told me that the sentry at the door reported firing.

I went to the top of the house, on which was a lookout. and heard a few shots, apparently in the direction of Peno Creek. With my glass I could see neither Indian nor soldier. I think I counted six scattering shots at first, succeeded by more rapid firing. I directed the orderly, then in front of the house, to notify the officer of the day; had the sentry call the corporal of the guard, and the guard formed immediately. Sent one man who was bringing boards into the unfinished part of the house to the quartermaster's office, to have wagons and ambulances hitched, and to immediately go and notify every unarmed man in the quartermaster's employ, to report at once to the magazine for arms.

Lieut. Wands, Capt. Ten Eyck, and another officer whose name I do not recollect, were in sight from the top of the house.

I directed Capt. Ten Eyck to be prepared to move at once. I called Lieut. Wands to the top of the house to watch the firing, and went in person to hasten and organize the detail that was to move. It moved in a very few minutes. I rejected some men from the detail after it was formed, taking those only who had most ammunition and had reported promptly, not waiting to have any boxes re-supplied.

Having sent already a messenger to the cavalry, I sent, (immediately after Ten Eyck moved) the remainder of Company C, 2d U. S. Cavalry, dismounted (nearly 30 men in all), having the new carbine, requiring them to fill their pockets with all the surplus ammunition they could carry.

In the first wagon that reported, I placed 3,000 rounds of Springfield and two cases of Spencer (ammunition), to give this command, and also Fetterman's, additional ammunition. I sent Williams, master of transportation, in charge of the wagons and ammunition, with 42 men; these quickly following the details that had already left.

The whole garrison was placed under arms; all work suspended; arms stacked before quarters, to answer to the assembly.

This occupied but a few minutes, and I joined Lieut. Wands upon the house to watch indications of the position of the parties out. There had been a short lull in the firing (namely, only scattered shots here and there), succeeded by a very brisk firing, apparently by file at first, and quite regular, and an occasional volley, followed by indiscriminate firing, gradually dying out in a few scattering shots. Being satisfied that the affair was occurring beyond the range of Brevet Lieut.-Col. Fetterman's instructions, I became apprehensive of disaster, and directed Brevet Capt. Arnold, post adjutant, to determine and report to me at once the number of men remaining at the post—soldiers and citizens—who were armed, to determine whether I had any force to spare for further operations outside.

He reported the number at 119, including guard.

I sent couriers to the wood party to withdraw it, timber or no timber, and, as before stated, notified Capt. Ten Eyck, by courier, and in writing, that their return would give me 50 additional men to spare.

From the character and position of the firing by Fetterman's men, I believe he must have fallen short of ammunition before the last catastrophe occurred. If he moved out without inspection of his command, he still should have had an ample supply for any contingency, in the relief and protection of the train, but it is no less certain that, as when he was out before, he wasted fire at long range.

While Capt. Ten Eyck was out, I caused to be examined the sergeants of the companies which had furnished him details of infantry and cavalry, and the aggregate of ammunition reported to be with the party of Brevet Lieut.-Col. Fetterman was 2,800 rounds. I had but a few days previously issued 3,000 rounds to each company, to be kept by the officers, or in the sergeant's room, and the general standard of supply to each man was 40 rounds. This occasionally was depleted by small expenditures with the wood train during the day, but my standing order forbade them to fire at any game whatever without special consent.

At the same time, the garrison was so organized that every officer and soldier, every citizen or citizens' employe and teamster, and every clerk in the sutler's store, had his loophole, or place at which to report, at a general alarm by night or day.

Upon my return from the pinery the night previous, it was uncertain whether the train would go out in the morning, on account of the snow, which I had found quite deep in the woods; but just before guard mounting, or nearly 10 o'clock a.m., I concluded to send it, with a strong guard, as before mentioned. It was nearly 11 o'clock when the picket reported the train corraled. Brevet Lieut.-Col. Fetterman moved with his infantry certainly within 15 minutes—I think less. Lieut. Grummond mounted so quickly as to join Col.

Fetterman at the river crossing, about 1,300 yards distant from the post.

Just before dinner call, or nearly 12 o'clock M., my attention was called to the firing.

Capt. Ten Eyck moved very rapidly, reaching the summit of the hill, when he first halted, in about half an hour.

Sample, the orderly, whom he sent back to me, arrived at headquarters a little after 1 o'clock—perhaps half-past. All firing ceased, as far as I could hear any, just before Capt. Ten Eyck's advance reached the top of the hills, so that the duration of the firing was somewhat less than one hour—I should judge about 35 to 45 minutes.

The garrison of Fort Phil Kearny was as follows: including myself, district, regimental, battalon and post staff, seven officers; and for duty, including those on extra or daily duty as clerks or otherwise, 308 officers and enlisted men.

The nominal aggregate present was 339, and the aggregate proper of the command, including 10 commissioned officers (absent) and soldiers absent, the sick, and those in arrest, was 398 men.

The number of serviceable horses at the post was 37, and unserviceable, 13.

Fort Phil Kearny was established amid hostilities. Fifty-one skirmishes have occurred. No disaster, other than the usual incidents to border warfare occurred, *until gross disobedience of orders sacrificed nearly 80 of the choice men of my command.* In the grave I bury disobedience; but I will vindicate the living, and stand by my acts and record. It will stand as a simple fact that in the face of constant night and day attacks, and in the heart of the Indian country, the posts ordered to be established (Forts Reno, Phil. Kearny and C. F. Smith) were established during 1866.

HENRY B. CARRINGTON,
Colonel 18th Infantry
Commanding.

List of victims of the Fetterman disaster, from the Official Reports:

COMPANY A, 2D BATTALION,
18TH U. S. INFANTRY
First Sergt. Augustus Lang

First Sergt. Hugh Murphy
Corporal Robert Lennon
Corporal Wm. Dute

Privates Frederick Ackerman
Wm. Betzler
Thos. Burke
Henry Buchanan
Maxim Dihring
Geo. E. R. Goodall
Francis S. Gordon
Michael Harten
Martin Kelly
Patrick Shannon
Chas M. Taylor
Joseph D. Thomas
David Thorey
John Thimpson
Albert H. Walters
John M. Weaver
John Woodruff

COMPANY C, 2D BATTALION,
18TH U. S. INFANTRY
Sergt. Francis Raymond
Sergt. Patrick Rooney
Corporal Gustave A. Bauer
Corporal Patrick Gallagher
Privates Henry E. Aarons
Michael O. Garra
Jacob Rosenburg
Frank P. Sullivan
Patrick Smith

COMPANY E, 2D BATTALION,
18TH U. S. INFANTRY
Sergt. Wm. Morgan
Corporal John Quinn
Privates George W. Burrel
John Maher
Geo. H. Waterbury
Timothy Cullinane

Co. H, 2D BATTALION,
18TH U. S. INFANTRY
First Sergt. Alex. Smith
First Sergt. Ephriam C. Bissell
Corporal Michael Sharkey
Corporal George Phillips
Corporal Frank Karston

Privates George Davis
Perry F. Dolan
Asa H. Griffin
Herman Keil
James Kean
Micheel Kinney
Delos Reed
Regimental Armorer
Thomas S. Madden

COMPANY C, 2D U. S. CAVALRY
Sergt. James Baker
Corporals James Kelly
Thos. F. Herrigan
Bugler Adolph Metzgar
Artificer John McCarty
Privates Thos. Amberson
Thos. Broglin
Nathan Foreman
Andrew M. Fitzgerald
Daniel Green
Chas. Gamford
John Gitter
Ferdinand Houser
Wm. L. Bugbee
Wm. L. Cornog
Chas. Cuddy
Patrick Clancy
Harvey S. Deming
U. B. Doran
Robt. Daniel
Frank Jones
James P. McGuire
John McColly
Franklin Payne
Jas. Ryan
Geo. W. Nugent
Oliver Williams

CIVILIANS:
Isaac Fisher
James Wheatley
Capt. W. J. Fetterman
Capt. Frederick H. Brown
Lieut. George W. Grummond

(General Carrington, after the death of his wife, married Mrs. Grummond in 1871.)

Chapter II

~

THE "WAGON-BOX" FIGHT

Thirty-two Against Three Thousand—An Unparalleled
Indian Battle

~

AS ONE sits at ease in a palatial Pullman car, or is whisked across country by auto, through what, seventy-five years ago, was known as "the Plains country," he little realizes the tremendous sacrifice of life, the unparalleled suffering, the terrible privation, exposure and hardships endured by "the men who made the West."

The author refers more especially to the men of the old Regular Army, who, for the mere pittance of $13 a month, marched, fought and bivouacked over the "Great American Desert," established forts in the face of almost certain death; fought the hordes of savage warriors in their own country; protected the slow-crawling prairie schooners and emigrant trains, and kept the line of travel open for the Overland stages.

It was the "Regular Army Man" who bore the brunt of the advance of civilization. All honor to those men! Let the memory of their brave deeds and gallant sacrifices be never forgotten, but kept constantly before the minds of the rising generation of school children, who know—alas, too little of the history of the winning of the West.

The year 1866 was known as the "bloody year on the Plains." The savages were almost constantly on the warpath; stage travel was, for a time, completely at a standstill. The

43

Chief Red Cloud, noted Ogalalla Sioux leader.

Indians were seeking to prevent the encroachment of the whites into their favorite hunting grounds, or the establishment of ranches in the fertile valleys of the many beautiful streams in the present state of Wyoming.

Travel into the gold fields of Montana was especially heavy, particularly so by way of the Bozeman Trail, which had just been opened. And the Bozeman Trail led through what was then the last and best hunting grounds of the Sioux and Cheyennes. The white-topped prairie schooners were, in the eyes of the red man, on a par with a red rag to a bull. The encroachment of the whites meant that the game would be frightened, and driven out of the country; and this meant the annihilation of the commissary of the Indians—and what man, red or white, will not fight for his subsistence?

Chief Red Cloud—that greatest of fighting men of red blood, in his regime,—keen, brainy, crafty—a born general in battle—realized far better than did any of his sub-chiefs, what this white invasion of the West would mean in a short time to the Indian—and it was to protect the last and choicest hunting grounds of his people that he began a war of extermination against the whites.

In those days, old Fort Laramie was the "jumping-off place." After that point was passed, skillful frontiersmanship was necessary to prevent a surprise attack, and complete annihilation by the red men. The government was appealed to for soldiers to protect the trails. and to insure safe passage for the thousands of wagon-trains bound for the Montana and Wyoming countries and the Northwest.

Briefly, it was finally decided to send an expedition, thoroughly equipped, to establish military posts along the route of travel to the Northwest of Fort Laramie, over the Bozeman Trail. To this end, Col. Henry B. Carrington, 18th U. S. Infantry, was instructed to proceed from Fort Kearney, Nebraska, with all the necessary troops and equipment, for that purpose.

It is not the intention of the author to here recount the complete experiences of the Carrington Expedition on its way to a land about as unknown as the heart of Africa. This unsettled country comprised the present state of Wyoming.

Carrington's instructions were to proceed to old Fort Connor, and there restock and rebuild that post, garrison it, and make it the southern post of the Bozeman Trail. He was then to proceed northward and build and garrison two more forts, about 100 miles apart. It was thus believed that protection could be guaranteed to the newcomers into the Montana country.

Carrington's Expedition left Fort Kearney, Nebraska, May 19, 1866, with the noted frontiersman, Jim Bridger, as chief guide. Fort Laramie was reached on the 16th of June. Here were assembled thousands of Sioux Indians, headed by Chief Red Cloud, to hold a "peace council" with some Commissioners from Washington, D. C. This was for the purpose of endeavoring to secure passage through the Sioux country, without molestation, and to gain the consent of the Indians to erect and maintain the proposed military posts.

But Chief Red Cloud and his "right bower," Young-Man-Afraid-of-His-Horses, refused to consider the proposition. Red Cloud charged the Government with *"You steal the country before the red man has a chance to say yes or no."* Both Chiefs stalked out of the council, shouting defiance, and refusing any of the presents which had been offered them, and swearing they would "kill every white man who passed beyond Crazy Woman's Fork of Powder River." They said they would not object to the garrisoning of old Fort Connor, but under no circumstances would they consent that Carrington build any more forts north of that point. It would mean "war to the knife" if he did.

But Carrington paid no attention to these threats. He was there under orders from Washington to go ahead—and go ahead he did. Fort Connor was garrisoned and provisioned, and the name changed to FORT RENO, after which Carrington started north to locate sites for the other two proposed military posts.

On July 14th, the expedition reached a point nearly one hundred miles north of Fort Reno, which appealed to Carrington as best located for the erection of the first fort. It was at the forks of the Big and Little Piney Creeks. That spot in the late 1870 period was a part of the ranch of Jacob Geier, and is situated about twenty-three miles southeast of the city of Sheridan, Wyoming. The following morning July 15th, logging parties were detailed, and the erection of the new post begun, which was to be named "FORT PHIL KEARNY."*

Among the soldiers who left Fort Kearney, Nebraska, with this expedition, was Sergt. Samuel Gibson. About 1915 the author became acquainted with Sergt. Gibson, then holding down a job in Omaha. The sergeant there recounted the experiences he passed through during those trying days, which are here related in his own language:

SERGEANT GIBSON'S STORY

I was born in England in 1849, and resided there until 1865, when my father and his family removed to the United States. In April, 1866, I enlisted in the United States Army at Cleveland, Ohio. I was assigned to Company C, Second Battalion, 18th U. S. Infantry, at Fort Kearney, Nebraska, in May, where I became a member of the Carrington Expedition.

We marched across the Plains to Julesburg, Colorado, where we crossed the South Platte river over hand on a thick rope stretched across the river—nine hundred of us.

From Julesburg we marched through Ash Hollow and across the Platte Valley to Fort Laramie, where we rested three or four days. At this point some Indian Commissioners

---

* Fort Kearney, Nebr., and Fort Phil. Kearny, Wyo., were spelled differently.

were holding a council with Red Cloud and "Young-Man-Afraid," Sioux chiefs, to obtain their consent to build some forts through the Indians' favorite hunting grounds along the Bozeman Trail, close to the Big Horn Mountains.

When Red Cloud was told that Carrington was the man who was going in command of the soldiers, to build those forts, he grabbed his rifle and shook it in the faces of the Commissioners, declaring that the soldiers should not pass through his favorite hunting grounds, and that he would kill every soldier, and wage a war of extermination against all white invaders.

But Carrington proceeded to carry out his orders. The expedition reached old Fort Connor (later called Fort Reno) on June 28th. Here we relieved two companies of the Fifth Infantry, and two troops of the 11th Ohio Cavalry. We left this post on July 9th, and arrived at the forks of the Piney Creeks on July 14th. On the 15th, Col. Carrington located the plateau on which we built historic Fort Phil. Kearny—and from that time on, our troubles commenced—and I don't mean maybe!

Not a hostile Indian had we seen until after we arrived at the Piney Creeks but as soon as we began to send our logging trains to cut and bring in the necessary timber for the erection of the stockade, barracks and other buildings, there was continual fighting. The Indians attacked our logging parties nine times between July 14th and 29th, and when we went into the pineries, seven miles distant, we never knew from one day to the next if we would come back dead or alive.

In August, two of our men, Gilchrist and Johnson, were lariated by the Indians while returning to the post from the hay camp. They were pulled from their horses, and tortured to death over a slow fire. This occurred about eight or ten miles down Big Piney Creek. We found their skulls and portions of their skeletons a week later.

That is how the red devils harrassed us every day while we were building the fort. They ran off our beef herd early in September; also twenty-five or thirty mules, and attacked every wagon train that came up the Bozeman Trail, sometimes keeping these trains corraled three or four days between watering places, so that men and animals suffered extremely from thirst. Every wagon-train on its way to Virginia City

Sergt. Samuel S. Gibson who died in 1932.
Taken on the steps of City Hall, Omaha,
Nebraska, in 1917, by the author.

or Last Chance Gulch, lost from two to half a dozen men, besides a great many draught animals.

Yet, in spite of all this, we had to keep going to the pineries every day for logs. Each morning our wood-train would go seven miles west of the post to the headwaters of Big Piney Creek (except Sundays). On that day we always had inspection of arms and clothing, in full-dress uniform.

On October 31, 1866, our log stockade was finished. It covered a space of ground six hundred by eight hundred feet. A beautiful flagstaff had been made by Drum Major

Barnes of the band, assisted by Private William Daley. On that day Col. Carrington gave us a holiday, and we witnessed the hoisting of the first garrison flag at Fort Phil. Kearny.

On December 6th, Lieut. Bingham and Sergt. Bowers were killed on the bluffs near Lodge Trail Ridge, in an engagement with the Indians, and Lieut. Grummond barely escaped with his life, the fleetness of his horse alone preventing his massacre.

On December 21st occurred the terrible Fetterman disaster. Col. Carrington was blamed by the Government, and a criticising public, for this disaster, whereas Fetterman alone was to blame for it. I happened to be on guard at the west gate of the fort on the fatal morning, when Fetterman and his men passed out the gate, and I distinctly heard Col. Carrington order Fetterman to follow the wood train and not leave it under any circumstances whatever.

That is how we lived and fought for twenty-six months, with nothing to eat but hardtack and sow-belly three times a day. We had no vegetables of any sort, and we lost over thirty men who died with scurvy during that terrible winter of 1866-'67. When the Piney Creeks froze up for the winter, we did not have a chance to take a bath until they thawed out the following spring, consequently most of the enlisted men were lousy most of the time we were at Fort Phil Kearny.

After the Fetterman disaster the Indians did not bother us again until spring. They had enough to do to keep their own camps warm without molesting us; but with the coming of spring they again started up their old tactics of the previous summer. Every time the logging parties ventured out, they would be attacked.

It was well along toward June when Gilmore & Porter's bull trains came up the trail with supplies for our post. When they did come, they were loaded to the guards with provender. But the thing that brought joy to our hearts was a huge lot of the new improved breech-loading rifles (Springfields,

50-caliber). These were the very first rifles of this type ever issued to troops in the Indian country. One hundred thousand rounds of ammunition accompanied these weapons. We now felt that we would stand a better chance in our battles with the savages. The guns we had been using were old antiquated muzzle-loaders, relics of the Civil War. The Indians knew this, and they also knew that once these old guns were fired, it took some time to reload them. Had it not been for these breech-loaders we had received, the Wagon Box fight would have ended with our scalps dangling at the belts of Red Cloud's savage hordes.

THE WAGON-BOX FIGHT

The firm of Gilmore & Porter had a contract to supply Fort Phil Kearny with logs for the sawmills and firewood for the winter. In order to protect their stock from night attacks by Indians, the contractors improvised a corral six miles west of the fort on a level plain. They removed the boxes from their wagons, fourteen in number, and formed them into an oval shaped enclosure into which their stock was driven every night. The pinery where the logs were being cut was at some little distance from the wagon box corral. Several tents were pitched just outside the corral where the woodchoppers and soldiers bunked. Seven thousand rounds of ammunition were arranged inside the corral, and every-body was instructed, in case of Indian attack at the pinery, to retreat to the corral, where it was considered that a good defense could be made until relief arrived from the fort.

It was early in July when the contractors formed the corral, and Company A of my regiment, the Twenty-seventh Infantry,* was sent out with the train, as a guard for the month, to do escort duty to and from the fort daily, and also to protect the woodchoppers in the pinery. Company A saw Indians but two or three times during the entire month of July. On July 31st, Company C, to which I belonged,

---

*(Ed. Note: Formerly a battalion of the 18th Infantry.)

Captain James W. Powell, in command of the defenders of the Wagon Box corral.

relieved Company A. Packing our wagons with a month's rations we marched out from Fort Phil Kearny, across Sullivant Hills, to the woodchoppers' camp near the lower pinery.

We pitched our tents around the outside of the corral. There were spaces between the wagon beds wide enough for a man to walk through, but not large enough for a steer to push outside. There were two of the wagon beds which had canvas covers on them—one at the extreme east end, holding the rations of the woodchoppers, and one on the south side which held our company rations and miscellaneous stores. There was also a wagon complete, with extra rations for the woodchoppers standing outside the corral at the west end, which contained the bedding of the woodchoppers. This wagon stood some ten feet from the wagon boxes which formed the corral. It had a canvas cover over the bows.

On August 1st I was with the detail guarding the woodchoppers at the lower pinery, and was on picket all day. Several of us, when questioned by the sergeant in charge of the detail as to whether we had seen any Indians, replied that we had not, but that we "thought we could smell them." The sergeant, McQuiery, gave us an incredulous look and gruffly exclaimed, "Smell hell!" with extreme contempt.

That night we, who had been on picket duty all day, formed the guard around the camp. Two sentinels were posted, one at the east end and one at the west end of the corral, with strict orders from Captain Powell to allow no one to enter the camp, and to challenge anyone or anything approaching; also, if there was the slightest suspicion in our minds, to open fire upon the approaching objects, or upon anything that looked like Indians.

The night was clear and starry above us, but toward the mountains and down the Big Piney valley it looked awfully dark and ominous. Private Jack McDonough's dog, "Jess," was round with the sentinels all night, and although we could not see or hear anything suspicious, the animal would run furiously down the hill toward the Big Piney valley every few minutes, barking and snapping furiously.

I have always since believed that Red Cloud's warriors were in the valley and around our camp all that night of August 1st, waiting for a chance to surprise us during the night or at daybreak, when we were supposed to be somewhat off our guard.

At daybreak on August 2d, the cooks were called early

to get up and prepare breakfast for the company. A detail of pickets was sent to the point on the banks of the Little Piney between the two camps. Our drummer-boy, Hines, beat the reveille first call, and fifteen minutes later the company fell in, and answered reveille roll call—some, alas, for the last time.

Breakfast was announced by Cook Brown calling "Chuck!" and immediately after, the company broke ranks and laid away their rifles. The whole company took breakfast, with the exception of two men still on picket around the corral. By this time the sun had risen, and we scanned the horizon and the foothills to the north and down the valley of the Big Piney.

We could not see the least sign of an Indian, although we learned afterwards that they were watching our every movement from points of vantage in the hills. I was told this some years later by Chief Rain-in-the-Face while I was sergeant of Company H, Twenty-second Infantry, at Standing Rock agency, during the Sioux Ghost Dance war of 1890-1891.

Immediately after breakfast the wagon trains started for their different destinations—one going to the fort loaded with logs which had been brought out of the pinery the day before, with a detachment of twenty men, commanded by Lieutenant Francis McCarthy and Corporal Paddy Conley, who accompanied the train as an escort. If my memory serves me right, Mr. Porter who owned the bull train and had the contract for supplying the wood to the quartermaster at Fort Phil Kearny, went along.

The other train pulled out for the lower pinery with an escort of thirteen men. Jack McDonough, Dave Moore, McNally and McCumber are the names of some of this escort, which was commanded by Corporal Riley Porter. With Porter was "Portugee" Phillips, who had carried the dispatches of Colonel Carrington from Fort Phil Kearny to

Horseshoe Station after the Fetterman disaster of December 21, the previous year. Phillips was accompanied by a man named Judd. Both Phillips and Judd had subcontracts from Mr. Porter, the contractor.

About this time, 6:45 a. m., I was ordered by the first sergeant to proceed, fully armed and equipped, and relieve Private John Grady as lance corporal in charge of the picket-post on the banks of the little Piney. Having relieved Grady, who instructed me to keep a sharp lookout for Indians, I fixed up a sort of shade from the hot sun with willows stuck in the ground and ponchos tied over the tops. I had laid under this canopy for perhaps fifteen minutes with a private named Deming, when suddenly guard Garrett yelled "Indians!"

Deming and I jumped to our feet, and sure enough, away to the west of us we counted seven Indians mounted, coming across the divide from the north on a dead run and in single file, riding toward the Little Piney and chanting their war song. As the Indians were coming in an oblique direction toward us, and as not a man in the company had yet fired a shot at an Indian from the new breech-loading fifty-caliber Springfield rifles with which we had just been armed, I sat down and adjusted my sights to seven hundred yards, and laying my rifle on top of a stone breastwork, took steady aim at the Indian in advance and fired. My bullet struck a stone in front of the Indian, ricocheted off and wounded his pony. The Indian was thrown off, but immediately sprang to his feet as his pony fell, and was taken up behind a mounted warrior who was following closely in his rear.

About this time Deming and I looked toward our main camp, and over the Big Piney, to the foothills toward the north, and there we saw more Indians than we had ever seen before. Deming exclaimed in an excited tone: "Look at the Indians!" and pointing toward the foothills across Big Piney Creek, he added: "My God! there are thousands of them!"

Hearing shots across the Little Piney, I ordered Garrett to watch for signals from the main camp, and sent Deming across the Little Piney to see what was going on at the other camp, which was a woodchoppers' camp consisting of seven or eight wagons. This camp was perhaps twelve hundred yards directly south of our main camp. Garrett and I watched the Indians coming across the foothills, like a big swarm of bees, on the north side of the Big Piney, feeling very uneasy the while about our failure to receive any signals to return to the main camp where the wagon boxes were corralled. Deming soon came back and reported that Indians had run off the herd, and that all the men, including four of our soldiers (Harris, Kittredge, Lang and Kilberg), who were guarding the small camp south of Little Piney, had run for the mountains, and that one of the civilians, a herder, was coming across the creek, leading his pony, to join us.

Looking toward the main camp we saw quite a commotion going on. The men were hurrying here and there. By this time the herder had come across the creek and joined us, and I told Deming and Garrett that we would start at once for the main camp, and that if the Indians got after us we would make a running skirmish for it. The plan was that we would stop alternately and fire two or three shots, following each other up closely, with myself in the rear.

We immediately started on a good brisk walk, but had retreated only about seventy-five or a hundred yards before the Indians commenced coming up out of the Little Piney Creek bottom by ones, twos and threes at different places. The first one I saw was coming up the bank of the creek sideways, and he carried an old Spencer carbine which he was waving excitedly. I immediately "pulled down" on him just as he was aiming at me. My bullet knocked him off his pony, and I heard his shot whizz past my head.

By this time Garrett had stopped and was down on one knee, firing at the Indians who had come up out of the creek

The great Sioux War Chief, Red Cloud, at 90 years of age, blind and infirm. Photo courtesy of Capt. J. H. Cook, Agate, Nebraska.

higher up to the west of us. I ran past Garrett toward camp, and saw Deming on my right, shooting at the Indians. At this moment the citizen herder, who was leading his pony by the bridle-rein, told me to stick my bayonet in the animal's flanks to make him go faster. I told him to turn the pony loose and shoot at the Indians, who had by this time increased in number at such an alarming rate that they seemed to rise out of the ground like a flock of birds. All of them were naked, with the exception of the regulation "gee-string" around their waists, while some of them wore gorgeous war-bonnets; others had a single feather in their scalp-locks. Their bodies were painted white, green and yellow, which made them look hideous in the extreme.

All of us were now on the dead run. Even the herder's pony was clipping it off, with half a dozen arrows sticking in his flanks, and it seemed as if hell had broken loose. The Indians whooped and yelled as they rode hither and thither and backward and forward in their efforts to surround us by circling, endeavoring thereby to cut us off from the main camp. Each one of us knew full well that if we were hit by an arrow or bullet it would mean death—or something worse if captured alive. We realized that if disabled our scalps would soon be dangling at the scalp-pole of some Sioux warrior. We had seen and assisted in collecting the bodies of our comrades who were so horribly mutilated at the Fetterman fight, and knew that a similar fate awaited us if we were cut off. We kept on running and shooting, expecting every minute to feel a bullet or an arrow in our backs.

We soon saw one of our men run out to meet us from the main camp. He dropped on one knee about a hundred yards from the main corral and opened a rapid fire on the advancing hordes of savages. Several fell from their ponies under his accurate fire. This man proved to be one of our *sergeants, Littman* by name, who, by his courage and thoughtfulness in coming out to meet us, and the rapidity and effectiveness of his fire, saved us from being surrounded and cut off by the red devils. We were thus enabled to reach the main camp in the wagon box corral, although we were in a completely exhausted condition. The civilian herder who was leading his pony, was the last one to enter the corral.

Upon our arrival, completely winded from our long and dangerous run, I immediately reported to Captain Powell, who was standing outside and on the south side of the corral, where he had evidently observed our retreat and pursuit by the Indians. To him, in a panting and exhausted condition, I reported why we had left the picket-post without orders, as it was impossible for us to hold it against such overwhelming odds.

Looking me straight in the eye, Captain Powell exclaimed: "You have done nobly, my boy. You could not have done better!" Then addressing the three of us, he said "Men, find a place in the wagon boxes. You'll have to fight for your lives today!"

We saluted and turned to obey his order, at the same time following his instructions to provide ourselves with plenty of ammunition.

To my dying day I shall never forget the fierce "do-or-die" look on Captain Powell's face that morning. Deming, Garrett and I split up, and each man carried into his wagon box plenty of loaded shells. The Indians were not aware that we had received new rifles, and supposed that after we had fired one shot they would be able to ride us down before we could reload.

Much has been said by historians and others who have written short accounts of this fight, regarding the wagon boxes inside of which we fought. Some have said that the boxes were made of boiler-iron, and others that they were lined with steel and had loopholes through the sides. All such statements were absolutely without foundation. They were the ordinary government wagon boxes, part of the same equipment used during the Civil War. They were built simply of thin wood, while some of them were make-shift wagons belonging to the contractor's bull train; the heaviest of them

Max Littmann, one of the defenders of the Wagon Box corral. Later a successful manufacturer of St. Louis.

being made out of one inch boards. There was not a particle of iron about them anywhere, except the bolts, stay-straps and nuts used in holding the rickety concerns together. I also have read in some accounts that the wagon boxes were "a kind of travelling fort supplied by the government." Any statement that the wagon boxes used as protection in this fight of August

2, 1867, were other than plain, ordinary wood wagon boxes, is a fabrication pure and simple, no matter on what authority given.

I soon found a place in one of the wagon beds on the south side of the corral, and here I found Sergeant McQuiery and Private John Grady. Grady was the only one to speak to me, inviting me to come in with them, saying: "You'll have to fight like hell today, kid, if you expect to get out of this alive." I was the youngest boy in the company, being eighteen years of age, and was always called "the kid," which appellation was given me by Dan Flynn, a member of Company H.

Leaning my rifle against the sides of wagon beds, I carried a hundred rounds of ammunition to my place, and then took a walk around among the men who were standing in groups inside and outside of the corral watching the Indians assembling all around us. I spoke to some of the men, but no one answered me, and the expression of their faces will haunt me as long as I live. I had been in a score of fights and skirmishes with most of my comrades since we began to build Fort Phil Kearny in July of 1866, and had been with some of these same men when we went out with Colonel Carrington on December 22d of that fatal year to bring in the remainder of Fetterman's command from Massacre Hill, where they were killed the previous day, and had then seen the stern, revengeful looks on their faces; but the looks in their eyes this morning was altogther different. It was a look, not of despair or desperation, but one of intense earnestness and resolution.

I saw Private Tommy Doyle piling up some neckyokes belonging to the bull train on top of one another for the purpose of forming a breastwork, between the ends of two of the wagon boxes. I saw another man, Sergeant Frank Robertson, an old soldier who had served in the old Seventh and Tenth Infantry, taking the shoestrings out of his shoes and tying them together, with a loop at one end, which he fitted over his right foot, and a smaller loop at the other end to fit over the trigger of his rifle. I did not ask him what he was doing, because the awful horror of our isolated position seemed to dawn upon my mind, but I knew too well the meaning of those grim preparations—that the red devils would never get old Frank Robertson alive!

I then joined a group of five or six men outside the corral at the southwest end, and in the midst of them stood Lieutenant John C. Jenness, who was watching the Indians through a field glass down the Big Piney valley to the north, and on the highest point of the hill on the ridge east of us. There seemed to be hundreds of Indians, all mounted on their finest and handsomest war ponies, riding here and there, chanting their war and death songs. In the valley, more were assembling. Lieutenant Jenness seemed to be watching the big bunch of Indians on the high hill about three-quarters of a mile distant, and I heard him say to Captain Powell, who soon joined us: "Captain, I believe that Red Cloud is on top of that hill," (pointing to the east). The captain made no reply, but hearing a commotion, accompanied by loud talking, among the men to the south of us, he turned and seeing the Indians riding furiously about the plains between Little Piney and Big Piney Creeks, he exclaimed: "Men, here they come! Take your places and shoot to kill!"

And those were the only words of command given by him, save once, during the entire fight.

Each man quickly took his place in the wagon boxes. Not a word was spoken by anyone, and the silence was awful. When I took my place in the wagon box occupied by Sergeant McQuiery and Private John Grady, both of them had their shoes off, and were fixing their shoestrings into loops to fit over the right foot and from thence to the trigger of their rifles,—to kill themselves when all hope was lost, if the Indians passed over our barricade by an overwhelming force of numbers, when every man would stand erect, place the muzzle of his loaded rifle under his chin and take his own life, rather than be captured and made to endure the inevitable torture. I had just taken off my own shoes and made loops in the strings when the firing began.

Resting my rifle on the top of the wagon box I began firing with the rest. The whole plain was alive with Indians, all mounted and visible in every direction. They were riding madly about, and shooting at us with guns, bows and arrows, first on one side and then on the other of the corral. Then they would circle, and each time come in closer, uttering the most piercing and unearthly war cries. Some of the more venturesome would ride in close and throw spears at us. Others would brandish their war-clubs and tomahawks at us, and others, still more daring, would ride within a hundred yards, then suddenly drop on the offside of their ponies, and all we could see would be an arm or a leg sticking above the pony's back, and "whizz!" would come the arrows! They paid dearly for their daring, for we had a steady rest for our rifles, the Indians were all within easy point-blank range, and we simply mowed them down by scores.

The tops of the wagon beds were literally ripped and torn to slivers by their bullets. How we ever escaped with such a slight loss I never have been able to understand. After we had commenced firing, a great number of Indians rode in very close—probably within a hundred and fifty yards, and sitting on their ponies waited for us to draw ramrods for reloading, as they supposed we were yet using the old muzzle-loaders, but, thanks to God and Lieutenant-General Sherman, the latter had listened to the appeals of Colonel Carrington, commanding Fort Phil Kearny the previous year, and we had just been armed with the new weapon, and instead of drawing ramrods and thus losing precious time, we simply threw open the breech-blocks of our new rifles to eject the empty shell and slapped in fresh ones. This puzzled the Indians, and they

Old Fort Laramie as it looked in 1902, years after its abandonment as an Army Post by the government. Photo by John Hunton.

were soon glad to withdraw to a safe distance.

The plain in front of us was strewn with dead and dying Indians and ponies. The Indians were amazed, but not by any means undaunted. They were there for blood, and came in such hordes that they were ready for any sacrifice if they could but capture our little party. They made heroic attempts to recover their wounded. It was their lives or ours. We had not forgotten Massacre Hill. We were not fiends, gloating over the suffering of their wounded, but that bloody day of December 21st was fresh in our minds, and we were filled with a grim determination to kill just as we had seen our comrades killed. There was no thought of wavering. We knew from their countless numbers that if they overwhelmed us they could easily capture the fort, but six miles distant, where there were helpless women and children. We were fighting for their lives as well as our own.

After recovering a great number of their dead and wounded at a fearful sacrifice of life, the Indians withdrew to a safe distance, but while recovering their injured we witnessed the most magnificent display of horsemanship imaginable. Two mounted Indians would ride like the wind among the dead and wounded, and seeing an arm or leg thrust upward, would ride one on each side of the wounded savage, reach over and pick him up on the run, and carry him to a place of safety. This was done many times, and we could not help but admire their courage and daring.

During a lull in the firing, we got a fresh supply of cartridges out of the seven cases holding a thousand rounds each, which had been opened by order of Captain Powell some time before the firing started, and had been placed about the corral at convenient places. We had to crawl on our hands and knees to get the ammunition, and I saw several of the men, crawling like myself, to get cartridges. None of them spoke a word to me, and the utter silence was uncanny.

When I got back to my wagon bed I heard some man in

the box next to me ask in a loud whisper for a chew of tobacco. While I had been getting my ammunition I asked a man named Phillips, who was also getting shells, if anyone had been shot. He shook his head and simply whispered, "Don't know." After I got back to my place I looked around and saw Captain Powell, who was in the second box west of me, with Sergeant Frank Hoover, and both of them were firing at some wounded Indians within sixty yards of the corral to the west.

Lieutenant John C. Jenness was leaning over the cover of the wagon bed at the west end of the corral, firing at some Indians on the northwest side, where they lay partially concealed under the brow of the hill where the land sloped down toward Big Piney valley. On the north side of the corral, in a very irregular form, the land on which we were encamped came to an abrupt termination, sloping down toward the Big Piney valley. The nearest point from the corral was probably seventy-five yards northwest, and extended a greater distance toward the east. It was behind this ridge where the Indians on foot had placed themselves in scores, all armed with rifles, and all one could see of them would be the two sticks across which they rested their guns. When they raised their heads to take aim we could see the single feather sticking up in their scalp-locks. It was these Indians who killed Lieutenant Jenness and Privates Doyle and Haggerty.

While watching Lieutenant Jenness I heard Sergeant McQuiery ask in a hoarse whisper if anyone had been killed or wounded. I answered that I did not know. The Indians, both mounted and on foot, were still trying to rescue their dead and wounded from the plain in front of us; and on the plain to the southeast a large body of Indians were signaling with pocket-mirrors toward the big ridge east of us, while couriers were observed riding furiously back and forth at break-neck speed, going and coming by way of Big Piney

Red Cloud and his wife. Courtesy of Capt. J. H. Cook, Agate, Neb.

valley. We did not know what to expect, but we knew they would attack us again soon. Something desperate had evidently been determined upon by the savages. All we could do was to wait and watch. Not a word was spoken. It was a moment of suspense that was simply terrible.

As we sat and waited for what we thought would be the finish of us, I looked along the wagon beds and saw my comrades sitting there watching the assembling of the Indians. Every man had his jaws firmly closed, with a grim determination to fight until we were overpowered. We did not know what time it was and nobody cared.

The fight had commenced about seven o'clock in the morning, and I did not hear any man ask about the time of day during the fight. Nearly all of us were bareheaded, as we had used our caps and hats to hold ammunition. The sun beat down with a pitiless glare that terrible August day, and it seemed like eternity to us all.

Suddenly someone on the northside of the corral yelled, "Look out! they're coming again!" We could see the Indians to the east, south and southwest of us galloping about and circling toward us, coming nearer and nearer. All at once some soldier shouted in a loud voice: "The tents!"

The line of tents were in front of us on the south side and had been left standing all the time of the first fierce charge, and we had simply fired through the spaces between them. No one had thought of pulling them down until that moment. Then two men leaped out of a wagon bed to the east of us, ran toward the tents but a short distance away, and began pulling them to the ground.

At this moment Private John Grady, who sat near me in my wagon bed, yelled: "Come on, kid!" As he leaped over the wagon bed I followed him, with the bullets zipping about us and the arrows swishing past and striking into the ground on all sides of us. We loosened the loops around the tent-pins at the corners, working together until all but the last of the tents dropped; and as Grady and I started toward the last one—an officer's tent, sixty or seventy feet in front of ours, to the south, we heard Sergeant Hoover shout: "Come back here! you'll get hit! Never mind the captain's tent! Get into your wagon box and shoot!" We dropped everything, and amid a perfect hail of balls and arrows rushed back and leaped over into our wagon beds again. How we escaped has been the mystery of my life, but neither of us were even hit.

With the tents down, we could see the Indians to much better advantage, and were enabled to deliver a more effective fire. The whole plain was again alive with countless swarms of the warriors, assembling for another grand charge upon us. Our fire was terribly destructive and deadly in accuracy, and we repulsed them again, but our gun-barrels were so overheated from the rapidity of our fire that the metal burned our hands, and we were obliged to open the breech-blocks during this lull to allow the barrels to cool off. During one of these momentary lulls Grady asked me to go after more ammunition. I crawled out of the wagon box westward, and saw several other men after more ammunition, and as I looked toward the west end I saw the body of Lieutenant Jenness lying where he had fallen, shot through the head and heart. Within a few feet of the corpse, Private Jim Condon was fighting behind a barrel of beans placed in the interval between Captain Powell's wagon bed and the one with a cover on.

Having secured the ammunition, I crawled back in my wagon bed. Here I told Sergeant McQuiery and Private Grady that Lieutenant Jenness had been killed, and of the manner in which he had apparently been shot. They both exclaimed: "Good God! Anyone else?" I answered that I did not know, and as the Indians were still making false charges toward us to recover their dead and wounded, we opened a desultory fire upon them.

About this time word was passed around that Privates

Henry Haggerty and Tommy Doyle had been killed on the north side of the corral. The brave little Jerseyman, Haggerty, had been shot through the left shoulder earlier in the fight, but the fact had been kept secret by the other men in the same wagon bed, lest some men become disheartened. The men in the box with Haggerty wanted him to lie down after getting shot through the shoulder, but with his left arm hanging useless at his side, he had used his good right, and kept on loading and firing for over two hours, until the Indians on the north ridge finally killed him by sending a bullet through the top of his head. Doyle had been killed some time after the first charge, while bravely fighting behind a breastwork of ox-yokes. He was struck in the forehead.

It was now becoming a question of water. Men were everywhere asking for it, and the supply was getting woefully scarce, and the suffering from the terrific heat and nervous strain was intense. Added to this, the Indians had rained fire-arrows inside the corral, which set fire to the dry manure within the enclosure, and the stench from this was abominable. I had filled my canteen in Little Piney Creek that morning and had brought it back to the corral on the retreat from the picket-post, so that we three in my wagon box had all the water we desired up to that time, and there was still some left. Grady took up the canteen and drank a mouthful, but immediately spat it out again, exclaiming that it was too hot for him. Sergeant McQuiery then washed out his mouth with some, remarking: "It is pretty warm, but water is too precious to waste just now."

Soon after this Sergeant Robertson started crawling on his hands and knees, coming from the east end of the corral toward the west end, poking aside with his head the arrows that were sticking up in the ground. When he arrived at the place where the body of Lieutenant Jenness was lying, he placed a wagon cover over it, and then returned to his wagon bed at the east end of the corral.

There was a barrel half full of water standing outside the corral at the west end when the fighting began. It was about twenty feet away from the wagon beds. During the fighting it had been struck by bullets and the water had nearly all leaked out. Under the covered wagon, close to the west end of the corral, were two camp kettles in which our coffee had been made for breakfast, and Brown, the cook, had filled them with water on top of the old coffee grounds, intending to use the coffee for the company supper. Private Jim Condon had seen the water leaking from the barrel, and had passed the word around the corral that the barrel was empty, or nearly so. Then Cook Brown volunteered the information that the camp kettles had been filled with water, and as they were but a short distance away, we immediately planned to secure them.

My comrade, Johnny Grady, who sat next to me in our wagon bed, was crazy for water. He said: "Kid, let's go get one of those kettles." I replied, "All right." We took a careful look about and then commenced crawling on our stomachs through the arrows that lined the corral, and as we reached the wagon bed with the cover on at the west end, Jim Condon, from behind the barrel of beans where he was fighting, cautioned us to be on the lookout or the Indians would get us sure.

The men on the north side seemed to divine our purpose, and word was passed along to keep up a steady fire on the Indians along the ridge. We crawled through the opening between the wagon beds, hugging the ground as closely as possible, and soon reached the place where the kettles stood without having apparently been detected. We each grabbed a kettle and then commenced crawling back, pulling the kettles along. We had gotten about half-way to safety, when "bang! bang! bang!" came several shots from the Indians to the north of us, and "z-zip! p-i-n-g-g-g!" we heard some of the bullets strike the kettles, but fortunately without injuring us. We both thought our time had come, but we finally got back inside the corral with those kettles of dirty black water. When I looked at mine, there were two holes clean through it, and consequently I had lost some of the water, but we left them both with Private Condon, who gave each man a good drink when he crawled out of his wagon box for it.

The time between each charge dragged heavily, and the day seemed almost endless. Yet, the Indians on the north side of us, hidden under the ridge, kept us constantly on the alert, and some of them at the east end of the ridge, about two hundred yards from the east side of the corral, would run out toward us once in a while, armed with spears and tomahawks, each carrying a big shield made of buffalo-hide. There they would brandish their weapons in a menacing manner and utter shrill war cries. There was one big giant of an Indian who had thus run out several times from the ridge to the east, and he always managed to escape our fire, until he apparently thought he bore a charmed life, and that we could not kill him. He was truly a magnificent specimen of Indian manhood, nearly seven feet tall and almost wholly naked. He had led all of the previous charges from the east end of the ridge, and must have been a subchief. The last time he appeared must have been about two o'clock in the afternoon, and this time he came out slowly but grandly, with his big buffalo shield in front of him, brandishing his spear and chanting a war-song. Then he would hold his shield on one side and run toward us, jumping into the air and alternating this movement by dodging to one side. The sight was fascinating, and we could not but admire his superb courage. Several of us had fired at him but without effect, when one of the boys at the east end remarked: "We have simply got to get that fellow, as he thinks we can't hit him." We carefully adjusted our sights, taking accurate aim, and just as he shifted his shield aside and began running toward us, we fired together, and he leaped into the air and came

The late Frederic Claus, one of the defenders of the Wagon Box corral.
1917 photo.

down as limp as a rag, fairly riddled with bullets. We all breathed easier after this warrior was killed, for his death seemed to put a stop to any more charges from that direction.

The Indians had withdrawn out of range, except those concealed under the brow of the ridge on the north side. These would take a shot at us every few minutes. The main body of Indians was around the big hill at the end of the ridge east of us, where Red Cloud was stationed in supreme command, and we could plainly hear him or some other chief haranguing them in a loud voice. Presently a great number of Indians rode down the Big Piney valley out of sight. Another party, several hundred in number, rode out on the plain toward us, evidently for another charge. We all knew that they had lost scores of their braves in killed and wounded, and in their maddened frenzy would make another attempt to overwhelm us by force of superior numbers, and would take horrible revenge upon us if they captured us.

It must have been after three o'clock in the afternoon when, straining our eyes for the sight of that line of skirmishers in the glorious blue uniform (which appeared later) we could distinctly hear a sort of humming sound, seemingly made by many voices, below us in the Big Piney valley. Some of us thought it was the squaws wailing over their dead warriors, and as the sound grew louder some of the men on the north side of the corral rose to their feet to see if they could discern anything below them in the Big Piney valley, but they had no sooner risen to their feet than others yelled at them, "Down, down, or you will get hit!"

As we waited in silent wonderment at this strange sound, unlike anything we had ever head before, the echo appeared to come from the northwest of the corral. The Indians to the east and south of us had come out on the plain, where they were circling and coming nearer all the time, brandishing their spears and war clubs at us and giving voice to their war cries. Those of the warriors who were armed with guns immediately opened fire again upon us, and we at once replied, killing and wounding many more of them. During this time, that awful humming, chanting sound grew in volume and intensity, coming nearer and nearer, now directly from west of us. The Indians to the south had withdrawn out of range, and seemed to be waiting for something to happen.

And something did happen! Suddenly there was a cry from the west end of the corral: "Here they come! We all looked in that direction, and saw a sight which none of those yet alive will ever forget to their dying day. It chilled my blood at the time. We saw the naked bodies of hundreds upon hundreds of Indians swarming up a ravine about ninety yards to the west of the corral. They were all on foot, formed in the shape of a letter V, or wedge, and were led by Red Cloud's nephew, who wore a gorgeous war bonnet. Immediately we opened a terrific fire upon them, under which nothing could stand, and at the very first volley Red Cloud's nephew fell, pierced by many bullets. Nothing daunted, the forces came on slowly, and in great numbers, the places of those who fell under our fire being taken immediately by others.

So close were the Indian hordes by this time that the heavy rifle bullets from our guns must have gone through two or three bodies. They were so near us that we could even see the whites of their eyes. As they swarmed toward us with shrill cries and piercing whoops, Private Jim Condon jumped to his feet from behind his barrel of beans, and shouted, as he waved his rifle over his head: "Come in, you blatherin' sons av guns! We kin lick th' hull damn bunch av yez!" Captain Powell, who was close by Condon, at once ordered him to lie down.

And now the Indians were so close that it seemed as if nothing could prevent their swarming over our barricade and into the corral, when it would have been all over with us in no time. Our fire was accurate, coolly delivered and given with most telling effort, but nevertheless it looked for a minute as though our last moment on earth had come. Just when it seemed as if all hope was gone, the Indians suddenly broke and fled. They could not stand before the withering fire we poured into their ranks. The several hundred mounted Indians, on the plain to the south of us, who were intently watching this foot-charge, never offered to assist their red brothers by making a mounted charge, but discreetly remained out of rifle range.

During those charges against our corral, Red Cloud who was in supreme command, stood (or sat on his horse) on top of the ridge due east of our little improvised fort. Some of the boys estimated it to be three-quarters of a mile away. After this last charge of the Indians on foot from the west, and while we were waiting to see what the red devils would try next, some six or eight of us elevated the sights on our rifles to the full extension of long range firing, and let loose five or six volleys at Red Cloud and his crowd on top of the hill, and we all fully believed, from the sudden scattering of Indians, that some of our bullets found lodgment and made "good Injuns" of some of them.

Suddenly the Indians on the big hill at the top of the ridge started down the steep decline into Big Piney valley by twos, threes and fours. We took a few long range shots at them, which served to accelerate their speed very effectively. We did not understand this maneuver for a few minutes.

Just then someone at the east end of the corral cried out: "Hark! did you hear that?" Everybody ceased firing, and in another moment we distinctly heard the boom of a big gun to the east of us. It was indeed heavenly music to all of us. It was the sorely needed relief from Fort Phil Kearny. They had heard the sounds of battle and started reinforcements, with a howitzer, to our succor. It was this big gun that was driving the savages off the big hill. The Indians on the plain south of us could also be seen disappearing into the pinery to the west. We knew what the commotion meant, but waited, with nerves and senses wrought almost to a frenzy. Suddenly one of the men jumped to his feet, shouting: "Here they come, boys! Hurrah!" and as we looked toward the east we could see those glorious old McClelland caps on the heads of our comrades as they appeared in a long skirmish line.

Then we all jumped to our feet and yelled. We threw our

caps in the air. We hugged each other in the ecstacy of our joy. We laughed, cried and fairly sobbed like little children in the delirium of our delight. The awful strain was over.

Captain Powell suddenly ordered everybody back into the wagon beds, lest another charge be made by the Indians before our rescuers should reach us. We obediently returned to our places, and sat watching the skirmish line advancing, while the boom of the big gun was the sweetest sound that ever fell on our ears. The gunners were throwing shells into a big bunch of Indians in the Big Piney valley.

The redskins began scattering rapidly across Big Piney Creek and were soon out of range. The skirmish line continued to advance, and in a few minutes we saw the main body marching in front of a small wagon train of ten or twelve six-mule teams of empty ambulances and wagons, with the big brass cannon in front of the team.

By this time everybody was talking and waving their arms as we recognized well known comrades from the fort. We recognized Major Smith as in command of the rescue party, and also our genial post surgeon, Dr. Samuel M. Horton, and when they arrived within two hundreds yards of us we ran out to meet them, and such a shaking of hands as there was. The first question he asked us was, "Who's hit? Who's killed—or wounded?" Our rescuers told us they had not expected to find a man of us alive.

Dr. Horton—God bless him!—for he was always so kind and considerate of every man, woman and child at the post. had his ambulance driven near to the west end of the corral, and with the consent of Captain Powell he gave every man— soldier and civilian—a big drink of whiskey out of a small keg which he had brought along.

Then we tenderly laid the body of Lieutenant Jenness in the ambulance, and the bodies of Doyle and Haggerty in one of the wagons, and having packed our tentage, bedding and rations in the empty wagons, marched back to the fort. When we arrived at the big hill at the west end of the ridge east of the corral, we halted, and as we looked back up Big Piney valley, we saw a long train of Indian ponies, three and four deep and fully a quarter of a mile long. They were carrying off their dead and wounded.

As we approached the commanding officer's quarters, he stepped from the house and halted us. We came to attention and the general removed his cap and complimented Captain Powell and all of us for our splendid victory against such overwhelming odds. He furthermore added that we had displayed such heroic courage and bravery that he would recommend every one of us for a medal of honor. The recommendation was made, but for some reason none of us ever received the medal.

As to the number of Indians killed in the fight, that is a hard question to answer. Captain Powell, in his official report, estimated the Indian loss at over three hundred killed and wounded, but we—the men of Company C—estimated that there must have been seven or eight hundred killed and wounded. The late General Grenville M. Dodge said that about thirty years ago, in an interview with Chief Red Cloud at Pine Ridge Reservation, the chief placed the total loss of the Sioux, Cheyennes and Arapahoes at over eleven hundred in killed and wounded. It was utterly impossible to keep any account of the individual Indians each man saw fall, because as fast as an Indian dropped, others would ride up and carry him away. Chief Rain-in-the-Face told me at Standing Rock agency in 1895, through an interpreter, that he did not care to talk about the Wagon Box Fight.

I have served in the army forty-eight years, taking active part in the Sioux campaign of 1876 and also in the Wounded Knee campaign of 1890-'91 at Pine Ridge agency, but never before or since have my nerves ever been put to the test they sustained on that terrible 2d of August, 1867, when we fought Red Cloud's warriors in the wagon box corral.

CHAPTER III

~

THE ISLAND OF DEATH

*How "Forsyth's Scouts" Fought the Cheyennes
at Beecher Island*

~

ON the afternoon of September 16, 1868, a heavily-armed body of 50 picked frontiersmen rode through a little ravine, which debouched into a valley some two miles wide and about the same in length, in what today is Yuma county, Colorado. A little stream known as the Arickaree fork of the Republican river wound its way through this valley, and on the south bank of the stream, about 4 o'clock that day, the plainsmen went into camp.

The leader of this bold and fearless band was a dauntless and dashing cavalryman who had distinguished himself during the Civil war—George Alexander Forsyth, commonly known among his friends as "Sandy" Forsyth. He had been an aide-de-camp of General Phil Sheridan, and was one of the two officers who made that thrilling ride with Sheridan when the latter saved the day at the battle of Winchester.

In 1868 the Cheyennes, Arapahoes, Sioux and Kiowas were devastating western Kansas, and from the middle of August until November the hostiles attacked over forty widely-separated places, in nearly every instance killing the settlers, burning cabins and stealing stock. The Indians were wild with rage over the progression of the Kansas-Pacific railroad through their hunting grounds, and time and again they had wiped out the different section gangs which were operating. But the building of the line continued, nevertheless.

"Sandy" Forsyth had been wanting to take the field in person against the hostiles, and finally General Sheridan acceded to his importunities by authorizing him to raise a company of fifty citizen scouts who were to go out against the Indians.

The company was organized the latter part of August. Scores of able frontiersmen offered their services, and from the number Forsyth selected his men—twenty being from Fort Hays and the remaining thirty from Fort Harker. The men were, of necessity, carried on the payrolls as quarter-masters' employes, as there was no government provision for the employment of scouts or civilian auxiliaries.

As officers to assist Forsyth were Lieut. Frederick H. Beecher, a nephew of the great Henry Ward Beecher, the noted divine, and First Sergeant W. H. H. McCall. The chief guide of the party was Abner Sharp Grover, one of the greatest frontiersmen of those days. The surgeon of the command was a Dr. John H. Mooers of Hays City, who was in private practice at that place, but who, when he learned of the organization of the scouts, volunteered his services. It took Forsyth just five days to pick his men and start on the march.

About the time the company reached its complement Forsyth received word from General Sheridan that a band of hostiles had begun depredations near Sheridan City, one of those mushroom towns along the line of the railroad, and a few days later another band appeared near Fort Hays and stole some horses. Forsyth was ordered to "get" these marauders.

Forsyth's command scouted the country for six days and finally struck a well-defined trail which grew warmer and larger as it was followed. It was plainly evident that the Indian force was large, and would greatly outnumber that of the scouts, but Forsyth had come out for a fight and was determined to have one, and so the command pressed on.

When they entered the little valley of the Arickaree on that hot September afternoon, the men were weary with hard riding, and the horses were sadly in need of rest. The grazing was most excellent and the scouts were hoping for a few hours' of recuperation.

Grover, the guide, had been making mental calculations from the Indian trail as to the probable number, and when questioned by Forsyth said:

"Countin' 'em as men, women and kids, I should say nigh onto four thousand, and that means we got to face purty close to 1,500 warriors."

Upon learning this, Forsyth had halted the command and explained the circumstances. They were right at the heels of an enemy that outnumbered them twenty to one. If anyone wanted to turn back, now was the time to do it. But not a man faltered. They had come prepared to follow their nervy commander wherever he chose to lead.

The scouts made camp forty or fifty yards back from the stream, which was bordered with thickets of alder, wild plum and willow. The bed of the river at this point was perhaps 140 yards wide. On the side where the command camped the land made a gentle incline down to the stream, while on the north it stretched away in a level expanse for nearly a mile, where the valley abruptly ended against a line of high bluffs. In the middle of the stream was a little island which arose a couple of feet above the shallow water. It was covered with a thick growth of stunted bushes, alders and willow at the upper end, while at the lower end it sloped away to the water's edge, and here stood a solitary cottonwood tree. As there had been but little rain for some time. the river bed for the most part was hard and dry, but for a space of a few feet on either side of the island the water languidly moved along at a depth of not over a foot. The banks of the river bed on either side commanded the island.

Preparations for the night were soon made. Forsyth personally saw to the making of the camp and posted the sentries. Every man was directed to hobble his horse and drive the picket-pin firmly into the ground, so that in case of a surprise by the Indians there would be no stampeding of the horses. In the event of a surprise every man was directed to seize his lariat with one hand, rifle with the other, and stand ready for orders.

Forsyth remained awake through the night, making the rounds as though he feared trouble. As the command was entirely alone and in the very heart of a hostile Indian country where white men had hardly before ever penetrated, and moreover was in close proximity to the enemy and liable to be attacked at any moment, it is little wonder that the intrepid commander used the utmost caution.

Shortly before daylight the command was aroused by a single rifle shot. Springing to their feet the scouts saw Forsyth, rifle in hand, peering up the southern bank of the stream, and instantly he shouted:

"Up men! The Cheyennes are upon us!"

*   *   *   *   *

At this point we turn to the thrilling story of "The Battle of Beecher Island," on the Arickaree Fork of the Republican river, as related by "Sandy" Forsyth's youngest scout, Sigmund Schlesinger, to the author.

SCOUT SHLESINGER'S STORY

Well, there I was, "Sig" Shlesinger, a friendless, seventeen-year-old boy, knocking around the Western Kansas army post of Fort Hays all my spare time during that summer of 1868. I was glad enough to get acquainted with some of the Government scouts, and listen to their tales of Indians and Indian fighting.

If I hadn't been too proud to let my father know of my misfortune, I'd probably have been back in my comfortable home in New York city

S. Shlesinger, youngest member of "Forsyth's Scouts," whose story is here recounted.

But my father had objected to my going west at sixteen to work for a merchant from Leavenworth, Kansas, who had taken a fancy to me while he was on a business trip to New York, and offered me employment. To be sure, the merchant and I had finally obtained my father's reluctant consent to my going; but when, after I had been working for some time in Leavenworth, my friend and employer had been suddenly killed in an accident, I had been too proud to tell my father that I no longer had a job.

Yet, I had to live. The Union Pacific railroad was then being built across the Plains. Hoping to find work, I had joined the wild throngs drifting toward the frontier along the surveyed line of proposed track.

I had moved along with the human tide—not a friend in all that motley crowd of rough-talking, pistol-toting flotsam and jetsam.

How had I managed? By tackling any and every job thrown my way—acting as waiter in a tent hotel, shoveling on the railroad, cooking for teamsters, night-herding mules, driving team to and from a stone quarry.

So I had moved along—westward, ever westward, until I found myself one day in Hays City. There I turned to peddling newspapers for a living.

And one of my newspaper customers was Gen. George A. Custer, out at Fort Hays, which was about a half mile from the little frontier town of Hays City. Custer was a live wire, and the Seventh Cavalry the idol of the frontier.

You can see why I hung around the army post all my spare time, and you can guess how glad I was to get acquainted with those scouts, who seemed to take a friendly interest in a lonesome boy. I listened eagerly to the tales of hair-breadth escapes, and occasionally they allowed me to accompany them when they were carrying dispatches. I was in my glory on such occasions.

And then, like a bolt from the heavens came the dire news that the Cheyennes had taken to the warpath, and were sweeping through Western Kansas like a whirlwind, leaving death and desolation in their wake.

"Heered the news, fellers?" asked Sharp Grover, one of the more experienced of the post scouts, speaking to a bunch of hangers-on in the post trader's store one morning in late

August. "Colonel Sandy Forsyth is oarganizin' a comp'ny of fifty men to go out an' sock it to them 'ere murderin' Cheyennes. Why, they killed eighty-four settlers jes' last month!"

"Who's a-goin' with Forsyth from here?" inquired one of the store clerks.

"Sez he'll take anybuddy that's got a hoss—an' the required amount of nerve. He sez the men usin' their own hosses'll draw seventy-five dollars a month, an' them what the Guv'ment has to furnish mounts fer will git fifty dollars."

"You goin', Sharp?"

"Reck'n I am. Jest been asked by the Colonel to go as his guide. I want to git a crack at them Cheyennes myself."

"Who's the other officers besides the Colonel?"

"Why, I heered that Lef'tenant Fred Beecher and a feller named McCall was the only other officers. You know Beecher —nephy to that 'ere famous sky-pilot, Henry Ward Beecher in New York. Right smart army man, Beecher is. And Doc Mooers, over town is goin' along as surgeon. Sez he wants a leetle excitement."

"Well, he's likely to git it a-plenty," observed a lounger. "None o' that fer ME! I ain't lost no Cheyennes."

"What's the show of joinin' Forsyth?" inquired another man.

"Well, he got thirty men over at Fort Harker, an' figgers on gittin' enough here to make up his fifty. I reck'n they's a good chance right now, if you want to join."

Here was my opportunity! A chance to see the most adventurous side of Western frontier life. I wondered if I would stand a chance of being accepted by Forsyth. I determined to find out at once.

"Where is Colonel Forsyth?" I casually inquired of Grover.

"Reck'n you'll find him over thar at headquarters right now. Whadda *you* want t' know fer, kid? Goin' to enlist?" and Grover guffawed.

My face grew hot, but I didn't answer. Presently, when

Grover got absorbed in conversation, I slid out the door and streaked it for post headquarters.

The commandant's orderly directed me to a room where he said Colonel Forsyth was receiving the enlistments for frontier scouting. Shyly I elbowed my way inside. Colonel Forsyth was pointed out to me at a desk, in conversation with several men, evidently also bent on enlisting. At length he was at liberty, so I approached and made known my wants.

"Why boy, you're not old enough," smiled the Colonel. "This sort of campaigning calls for experienced frontiersmen. What could *you* do in an Indian fight?"

I assumed a bold front. "I'll do as well as any man in your command," I exclaimed. "Besides, I'm out of work, and there's nothing to do here. I can shoot, and I can ride—ask Mr. Parr. Here he is right now, just coming in."

"What do you know about this youngster, Parr?" and Colonel Forsyth turned to that individual, one of the older of the post scouts.

"Why, the kid has done quite a bit of ridin' 'round with some of us post scouts, Colonel," volunteered Parr. "I think he'll make good. If you want to take him along I'll let him have one of my hosses—fer twenty-five dollars a month, to be deducted from his pay."

"Well," mused the Colonel, stroking his chin meditatively, "I'm in a hurry to get away, and want to make up my quota within another twenty-four hours," and then, turning to me he added, "All right, my lad, I'll take you—but remember one thing—there'll be no backing out after we get away from here."

"Huh, he'll be a-hollerin' for his ma at the first sight of a redskin," sneered a rough mule-skinner. "The idee o' takein a kid like that—huh!"

I wanted to make a sharp retort, but swallowed my wrath.

"Report here day after tomorrow," ordered Colonel Forsyth, after I had signed the muster rolls.

I walked out of the room on air! I was filled with enthusiasm over the expected adventure—probably because I did not know what was coming.

That afternoon as I was sauntering restlessly about the post, a boy a year or so older than I, spoke to me. He said his name was Jack Stilwell, and that he, too, had joined Forsyth's Scouts. He had seen me talking to Colonel Forsyth, and understood that I was going with him.

"Yes, I am," I admitted. "Have you had any experience in Indian campaigning?"

"Well, not much," he replied, "but I've been knocking around on the Plains for the last three years, and am pretty well used to roughing it. I'm glad you are going. You and I are the only kids in the bunch, I understand, and we'll have to stick together. Come on over to my hang-out for awhile."

I was glad of the chance to become better acquainted with Stilwell, for I liked his looks. We went over to his quarters, and I helped him sew a collar on a buckskin shirt he was going to wear on the expedition.

"We're likely to see some pretty hot work before we get back," volunteered Jack. "The Cheyennes are raising the very mischief over in the Saline and Solomon River valleys."

After some further discussion I left to get my own outfit in shape.

Early on the morning of the second day, we all assembled at Colonel Forsyth's headquarters. There were men from all walks of life, many of whom, like myself, were out of work, and ready to tackle anything that promised to keep them in rations, and give them a little extra money.

The full complement of fifty men had been raised. Each was fitted out with a horse, saddle, bridle, haversack, canteen, blanket, knife, tin cup, a Spencer seven-shot carbine, and a heavy Colt revolver. We had a baggage train of four mules loaded with rations, extra ammunition and surgical supplies, but carried no tents or like equippage.

"Now, men," announced Colonel Forsyth, as we stood at

attention, "we're going to start in a northwesterly direction, and see if we can strike any war parties. Now, remember—this is no Sunday school picnic you are going on; so if any man here feels that he isn't going to be able to stand the gaff, now's the time to speak up."

Feb'y 4'/20

To whom it may Concern:—

The story of the Indian fight at Beecher Island as given by me to E. A. Brininstool for publication is strictly in accordance with the facts as they came under my observation while we were fighting for our lives against overwhelming numbers

S. Shlesinger

Shlesinger affidavit authenticating his article.

Silence followed this little speech. Nobody cared to back down at that stage of the game—and so we were off.

We traveled all day, going into camp on the Saline river late that night. I was simply "all in" when we went into camp, though Jack Stilwell had ridden through the day with the ease of a seasoned campaigner.

Too tired to eat any supper, I threw myself on the ground for a rest; but I was soon detailed for guard duty. I must confess that I had no sooner been directed to my post than I dropped exhausted on the ground, and fell asleep. Had there been a thousand Indians near, they could have sneaked past me into camp without difficulty. Fortunately, I awoke before my relief came, and so escaped censure.

"You'll get hardened to things in a few days," grinned young Stilwell, as with many groans I clambered awkwardly into my saddle that next morning. "Keep a stiff upper lip, kid," urged Jack.

For several days we scouted the country without detecting any Indian signs. But about the fifth day Grover, who had been riding some distance in advance, came galloping hastily back to the command.

"Colonel, I've found a fresh trail!" he exclaimed. "Big party, sure as shootin'."

"How many?" demanded Colonel Forsyth.

"Nigh onto fifty, I reck'n; draggin' plenty of tepee poles; trail ain't more'n a day old."

Grover turned his horse and the entire command rode swiftly forward.

Sure enough, there was a fresh trail!

"What do you think of it, Farley?" queried the Colonel, turning to Lewis Farley, the oldest man in the command, and accounted the best shot among them. "You should be able to give a pretty good estimate as to their number."

Farley dismounted and scanned the ground with the practiced eye of a veteran plainsman.

"Sharp ain't very fur wrong," he finally remarked. "Only I think thar's more'n fifty of 'em—nearer a hundred, if I'm any judge. Lots o' ponies along with that 'ere bunch, too. They've got their families with 'em, too, or they wouldn't be draggin' so many tepee poles. That means it ain't a reg'lar war party."

"All right—lead ahead, Grover," commanded the Colonel.

Half a mile further Grover was seen to rein in his horse sharply and scan the ground.

"Another trail right here leadin' into this one from the east," he exclaimed as we rode up. "That first party has been joined here by all of twenty-five others. Thar's some deviltry afoot, you can gamble on that!"

"Looks to me like all the Injuns have started out on a general raid," commented George Culver.

"I don't exactly agree with you, Culver," spoke up old man Farley. "Injuns don't have their families along when it's a war party."

"Maybe they're just out on a big buffalo hunt, dad," suggested "Hutch" Farley, son of the veteran frontiersman.

"Well, whatever it means, we're here to find out," announced Colonel Forsyth. "Lieutenant Beecher—and you, McCall and Farley, I'd like to have you ride in advance with Grover and myself. Keep pretty well together, men," he warned, turning in his saddle. "No knowing how soon the ball will open."

With every nerve keyed to the highest pitch, we rode steadily along the trail. Another mile, and a trail from the west entered.

"There's a hundred head of ponies in that there trail," declared Lewis Farley, after he and Grover had studied the tracks. "It's my opinion that these Injuns have an understanding to meet some'rs not more'n fifty miles from here, for some sort of a pow-wow."

Grover nodded approval. "We're goin' to bump into that gang afore another twenty-four hours," he soberly announced, "and we'll have a big fight on our hands."

"Jack," I asked Stilwell in a low tone, "do you really think we're going to have a big fight?"

Stilwell looked steadily at me. "Anything that old man Farley or Sharp Grover tells you, you can bank on," he replied. "Why?—Are you getting scared?"

"W-e-l-l, I don't know as it's exactly that," I remarked. "I'll try to keep my end up if it comes to a show-down."

"That's the way to talk, Sig," Jack exclaimed. "Keep a stiff upper lip. We've got a lot of good fighters in this bunch, and we can make it mighty hot for any bunch of Indians we run into."

No fires were lighted that day when we stopped for noon lunch. Each man hastily swallowed a cold bite, and we were again in the saddle.

As the afternoon advanced, other trails began leading into the main trail until it resembled a broad and well-beaten highway; and Grover and old man Farley agreed that there were not less than five hundred Indians ahead of us. Those of the party possessing field glasses were continually scanning the country. Colonel Forsyth, Grover, Farley and McCall, from behind every hillock and knoll, first carefully inspected the country ahead before allowing the command to move up.

We were a sober crowd. All joking and bantering had ceased, and we talked only in low, guarded tones.

The trail we were now following finally led up the broad valley of a little stream known as the Arickaree Fork of the Republican River. At that season of the year, the water was low, and flowed in a sickly, slow-moving current, and there were sand bars and gravelly shoals in plenty.

It was mid-afternoon on the 16th of September. Our horses were jaded from long and hard riding, and about four o'clock Colonel Forsyth ordered a halt.

"We'll go into camp right here, men," he ordered. "It looks liks good grazing hereabout, and we've had a pretty strenuous day of it."

We were on the south bank of the Arickaree. Camp was made opposite a flat plateau that formed a small island by the overflowing of the stream in flood season. But a few inches of water meandered past, and the stream divided at the upper end of the tiny island, and rippled smoothly by on each side, until it again entered the main stream, perhaps a hundred yards below.

Danger seemed hovering near. Jack Stilwell smiled grimly when I told him that I could almost feel arrows sticking in my back, and a scalping-knife encircling my head.

"See here, Sig," he exclaimed, as we were picketing our

horses, "there ain't no question but that we're marching right into a hornet's nest, but keep your nerve. This ain't no tenderfoot outfit, aside from you. Sharp Grover is the best plainsman in this region, and old man Farley ain't a whit behind him. Don't ask any fool questions, but pin back your ears and listen when you hear them two say anything."

Our supper was eaten in silence, while strong pickets were posted to guard against surprise. We did not know it then, but that was the last meal we were to have for many a weary day. As I watched the purple twilight tinge those low Colorado hills, and the evening shadows deepen, I wondered what my parents in far-away New York would have thought, could they have known what I faced.

I rested but fitfully. Jack Stilwell slumbered heavily at my side, but Jack was not new to the dangers of the Western Plains, and sleep, to him, came easily.

Colonel Forsyth himself took no rest, but all through the night noiselessly passed from picket to picket, cautioning in whispers the utmost vigilance. And twice during the night I saw him talking with old man Farley.

We later learned, from some of the Cheyennes, that for over forty-eight hours their keen-eyed scouts had been watching our every movement. They had noted the strength of our little command, and had kept just far enough in our advance to invite pursuit, with the expectation that an opportune moment might come when they could turn and strike a crippling blow.

And it developed that had we continued to advance but a short half-mile farther we would have fallen into an ambush so cunningly devised, so ingeniously prepared, and so favored by the topographical formation of the country, that probably not a man jack of us would have escaped! But a watchful Providence spared us from Indian wrath at that time.

The first faint flush of dawn was tinging the eastern sky, when Colonel Forsyth who stood talking with one of the sentries, his keen eyes roving hither and yon, discerned silhouetted against the skyline, the feathered war bonnet of a hostile Cheyenne.

"Quick, Alderdice, let him have it!" exclaimed the Colonel, at the same time grabbing his own rifle and letting drive a shot.

As the "bang! bang!" of the cavalry carbines echoed through the camp, and up and down the valley of the Arickaree, the whoops of a party of the savages brought every man to his feet. Like a whirlwind the Indians scudded toward our horse herd, yelling as only savages can yell, rattling dry hides and ringing bells in an endeavor to stampede the animals and set us afoot! Some of the pack mules, loosely picketed, broke away and galloped off, but the picket pins of the others held. The little party of Indians disappeared in the gray of approaching dawn on the trail of the stampeded mules.

"Run in those horses and saddle up—quick!" shouted Colonel Forsyth. "And stand by, ready for action!"

Just then Jack Stilwell stood at my side. "Well, kid, they're here—our Indian friends," he coolly observed as we awaited further orders.

I nodded—but I WAS scared!

Scarcely had our little command assembled, ready for action, when Sharp Grover uttered an exclamation of alarm, and grasping Colonel Forsyth by the arm he pointed down the valley. "My God, Colonel, LOOK—jest LOOK at the Injuns!"

The morning sun, just beginning to lighten surrounding objects, revealed a sight that few men have looked upon and lived to record it.

As suddenly as if the very hillside rocks had been transformed into human beings, out from the tall grass across the rippling Arickaree, swarming down the slopes in our rear, springing from the little hollows, and advancing in hordes

upon us from every direction, came Indians in massed formation—hundreds upon hundreds—both on foot and pony-back.
We were trapped! Every avenue of escape seemed closed!

"JACK!" I exclaimed as I gasped the words, "It's all over
with us now!"

We were facing death in its most hideous and awful form!

But nothing could shake Colonel Forsyth's courage and
coolness. Turning to Grover he camly remarked, "Well,
Sharp, we've run our heads into a noose—eh?"

Site of the Beecher Island fight. In 1868 the Arickaree divided, forming
a small island where the trees and marker are shown. Photo by
Brininstool, 1917.

Before Grover could reply, young Jack Stilwell exclaimed:
"LOOK, Colonel—the Indians have overlooked that little
island. We can stand 'em off there!"

"By the Mighty, boy, that's a bright idee," exclaimed
Grover.

"It's our only chance," seconded old man Farley.

"To the island, men," shouted Forsyth. "QUICK! Don't leave an animal behind!"

Before the Indians could comprehend our move, we were dashing madly through the shallow Arickaree. Not one of the riding animals had been left behind; but the pack-mules were gone, and we had no time to think about the rations and surgical supplies. All these fell into the hands of the Indians, and the lack of them later caused untold suffering and agony.

We gained the little island without the loss of a single animal or man. Here Colonel Forsyth gave sharp, hurried commands.

"Fasten the horses to the bushes, men—they'll all undoubtedly be shot down anyway. Form a circle, and get under cover quickly! We'll have to dig in for our lives!"

Like fiends we fell to, while some of the best shots were hastily ordered to points of vantage to cover this work. There was nothing but our hands and the knives at our belts with which to work, but the soil was soft, loose sand, and the light sod was easy to cut. Kicking with toes and heels, and working with knives and hands, we soon had shallow holes that afforded us slight shelter.

The Indians were plainly filled with disgust and anger at their failure to take possession of the island themselves. Their rage expressed itself in wild, blood-curdling whoops and yells. We could see their chiefs riding furiously about, giving sharp orders, and disposing of their warriors at every vantage point, making instant preparation for attack.

"Don't fire a shot until I give the order!" Colonel Forsyth commanded. "Keep cool, lie low, and make every shot count!"

"It's old Roman Nose's outfit, Colonel," I overheard Sharp Grover announce. "Them's the Northern Cheyennes he's got there—six or eight hundred of 'em. See—they are gettin' the women and kids away out of rifle-shot on them hills to the south. We ain't goin' to have long to wait fer the ball to open!"

Jack Stilwell and I were, as usual, side by side. The remarkable coolness of this eighteen-year-old youth was mighty comforting to me. He patted the top sods of the little trench with the stock of his carbine.

"There, by hokey!" he exclaimed. "NOW, Mister Roman Nose and all the rest of you, come right ahead, and we'll give you the darndest lickin' you ever had! Keep your grit, kid," he added turning for a look at my set face. "We ain't licked yet, by a long shot!"

I nodded feebly. Then I ran my eye over the balance of the command, waiting for the first charge from the savage foe. Carbine barrels were pushed across the sod tops of the hastily-constructed trenches, and triggers clicked as hammers were raised.

And then, with the fury of a prairie cyclone, with unearthly yells, with fluttering war bonnets nodding in the breeze, with the first rays of the morning sun shining on silvered bracelet, gleaming spear point and glistening ornament, there came the thudding of hundreds upon hundreds of pony hoofs that seemed to shake the very earth, while piercing war cries echoed up and down the valley of the Arickaree! In front of this line of painted and war-bedecked foemen, the giant form of the great chieftain, Roman Nose, towered high. He sat his gaily-caparisoned mount with the grace of a Centaur, and shook his heavy, long-barreled rifle above his head as if it were a wisp of straw!

"STEADY!" roared Colonel Forsyth. "Not yet, men!" as several half arose from their trenches and threw their carbines forward.

Down the slopes and into the shallow stream poured the yelling savages, every mother's son of them quirting his pony at every jump, and every moccasined heel drumming at heaving flanks. Now they were a hundred yards away—now fifty —twenty-five—

"NOW!" shouted Forsyth. "NOW!" echoed Lieutenant Beecher.

Out from our sod-lined sandy shallows boomed billows of death into the painted, pony-riding hordes. Horses fell, screaming; and as the levers of our Spencers clicked back and forth, naked bodies swayed and toppled to earth.

No living thing could withstand such a seething hell of flame and lead! With wild cries of rage, the onrushing savages broke at the edge of the island, deflecting to each side and passed like a tornado!

"Mighty pretty work, kid!" shouted Jack Stilwell into my ear. I nodded. I was nerved now, and no longer did my hands tremble. The first shock of battle seemed to have suddenly transformed me into a man, cool, courageous, alert.

"Can they do better than that, Sharp?" called out Colonel Forsyth in anxious tones.

"I've been on the Plains, man an' boy, fer the last twenty year, Colonel, an' I never saw a more des'prit charge, ner one so well met," was the reply of the old scout.

"All right then," nodded the Colonel. "I guess we are going to be able to stand them off."

But that first charge had by no means left the command unscathed. Our devoted surgeon, Dr. Mooers, had received a ball in the brain, and never spoke another rational word, although he lived three days.

And now Lieutenant Beecher dragged himself painfully to Forsyth's side, as he exclaimed between gasps, "I've got my death wound, Colonel."

"Oh, it can't be that bad, Beecher," exclaimed Forsyth in distressed tones. "Where are you hit?"

"Right here in the side—no use—I'm dying—goodnight—" and our brave lieutenant stretched himself out at Forsyth's side, face downward on his arm, murmuring, "My poor, poor mother!" He soon lapsed into unconsciousness, and so remained until sundown, when death relieved his suffering.

During the first breathing spell, while the savages were congregating again for another onslaught, we dug, with feverish haste, deeper into the loose sand.

"I'm going to get old Roman Nose next time," muttered Stilwell, refilling the magazine of his carbine "Let's both fire at him together. If we can just knock out that chief, we will be pretty apt to discourage the whole gang."

"I'm with you, Jack," I nodded.

Shrieks and wails were echoing from the bluffs, where the squaws and children stood watching this strange, unequal contest. Many a husband, many a sweetheart had, in that first wild charge on the Arickaree, gone down to death.

The sun had now risen, showing the broad valley filled with the Indian hordes. Only for a fraction of a second did any of us dare lift our heads above our shallow defenses for a peep at the enemy.

The wrath of the savages at their first failure was plainly evident. That they would do better in the next and succeeding charges, we well realized.

Roman Nose was a born general. His dispositions were made with the skill of a well-trained military commander. Again placing himself at the head of his forces, he suddenly gave vent to a war-cry which echoed in weird cadences over the Arickaree Valley. And then they charged!

Once more waves of death billowed across our sod-topped defenses. Jack Stilwell, alert and cool, exclaimed, "NOW, Sig, let him have it!" The front sight of my carbine had been covering the broad chest of the chief, and our two reports blended into one. Our bullets went true to the mark apparently, for Roman Nose swayed, and was about to fall, when two daring warriors dashed to his side on their ponies, and supporting him between them, bore him from the field.

Wild yells of rage followed, and from every vantage point little wreaths of smoke marked the spot from which bullets came crashing against our defenses. The loss of Roman Nose seemed to dishearten the Cheyennes; but to our dismay Colonel Forsyth himself now lay groaning in his pit.

"Are you hurt, Colonel?" exclaimed Sharp Grover, bending anxiously over our leader.

Artist Zogbaum's conception of the defeat of Roman Nose by Colonel Forsyth at Beecher Island Battle in September, 1868. Reproduction by courtesy of the Library of Congress.

"Yes, they've got me—right in the thigh, and my left leg is broken below the knee. That last volley they fired has put me out of the game," he gasped grittily. "But never mind me, and don't tell the men. This is no time to lose our nerve. Anybody else hurt?"

"Old man Farley's shot through the thigh, too—a mighty serious wound, I'm afraid," reported Scout Thayer. "And Culver and Wilson are both dead—or at least dying. Hutch Farley and Barney Day both have got some bad nicks. And eight or ten others have got some sort of wound."

This was serious. There was no way of aiding the wounded, who were already moaning for water. WATER! Right there within twenty feet, in plenty, but not a man of us dare step over our trenches to obtain the precious fluid! And bandages were not to be had, unless we tore up our clothing, all due to the fact that the Indians had gobbled all our surgical supplies in that first attack on our camp before we gained the island, when they stampeded our pack-mules.

"I'm going to dig down here in my pit," suggested Scout Burke, "and see if I can't strike water."

"Mighty good idea, and I'll help you," I volunteered, and, laying aside my carbine, I joined Burke. In ten or fifteen minutes we had reached damp sand, and shortly thereafter water began to percolate through. It was muddy, but a God-send, nevertheless! And every uninjured man gave gladly underclothing, shirts—anything that could be used for bandages.

Now the savages employed different tactics. There were no more pony-back charges. They scattered out, and creeping to various points of vantage, began regular sharpshooter and sniping methods. Our men responded slowly, firing only when they were sure of a target.

And thus the long afternoon waned. Hunger began to be felt, as we had eaten nothing since the evening before. But rations we had not—not even hardtack, as the Indians had also gobbled the mule carrying our food supplies, at their first attack on our camp.

"It'll have to be horse-meat, boys," remarked Colonel Forsyth with a wan smile. "Better cut off a good supply of steaks from the best of the dead animals, and bury some of it good and deep in cool sand. We're in for a siege here, and we can't expect any relief unless somebody can get through the lines of the savages tonight and start for Fort Wallace. How far do you calculate it is, Grover?"

"Nigh onto a hunderd'n twenty-five miles, I reck'n," responded the scout. "But good Lord, Colonel, no man could ever git through their lines. Why, man, as quick as it gits dark they'll throw a cordon around this little island so tight that even a skeeter couldn't fly through."

The outlook was a gloomy one. We feasted on horse flesh that night, half-roasted over tiny fires in our trenches. And then Colonel Forsyth called us around him for a serious consideration and consultation; and outside the weird, uncanny death-songs of the Cheyenne squaws made the hours a bedlam.

The story of the Arickaree battle has been told and retold around many a frontier campfire, and on many an army campaign, but to me, who SAW IT in all its hideous reality, it has seemed since that long-ago day like some horrible nightmare.

"Men," soberly spoke Colonel Forsyth, his face white and wan from the suffering he was enduring, "somebody must go for aid. There is about one chance in a thousand that whoever leaves this spot will get half a mile away alive. I shall not order anybody out; but if there's a man in this command with the required nerve to make the attempt, let him speak up."

He gazed searchingly into the line of haggard faces about him. For a moment nobody spoke, and then,

"I'll go, Colonel, for one," and young Jack Stilwell quietly stepped forward.

There was a murmur of disapproval.

"Why, boy, you never could make it," exclaimed Grover. "That's a job for a man, and a man who knows Injuns."

"Maybe you'd like to go yourself, Sharp," suggested another of the command, as he suggestingly poked Stilwell in the back, with a wink.

Grover's sharp retort was cut short by old Pierre Trudeau, a trapper close to sixty years of age. "I'll go, Colonel, with the kid—and I knows Injuns," he quietly remarked.

"There really should be two," explained Colonel Forsyth. "For one thing, it's a better protection. Again, if one isn't able to keep up, he can turn the message over to his comrade."

"Jack, you shouldn't go," I exclaimed in alarm, as he passed me to replenish his ammunition. "But if you're bound to go, let me go with you."

"Not on your life, kid," Jack shot back. "I admire your grit, but I want a man who knows something of this country, and old Trudeau has hunted and trapped all over this region. Besides, he speaks Cheyenne, and I've got a scheme that ought to work if we happen to bump into any of those Indians. What do you think of our trying this, Colonel?" and Stilwell unfolded his plan to our wounded commander.

"There's a couple of dead Indians with war bonnets on lying out there at the upper end of the island. They were killed too close in for the others to rescue their bodies. As soon as it's good and dark, we'll sneak up there and get their clothes and moccasins, put on the feathered head-dresses and make the attempt. I believe we can reach Fort Wallace if old Pierre can keep up with me after we get through the Indian lines—*if we do.*"

Colonel Forsyth smiled and nodded approval. "That's a mighty bright idea, my lad," he exclaimed. "You've got a mighty good head on you for a youngster." Then he added very soberly, "Of course you know what to expect if you are captured."

Jack nodded. "I've been on the Plains since I was fourteen, and I know all about what to expect if we fall into Indian hands. But I don't intend to be taken alive," and he patted the holster of his six-shooter.

It was well along toward midnight when Stilwell and Trudeau, disguised in the Indian toggery, were ready to start. They had darkened their faces with smut-coals from the fires, and at a little distance their disguise was nearly perfect.

Meantime, Colonel Forsyth had written a hasty note to Colonel Bankhead, commandant at Fort Wallace, explaining our predicament, and asking that immediate aid be rushed to us.

"Now, Stilwell—and you, Trudeau," cautioned Colonel Forsyth, "exercise the greatest caution, and go slow until you are sure you are clear of the Indians. After that, travel as fast as you can. Barring accidents, you should reach Fort Wallace in five days; but I advise you to do your traveling at night—for the first forty-eight hours, anyway. And now, goodby and good luck, and God bless you both."

"Goodby, Jack," I whispered as he wrung my hand. Tears stood in my eyes. Jack, too, turned his head away.

And then, with whispered farewells, he and Trudeau slipped away silently out into the darkness.

For an hour we listened intently, with nerves at the breaking point; but not a sound did we hear, though we knew the savages would be on the alert for just such a move as had been made. After awhile we dared hope and pray that our two courageous couriers had at least made a safe start.

In all the history of heroism on the Plains, no undertaking teems with more thrilling interest than that hazardous journey through one hundred and twenty-five miles of Indian-infested country, entered upon by young Jack Stilwell, the eighteen-year-old hero of the Arickaree and the plucky Pierre Trudeau. It stands out as an example of the pluck and fortitude of the youth of the West in early days.

"Now, men," suggested Colonel Forsyth, "suppose you see what you can do for your wounded comrades. There's water —such as it is—and cold-water bandages will put us all in better condition.

And so we cared for the suffering ones, and worked through the long, anxious night strengthening our defenses, listening intently for any demonstration from the foe, and hoping and praying that our messengers were safe.

Slowly the blackness of night wore away, and the flush of dawn tinged the eastern horizon. Another day of horror was about to unfold. Four of our comrades lay dead—Culver, Wilson, Dr. Mooers and Lieutenant Beecher. Lewis Farley and Barney Day were steadily sinking, and others were more or less wounded.

Scarcely had the hot sun illumined the valley of the Arickaree, ere the Cheyenne sharpshooters again commenced activities. Creeping stealthily from cover to cover, they showered arrows and bullets against our flimsy barricades.

If they could only draw our fire and clean us out of ammunition, our weakened condition would soon be such that another charge would settle the matter. Already the unattended wounds of our comrades were beginning to develop blood-poisoning; fever had stricken them; and the total lack of skilled surgical care, the stench arising from the bodies of the dead, both men and horses, festering in the glare of the hot September sun; the lack of decent food; the need of drinking muddy water and eating putrid horse flesh—these things were sufficient to dampen the fighting spirit of the most courageous!

How long could we hold out? The horrible fear that our couriers might have been captured and tortured, kept us in feverish suspense. Death stood by our side in those shallow trenches along the Arickaree, and the shadows seemed fast closing around us.

And so, the second day passed!

Night descended—the gloomiest in all my life's history! Then again Colonel Forsyth called a council. Were there any more of the scouts would risk the horrors of capture and death in an attempt to reach Fort Wallace?

"Of course Stilwell and Trudeau *may* get through," the Colonel explained, "but if they don't—"

Allison Pliley and Jack Donovan, men skilled in frontiersmanship and Indian warfare were the second pair of heroes who offered to make the supreme sacrifice if necessary.

"Remember, boys," spoke Colonel Forsyth weakly, "you can't get to Fort Wallace any too soon. It looks as though the end is in sight for us—but we can stave the savages off for awhile if we know there is a possibility of relief getting here."

Out into the gloom of the night slipped Donovan and Pliley, carrying the God-speed of all of us. And we who remained, again settled down to watchful waiting, tortured by dreams of well-laden boards, awakening to the nauseous stench of decaying horse-meat, our only remaining food.

The following morning as I sat dozing in my trench, carbine at my side, I caught a flash of gray near one of the dead horses, fifty feet away. In a trice my carbine was at my shoulder and a random shot fired. Something fell, kicking and struggling. Worming my way through the bushes I found that I had killed a gaunt coyote. It made but a scant meal for so many, but even "coyote soup" will sustain life for a time. Another scout located a thicket of wild plums at the end of the island. Cranberry sauce and turkey are a fine combination, but we who ate roasted coyote and stewed plums on the Arickaree, in 1868, recall that it was a dish fit for the gods.

And so the days slipped past, until six had come and gone, and still there was no sign of the relief parties. The Indians had been leaving, a few at a time, and only a small number remained to harrass our position and keep us under cover.

Hope had now fled. We were convinced that neither of the two sets of scouts had been able to reach Fort Wallace. Death by starvation seemed a foregone conclusion.

And then the courageous Forsyth—all but in the grave— once more called us together.

"Men," he said faintly, "there are quite a few of us who haven't been hit by Indian bullets. It's only fair that *you* be given a chance for your lives. I don't believe the Indians are going to bother us any more; but we who are so badly wounded, cannot possibly get out of this if no relief comes. We must remain and take what the fortunes of war hand us. Tonight, however, I want you unwounded men to leave this hell-hole—and nobody will censure you in the least."

It was a most astonishing proposal. We looked at each other in grim silence. Life was sweet to every one of us, and we might be able to make our escape. But then we turned and looked at our groaning, fever-stricken, wounded companions.

LEAVE *THEM?*

"NEVER," shouted Grover. "We've fought together, and by heavens, if need be we'll die together!"

Cheers greeted this enthusiastic outburst. "NEVER!" we all shouted in unison. "We'll all die with you before a man of us will desert you, Colonel!"

Tears stood in the eyes of our beloved commander.

"Thank you, boys," he exclaimed brokenly. "I was only suggesting what seemed fair and just to me."

The twenty-fifth of September was peeping over the horizon. Eight days of horror had enveloped us. We were now at such a starvation stage that but little resistance could have been offered had the Indians again descended upon us.

"Come on, kid," Grover spoke to me. "Let's see if we can scare up any game. There ought to be some more coyotes around, if dead horses are any attraction fur 'em."

And so, carbines in hand, Grover and I wandered off to

the mainland. But we found no game—not even a jack-rabbit!

Weak and discouraged we turned back toward the island; but as my eyes wandered along the line of bluffs a mile ahead, I thought I discerned moving objects. I stopped short, my heart beating wildly! Could it be the Indians returning with a larger force to wipe us out?

"LOOK, Grover!" I exclaimed, pointing. "There comes the Indians again! Let's get back to the island and warn the command."

Grover stopped short, his eyes glued on the bluffs. Then he gave a frenzied shriek of joy.

"By the mighty, kid," he shouted, "that is an army ambulance, and those are mounted troops. We're saved! The boys have made it all right!"

SAVED—SAVED! Then and there, I dropped on my knees and thanked God for his kindly deliverance.

We hobbled back to the island, shouting the glad tidings. Already the command was making ready for what they thought would be another Indian assault. But when Old Glory and those faded blue uniforms came marching across the Arickaree Valley at double-quick, sobs, tears and even laughter and hysteria mingled!

It was Colonel Carpenter's command of the Tenth Cavalry. They had been out on a scout from Fort Wallace, and there, at Carpenter's side with his head proudly in the air, rode gallant Jack Donovan. The following day, Colonel Bankhead arrived, with Jack Stilwell guiding the party, and our horrible experiences were at an end.

It was a happy experience for Jack Stilwell and me, as we sat with the others around a blazing campfire that evening, with full stomachs. I thrilled as I listened to the recital of the adventures that he and Trudeau had experienced after leaving the island. It was as though a special Providence had watched over them.

"We're going to start back for Fort Wallace just as soon as the wounded are able to travel," Jack confided to me. "Colonel Bankhead won't lose any time in getting those wounded men into the hospital."

"And then, what, Jack?" I queried.

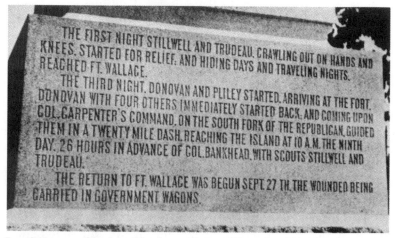

Inscription on Beecher Island monument. Photo by Brininstool in 1917.

"Well, I'm going to stay with the scouts. This frontier life is just what I was cut out for. What are you going to do?"

"I'll head for New York, and the old homestead, Jack," I replied. "This has been my first and last Indian fight. The East will look pretty good to me, after all I've been through with Forsyth's Scouts."

* * * * *

THE ADVENTURES OF SCOUTS STILWELL AND TRUDEAU

All day long the Cheyenne sharpshooters along the banks had alternated their devastating fire with three separate and distinct mounted charges against the beleagured scouts on the island. The loss of their Chief, Roman Nose, coupled with the destructive volleys from the scouts, resulted in decreasing aggressiveness on the part of the Indians. The final assault was made about 6 o'clock by the entire force of Cheyennes, both on foot and horseback, but it was quickly repulsed.

The sun dipped low on this awful scene of carnage before the scouts were able to take stock of their own losses and condition. Lieut. Beecher had just breathed his last. Surgeon Mooers was unconscious from a ball in the forehead and in a dying condition, and twenty-three others were more or less severely wounded. The only food they had was the scanty supply in their haversacks, but there was an abundance of water to be had by digging through the sand until it seeped up through. It was, of course, fatal to go to the edge of the island for the precious fluid.

Medical attention was the main thing of importance, but there was no one to take the place of the dying surgeon, and they were forced to administer to each other as best they could. Forsyth's wounds were giving him excruciating pain, and again and again he begged the men to cut the bullet out of his thigh, but no man would undertake the task for fear of cutting an artery. Finally, in desperation, Forsyth ordered one of the men to bring his razor from his saddlebags, and two of the men pressed back the flesh about the wound and he extracted the ball himself, getting almost immediate relief.

It was plainly evident that help must be summoned at once. The nearest point whence relief might be expected was Fort Wallace, over 100 miles to the southeast. Volunteers were called for, and every uninjured man responded, begging to be allowed to make the attempt to steal through the Indian lines and bring relief from the fort. Forsyth finally selected a beardless youth of 19 named Jack Stilwell, but a veteran in skill and frontiersmanship, and Pete Trudeau, a man well along in years, but with good judgment and plains experience.

The men knew that their chances of getting through the lines of the Indians were exceedingly slim, and even if they

Jack Stilwell, one of Forsyth's Scouts.

succeeded they must travel through a country infested with hostiles and comparatively open, where a walking man could be seen for miles. They figured it would take them four or five days to reach the fort if they succeeded in getting through the Cheyenne cordon.

Darkness fell by the time the two intrepid scouts were ready to depart. Forsyth gave them the only map of the country he possessed, and a note to the commander at Fort

Wallace, Colonel Bankhead, urging him to come to the relief of the scouts with all possible speed. With merely a few more cartridges in their belts and a small supply of food, they were ready.

Bidding their comrades be of good cheer, the two scouts removed their boots, carrying them in their hands until they could gain the opposite bank, and slipped into the shallow water. Stilwell had selected what was thought to be the most dangerous plan—crossing the river and going directly to the high bluffs where the main encampment of the Indians lay. His idea—and Forsyth agreed with him—was that the Indians would be less vigilant on that side, and never dream that anyone would attempt such a bold and daring thing. The remainder of the scouts listened intently for an hour well knowing that if Stilwell and Trudeau were captured the Cheyennes would apprise them of it by the whoop of exultation, but the hours slipped away and not a sound was heard.

Working their way stealthily through the shallow Arickaree, the two scouts gained the opposite bank without being detected. Here they slipped on their boots and then began crawling on their stomachs for the bluffs. Once across the bluffs they were sure they could make comparative fast time. When they were within a hundred yards of the outer edge of tepees an Indian dog came bounding toward them. The animal made a snap at Trudeau, and the old scout grabbed the cur by the throat, stifling the bark the animal was about to utter, and he held on like grim death until the body became limp and lifeless.

When daylight came they had progressed but three miles, but they discovered that the country was swarming with hostiles, and that traveling by day would be out of the question. However, they did not arrive at this conclusion until they had had a thrilling experience. Stilwell detected a body of Indians riding their way, and the scouts sank low in the grass, near an old buffalo wallow, just in the nick of time.

Within the wallow they discovered the skeleton of a buffalo, with shreds of the hide sticking to the ribs. The Indians continued to advance, and the scouts worked their way inside the foul skeleton and lay breathless, waiting for developments. The Indian cavalcade halted when within less than 100 yards of their retreat. Here they paused and scanned the country closely for some time, finally giving orders to one of their number, who remained on guard, while the others withdrew. For more than an hour the solitary Indian lolled on his horse, occasionally allowing the animal to graze within fifty feet of the strange hiding place of the scouts.

But their horror was increased when a strange buzzing sound was heard close at hand, and a huge rattlesnake crawled from the buffalo skull and came toward them. The situation was desperate indeed. If they made the least noise they knew the Indian would immediately detect their presence and communicate it to his companions. Trudeau, however, on this occasion was equal to the emergency. He was chewing tobacco at the time, and when the reptile crawled within "range" he ejected a mouthful of the strong tobacco juice into the eyes of the rattler, and it slid swiftly away.

The Indian finally left to rejoin his companions, and the scouts crawled from their unsavory retreat; but to continue in the daytime was now found to be out of the question. They located a thicket of bushes into which they crept, where, overcome with fatigue, they slept. Their trip was replete with thrilling experience, but on the fourth day, late at night, they reached Fort Wallace.

~

CHAPTER IV

THE RESCUE OF FORSYTH'S SCOUTS

How Col. L. H. Carpenter, 10th Cavalry, Relieved the
Beecher Island Heroes

~

ONE of the most important military posts on the frontier in 1868 was Fort Wallace, located on the western border of the present state of Kansas, at a time when hostile Indians—particularly the Northern Cheyennes, were raiding the then sparsely-settled frontier sections, paying special attention to the Saline and Solomon River valleys.

By September, 1868, these Indian depredations had reached such proportions that the Government was obliged to step in and attempt to subdue these fierce warriors. Consequently, Col. George A. Forsyth was instructed to recruit a company of fifty frontiersmen to scout the country, and assist in subduing the refractory Cheyennes.

The exciting story of Forsyth and his hard fighting veteran scouts, up to the time of their rescue by a detachment of the Tenth Cavalry, is recounted in the preceding chapter.

Perhaps the most dramatic events during the siege center about the adventures of the two separate pairs of scouts who successfully ran the gauntlet of the besieging Indians in a successful effort to secure help from Fort Wallace. The first pair, Pierre Trudeau and eighteen year old Jack Stilwell, moved out under cover of darkness the first night after the attack. Two nights later, two other scouts, Jack Donovan and Allison Pliley, volunteered to make the attempt to break through the cordon. As it turned out, both pairs were successful, but Colonel Henry Bankhead, commanding officer of Fort Wallace, distant about 125 miles, was not the first to relieve the scouts. That distinction fell to Colonel Louis H. Carpenter, 10th Cavalry, stationed at Fort Wallace, under the following circumstances:

Reports having come to Fort Wallace that the Indians were seriously interfering with travel on the Denver road, Col. Carpenter was ordered out on September 22d, (five days after the siege of Forsyth and his men began). He was instructed to proceed to a point where the Denver road was crossed by Sandy Creek, distant from Fort Wallace about sixty miles. His command consisted of about seventy men of H. Troop, Tenth Cavalry, being augmented by about seventeen frontiersmen, who went along as an auxiliary force. Colonel Carpenter was instructed to scout the country in every direction for hostile Indians, and endeavor to protect wagon-trains and others bound for points further west.

Carpenter's command expected to be in the field at least thirty days, consequently thirteen wagons were furnished in which forage, tents, food, extra ammunition, etc., were carried. The officers who accompanied him were Lieutenants Charles Banzhaf and L. H. Orleman, with Dr. Jenkins A. Fitzgerald of the medical corps, as surgeon.

After an all-day's march from Fort Wallace, Carpenter's command made camp near Cheyenne Wells, a station on the Denver road. Nothing of a hostile nature had been encountered. Early the following morning, the command again took up its march toward the west, finally arriving at a point on the old stage road some forty-five miles from Fort Wallace.

As the command was on the march the following day, about 11 o'clock, a lone horseman was observed in the distance coming toward them at full speed. It proved to be a courier from Fort Wallace, bearing a dispatch to Colonel Carpenter, which read as follows:

"COLONEL:—The commanding officer directs you to proceed at once at a point on the Dry Fork of the Republican, about 75 or 80 miles north northwest from this point, 30 or 40 miles west by a little south from the forks of the Republican, with all possible dispatch.

"Two scouts from Col. Forsyth's command arrived at Fort Wallace this evening, and bring word that Forsyth was attacked on the morning of Thursday last by an overpowering force of Indians (700), who killed all the animals, broke Col. Forsyth's leg with a rifle ball, severely wounded him in the groin, wounded Dr. Mooers in the head and Lieutenant Beecher in several places. His back is supposed to be broken.

"The men bringing the word, crawled on hands and knees two miles, and then traveled only at night, on account of the Indians whom they saw daily.

"Forsyth's men were entrenched in the dry bed of a creek, with a well in the trenches, but had only horse flesh to eat, and sixty rounds of ammunition left.

"Gen. Sheridan directs that the greatest dispatch be used, and every means employed to succor Forsyth at once. Col. Bradley, with six companies, is now supposed by Gen. Sheridan to be at the forks of the Republican.

"Col. Bankhead, with 100 men, will leave here in an hour, with two mountain howitzers.

"Bring all your scouts with you.

"Order Dr. Fitzgerald at once to this post, to replace Dr. Tanner, who accompanied Col. Bankhead, for the purpose of dressing the wounded of Forsyth's party.

"I am, Colonel, very respectfully your obedient servant,

"HUGH JOHNSON
"First Lieut. 5th Inf.
"Act. Post Adjt."

Here indeed was an alarming piece of news! Col. Carpenter at once ordered his command to a halt, and called all the men about him, to make them acquainted with the situation. He knew Forsyth, knew that he had raised a company of Indian fighters, and was supposed to be in the field against the hostiles, although in what section of country he was operating was problematical.

Although Carpenter had a map with him, it was very unreliable, no accurate surveys of that part of the country ever having been made. Nobody in his command was familiar with the country as described in the courier's dispatch, and just how to locate Forsyth was a serious question to Carpenter. Neither of the two scouts, who had come in from Forsyth, had been sent along with the courier to act as guides to the spot, they doubtless being "all in" physically, and not able to make the return trip.

Careful inquiry among the command developed the fact that not a man had ever been in that part of the country to the north. It was, in fact, a "terra incognita," frequented only by roving bands of Northern Cheyennes, and some of their allies among the various branches of the Sioux.

After some quick thinking, Carpenter decided to take all his wagons along. If the wagons were returned to Fort Wallace, it would require several men as escort, and he had none to spare. Further, the supplies were in the wagons, and these would be sorely needed by Forsyth's men, if found alive. Again, the wagons would serve excellently as defenses in case his forces were attacked while enroute to Forsyth's relief.

An examination of the map in Carpenter's possession showed that a point "north northwest" from Fort Wallace, was about ten degrees north of his present location, and it was determined to start out on that course, and trust to future developments.

The order directing Dr. Fitzgerald to return to Fort Wallace with the courier was deemed rather unwise under the circumstances. It would leave Carpenter's command without a surgeon, should he be attacked, and this was not to be considered. Dr. Fitzgerald undoubtedly would be greatly needed to assist in caring for Forsyth's wounded scouts. Moreover the doctor himself was more than eager to go along and assist in any possible way. It was therefore decided to retain him. He certainly would be needed, should Carpenter, by chance, reach Forsyth before any other rescue party arrived.

Only a few brief commands and instructions were necessary to the eager and enthusiastic troopers and scouts. Every exertion must be made to relieve the distressed and besieged scouts as quickly as possible.

The task of laying out and running the course to be followed was entrusted to Lieutenant Orleman; and the troopers and civilian frontiersmen at once mounted, left the wagon behind, and struck off across the open country to the north. The teamsters were ordered to keep all the wagons well in hand, and close to the troops, ready to be parked at a second's warning in case of an attack. The mules were all strong, husky stock, well able to be pushed to the limit of endurance.

The command led off at a gait of about five or six miles an hour. The country was a good one to travel over, and no great difficulty was experienced in getting the wagons along. Fully 35 miles were covered before the command camped for the night near some waterholes.

The following morning, at daybreak, with a hasty breakfast dispatched, Carpenter's command was again on the move. After going some twenty miles, they arrived at a large and imposing-looking dry river bed. Here a brief halt was made to study the situation.

The dispatch stated that Forsyth was on the Dry Fork of the Republican. But there was also a South Fork, a North Fork and the Arickaree Fork, and none in the command was able to tell which was the "Dry Fork" referred to. It was therefore quite necessary to investigate this stream.

Accordingly the command scouted up it some fifteen miles, but no trail of any sort was discovered, and the command headed northward again. Soon they encountered another stream, with much water flowing in it, which meandered through a wide, grass-covered valley. This seemed a more probable spot to pick up the trail; nor was Carpenter disappointed.

The Beecher Island monument, with stream (Arickaree Fork of the Republican River) in foreground.
Photo by Brininstool, 1917.

Scarcely had the command entered the valley before a heavy Indian trail was encountered. Evidence showed that fully two thousand Indian ponies had passed over the ground but a short time before. How Carpenter's command missed being discovered by this large war party was a marvel!

Indications showed that the Indians were traveling down the valley. The command was now on the alert! An encounter with the savages might be expected at any moment. It was therefore decided to park the wagons here in a defensive position on the banks of the stream, detach a small party and scout the immediate country thoroughly before proceeding with the wagon-train.

With a picked force, Carpenter rode to a high hill from which a good view of the country could be had for many miles in every direction. Suddenly one of the troopers called Carpenter's attention to several Indian scaffolds such as were used on which to place their dead. These were located on a near-by hill, and the command rode over to make an examination.

Indian bodies they were, and when several had been pulled down and inspected, their skin wrappings disclosed several warriors who had died from gun-shot wounds. There were five of these bodies, and all had died recently.

It therefore seemed certain that these Indians had been killed in a fight at no great distance from their burial place. Apparently it had been about five days since these warriors had met death, and as the fight with Forsyth's command was probably the only one that had taken place recently in that part of the country, it seemed logical that the besieged scouts were at no great distance.

While Carpenter's men were speculating, their attention was drawn to a large white object in a ravine across the valley. This was investigated. It turned out to be an Indian tepee made of freshly-tanned buffalo skins. Entering this lodge, Carpenter found the body of an Indian lying on a small platform, wrapped in buffalo hides. He apparently had been a man of prominence, as many Indian trappings and articles of war were found at the head and feet. It was supposed he was a chief of some standing. He, too, had been killed by a bullet.

Shortly thereafter, a scout who had been sent down the river to examine the Indian trail, dashed up with the information that the trail left the river some miles below, and trekked across country toward Beaver Creek. No Indians had been encountered, however, or seen. Nearby evidence showed that quite a large body of Indians had been camping there for probably a couple of days, preparing these bodies for burial in the method common among all tribes at that time—elevated in trees or on scaffolds or platforms.

That there had been considerable of a battle seemed certain, and that Forsyth's men, or some other command, had gallantly defended themselves, and inflicted some punishment to the foe, was likewise apparent.

Returning to the parked wagon trail, a council was held. From all indications the savages had satisfied their desire for scalps, and were now leaving the vicinity of their recent fight; and it seemed likely that to follow on their trail would only take the command further away from Forsyth's party, instead of to them.

While further discussing the probable location of the besieged scouts, darkness fell, and the command was obliged to camp for the night. It was a night of eager expectancy, for without a doubt the Forsyth party would be located the following day.

While breaking camp the next morning, some mounted men were observed away off on the hills to the south. Signals were exchanged, and presently the strangers rode down to Carpenter's camp. There were five men in the party, one being Scout Jack Donovan, who had left Forsyth's command the second night of the siege and started for Fort Wallace.

He had been accompanied by another scout, Allison Pliley. These two scouts had reached Fort Wallace shortly after the departure of Col. Bankhead's party. Donovan succeeded in getting several men to accompany him, and had started back, but not knowing the country, had taken the wrong course, and only by sheer good luck had fallen in with Carpenter's command. Pliley had remained at Fort Wallace, physically unable to make the return trip.

Donovan seemed to be of the idea that the present location of the Carpenter command was on the south fork of the Republican River, and that Forsyth's men would be located more to the north.

Examination of the trail of the Indians disclosed that the main body, at least, had traveled eastward, and that there would be little to fear from that direction.

Donovan's pitiful story of the condition of his comrades was such that Carpenter selected thirty of the best-mounted of his command, and, with an ambulance, in which wood for fires, rations and surgical supplies was placed, left the remainder of the troop and the wagons, to follow at a more leisurely pace. It was hardly expected that any of Forsyth's men would be found alive; but immediate investigation must be made at all hazards.

The back trail of the Indians disclosed that their force must have been an exceedingly heavy one. Carpenter and his picked force marched for some 18 miles, coming at length to broken and rugged ground, which was evidently taking them to breaks of another large stream.

At length, in turning a spur in the rugged buttes, a green, fertile-looking valley appeared in sight, down which a considerable stream of water ran east and west. Off in the distance could be seen something resembling an island in the stream, and Donovan excitedly recognized it as the spot where Forsyth and his men would be found. Moving objects could be seen near the island, which betokened the presence of at least some of Donovan's companions.

The immediate country was rough and rugged, and much care was necessary in getting the ambulance down to the bed of the stream. As the command laboriously picked its way over the rough ground, several man down the valley were observed to run toward the center of the little island, doubtless mistaking the strangers for a new foe. But presently Carpenter's command was recognized as friends—and the awful strain was over.

For eight days Forsyth's command had successfully withstood the siege, having nothing to eat meantime but the putrid flesh of the dead horses, which lay all about them, eked out with a few wild plums found in the thickets along the banks of the stream, which turned out to be the Arickaree Fork of the Republican River.

The Forsyth command was in a most deplorable condition. Several had been killed, and the wounds of others, dressed only with water, were festering, and in a fevered condition. Blood poisoning had developed in some cases, notably that of Colonel Forsyth, who, however, never lost his nerve, pluck and fortitude for an instant. His men were well trenched and could only have been reduced by starvation.

Lieutenant Banzhaf and the remainder of Carpenter's command, with the wagontrain, shortly arrived. Tents were erected in a grassy glade at some distance from the scene of the fight, and the wounded men were tenderly conveyed to the emergency field hospital, and soon Dr. Fitzgerald was attending to their injuries. One of the scouts, Lewis Farley, had been so seriously injured in the thigh that amputation was necessary; but the ordeal was too much for this elderly scout, and he died shortly after the operation.

The following morning Carpenter began to watch for the arrival of Bankhead and his troops, which were reported to have left Fort Wallace, 100 men strong, about midnight of the 22d, which would be about twelve hours before Carpenter was apprised by courier of the siege of Forsyth's men. Bankhead was further assisted by young Jack Stilwell, one of the two scouts who had left Forsyth the first night, and who was acting as guide for the Bankhead party. However, he had apparently carried Bankhead in the wrong direction. Carpenter therefore sent scouts out in search of him, and about twelve o'clock on the 26th, Bankhead arrived.

Two or three days later, the wounded were able to travel, and all were carried back to Fort Wallace. Here, for three months, Colonel Forsyth lay in a most critical condition, stubbornly refusing to allow amputation of the limb in which he had been so dangerously wounded. Dr. Fitzgerald stated that if medical attention in his case had been delayed another twenty-four hours, he would not have lived. Indeed, it was only through the most careful nursing that Forsyth did live; but he eventually recovered, and lived to take an important part in the Ghost Dance trouble of 1890, at Pine Ridge, South Dakota, although to the day of his death the glancing blow of the rifle ball he had received against his skull, caused the most violent headaches.

Forsyth was brevetted a brigadier-general shortly after the battle in which he and his men had put up one of the most stubborn fights in all the annals of Indian warfare on the plains.

Today the battlefield on the Arickaree is sacred and hallowed ground. The government had made it a National Park. Every year on the 17th of September, and while any of the Scouts were living, a reunion was held on the little island-section, augmented by thousands from near-by towns and villages. A beautiful $5000 monument was erected on the spot by the states of Kansas and Colorado, and the place named "Beecher Island" in honor of the brave Lieutenant Beecher who lost his life in the engagement. But in 1935 the monument was destroyed by the flood-waters of the Arickaree, although another was erected on higher ground. Today quite an imposing little settlement has been started at the historic spot, which includes a gasoline station, general store, a large cement-made auditorium seating 2500 and other improvements. Every Sunday, church services are held there, with a large Sunday-school for the children of that section.

The shifting sands of the Arickaree long ago closed the south channel of the stream so the "island" itself no longer exists, and cattle stand knee-deep in the shallow Arickaree. Congress has set aside 120 acres of land on the site. The exact location of the "Island of Death" is in Yuma County, Colorado, fifteen miles from the thriving little city of Wray, on the Burlington railroad.

~

CHAPTER V

THE "DULL KNIFE" OUTBREAK & TRAGEDY

*The True History of a Wronged and Outraged Indian Tribe
and the Most Masterful and Stubborn Resistance
in the History of the American Indian*

~

THE primary cause of every Indian war in which the United States ever engaged was the greed of the white man for the lands occupied by the red men. In other words, the entire avaricious situation can be summed up in five words: *"The white man wanted it!"*

Such was the cause of the great Sioux war of 1876. The Indian troubles of that year were all due to the previous invasion of the Black Hills of South Dakota by white men in search for gold.

In 1874, Gen. George A. Custer and the Seventh Cavalry were ordered into the Black Hills by the United States Government "on an exploring expedition." The Black Hills, which were included in the Treaty of 1868 with the Sioux, were a veritable paradise for that tribe. It was a portion of country set aside by the Government, which specifically stated that *"No white man shall ever be permitted to pass through or settle therein without the consent of the Indians."*

Custer's report of his alleged "expedition" electified the country. He had discovered gold in the Black Hills—and when gold is discovered anywhere, what barrier can stem the crazy human tide that will, by hook or crook, go where it has been found? By hundreds and thousands, miners, adventurers, crooks and gamblers began pouring into the forbidden territory. Troops were powerless to stop the mad rush into the newly-discovered diggings.

The Sioux remonstrated—*and rightly!* This was their own country—their home, which had been ceded to them by Uncle Sam himself—the "Great Father"—and they wanted no white man to occupy any portion of it. They therefore appealed to the Government to drive out the white invaders of their homeland.

A very feeble attempt was made by the Washington authorities to stop the mad rush; but the troops were powerless—at least, such was the excuse! What, then, could the Sioux do but take the matter into their own hands? What man will not fight for his home and country?

The Indians banded, and attempted to drive the white invaders out. Did Uncle Sam declare the Indians to be within their rights? *Far from it!* It was "just another Indian outbreak!"

Among the leading red men who thus fought for their homes and families, was Dull Knife, of the Northern Cheyennes, a chief whose magnificent generalship and dashing leadership was never at any time overshadowed by any of the noted United States army officers who were sent into the field against him. The Sioux and Cheyennes were allied by tribal intermarriage.

Dull Knife was a born fighter—a leader of men—keen, shrewd, diplomatic, a "red Napoleon of the Plains", with a brain that would have done credit to a Washington or the great French general he so closely resembled in his leadership.

The Indian Campaign of 1876 was a fizzle from start to finish, with the exception of the attack on Dull Knife's village in the Big Horn Mountains of Wyoming, in late November, by troops under command of General Ranald S. Mackenzie.

Dull Knife (right), Northern Cheyenne Chief, with Little Wolf.

The campaign began with a partial victory for Col. J. J. Reynolds, operating under General George Crook, when Reynolds attacked the village of Crazy Horse, on Powder River, March 17th; but he allowed the pony herd of some 800 animals to escape, for which he was later court-martialed. The campaign continued with a virtual "knockout" for General Crook at the battle of the Rosebud, June 17th, and it ended most disastrously one week later, June 25th, with the total annihilation of General Custer and his entire command of five troops, on the Little Big Horn river, forty miles north of Crook's battlefield.

The only "ray of hope" throughout the whole spring and summer campaign was when Colonel Anson Mills fought the forces of Crazy Horse at Slim Buttes, Dakota Territory, September 9th—and that "victory" was nothing worth bragging about, Crook losing nine men killed and about thirty-five wounded in his "Battle of the Rosebud." He thereupon retreated to his base on Goose Creek, near the present location of the city of Sheridan, Wyoming, instead of continuing on and joining Terry, Gibbon and Custer, as he had been expected to do.

All this while these various Indian tribes were on the warpath—driven there by desperation due to hunger, trickery and deceit of the Government in allowing the whites to invade their homelands. The Indians had no wagon-loads of supplies follow-in their wake, as had the army. They had to live off the country through which they passed in their forays, being entirely dependent on the game therein, or such animals and stock as they gobbled from the white invaders.

The situation could, therefore, end in but one way: They were virtually starved out and compelled to surrender. The Government grabbed the Black Hills and all the territory from the Indians, which had been included in the Treaty of 1868, and the red man was left holding the sack—*and it was a mighty empty sack!*

With the capture of Dull Knife and the surrender of Crazy Horse, the last Indian war of any consequence (outside of the Apache campaigns of the '80's) came virtually to an end. It would be only sarcasm to mention the Ghost Dance uprising of the Sioux in 1890-'91 as a "war." That brief, pitiful affair was a massacre, pure and simple—and the less said about it, the better (for Uncle Sam's reputation!).

The Government now had these thousands of surrendered hostile Indians on its hands. What was to be done with them —a people as simple-minded as children, when it came to making a living under the white man's ruling.

Crazy Horse's band, and those of the surrendered Sioux under Red Cloud and Red Leaf, were rounded up on a reservation near old Fort Robinson, Nebraska. At Camp Sheridan, forty miles northeast, were thousands of other branches of the Sioux, under Chief Spotted Tail. But "Old Spot" (wily diplomat that he was) was now a faithful ally of the government, and it was due largely to his wise diplomacy, keen sagacity and forceful management of his Indians, that trouble was kept within bounds.

Dull Knife's band—which had intermarried with the Sioux —wanted to live on the same reservation with them, but the government would not permit it. Dull Knife, "the disturber, the fighter," must be separated from the lately-surrendered hostile Sioux. Uncle Sam declared it would never do to allow two such great Indian generals to live together, where they might plot, plan and scheme new ways of fighting their hated white foe. So it was finally decided that Dull Knife and his Cheyennes should be sent down into the Indian Territory, several hundred miles away to the south.

But this was a climate to which these Indians were totally unaccustomed. It was much lower in altitude than their own land; it was enervating; sickness developed among them; fever broke out, and the Cheyennes began to die off like flies. Twenty-eight of their best fighting warriors died the first year, not to mention the mortality among the women and children, which was very great.

Dull Knife and his sub-chiefs, Old Crow, Wild Hog and Little Wolf, pleaded in vain for relief. Why did the Great Father insist upon keeping his children, his wards, in such an unhealthy climate? Why could they not return to the north, where the climate was such as they were accustomed to? Dull Knife reiterated that his people would never again take to the warpath if their request were granted. But for the sake of their wives and little children (whom they loved just as dearly as did the white man his own) would not the government allow them to return to their own country, where they had always lived, and to which they were accustomed?

But this pitiful plea of the Cheyennes was met by the government with a stern refusal. Dull Knife's people must content themselves where they now were. They had caused Uncle Sam trouble enough (though only fighting for their homes and families). The old and most decidedly untrue àdage that "the only good Indian is a dead Indian," (alleged to have been propagated by Gen. Phil Sheridan) seems to have been the feeling running rampant in Uncle Sam's breast, from the landing of the Pilgrims, even down to the present day!

Hence it was that Dull Knife's band did what any red-blooded people would have done under similar conditions—they decided to fight it out. And fight it out they did, in a manner which has won for them a record never surpassed in any Indian campaign in United States warfare, for sheer reckless bravery, keen strategy, boldness of execution and dashing generalship! The trails traveled in their masterful retreat were red with blood, and many a ranch was left in ashes and plundered of its horses to aid in carrying this dauntless little army of Cheyenne fugitives to the goal they sought —asylum with Sitting Bull and his Sioux in far-off Canada— before being brought to bay and exterminated.

Once determined to break away from the hated spot, where they were held against their will, and dying by inches, as it were, Dull Knife and his fighting chiefs lost no time in putting their plans into execution.

On the night of September 8, 1878, the Cheyenne camp, pitched some little distance from Fort Reno, away down in the Indian Territory, in a quiet valley, did not present its usual activity of romping children, chattering squaws and lively young bucks—at least so thought the sentries who were posted where they could keep vigilant watch on all the movements of Dull Knife and his people. But had those sentries passed among the tepees, they would have observed an unusual stir and much excited whispering among the inmates.

The pony herd was quietly driven in, and after darkness had settled down, the animals were quickly packed, saddled and made ready for a journey of no small proportions. Tepee coverings were stripped, packed and loaded onto the travois, but the poles themselves were left standing. This was to be a flight, and there would be no chance to pause and set up tepees at night.

And then, when everything was in readiness, Dull Knife placed himself at the head of his devoted little band, and away they started northward, men, women and little children. And the Cheyennes were miles away when the rising sun displayed to the astonished sentries nothing but an array of standing tepee-poles, minus their coverings!

Now, indeed, there was "hell to pay!"

A couple of troops of cavalry were at once dispatched on Dull Knife's plain trail, with orders to round him up and bring him and his tribesmen back to the reservation. Of course it would be a simple matter to capture this small band of erratic runaways! There would be no fighting—at least so thought the commanding officer of Fort Reno.

But this time he "reckoned without his host!" Dull Knife was again on the warpath, and although the troops sought in vain to run down the fugitives, they rode back to the post without having brought the daring Dull Knife to bay.

Immediately the commanding officer made the wires to Washington hot with messages. "We must have more troops if Dull Knife and his people are to be brought in," seemed to be the burden of his complaint. This sending out more troops was an easy matter, as the campaign of 1876 had developed men who were now inured to all sorts of hardship, incident to an Indian "outbreak."

Two thousand of Uncle Sam's best fighting men responded. Troops from all near-by posts were ordered out, and General Pope, who commanded the Department of the Missouri, was in full charge of active operations against this supposedly-insignificant, but desperate, band of Cheyenne fugitives. On the 12th of September, Pope wired Gen. Phil Sheridan as follows:

"The following dispositions have been made to intercept the Northern Cheyennes: One hundred mounted infantrymen leave by special train tomorrow for Fort Wallace, to head off the Indians if they cross the railroad east or west of that post. Two companies of infantry leave Fort Hays this evening to take post at two noted crossings of Indians on the Kansas-Pacific railroad, between Hays and Wallace. One infantry company from Dodge is posted on the railroad west of that point. Two cavalry companies from Fort Reno are close on the Indians, and will be joined by the cavalry company from Camp Supply. Colonel Lewis will assume command of them as soon as they reach the vicinity of Dodge. The troops at Fort Lyon are ordered out to watch the country east and west of that post, and are ordered to attack the Indians at once wherever found, unless they surrender, in which case they are to be dismounted and disarmed. Whatever precautions are possible should be taken on the line of the Platte."

The Department of the Platte was not idle, meantime. Troops of the Fourth, Ninth and Fourteenth Infantry were rushed to Sidney, Nebraska, over the Union Pacific, at which point a special train kept steam up day and night to rush troops east or west as needed. These troops were under the immediate command of Major T. T. Thornburg, who was killed later in the Ute war.

But in spite of all this unwonted activity, Dull Knife and his little fugitive army kept going straight ahead, like a bull going through the brush fence, and meeting with but little opposition. Day and night he urged his followers on, pausing only long enough to clean out an occasional ranch for supplies and fresh horses. Fifty, sixty, seventy miles a day did his devoted band travel, although impeded with scores of little children and aged and infirm old people. It was a thousand miles to Sitting Bull, in far-away Canada, and would require a brave, resourceful heart, and the brain of a born general, to outwit and lead his followers through the cordon of troops which were being hastily thrown around him—but on he went, nevertheless!

It was about a week after Dull Knife's flight before he encountered any real opposition. But of course he could not possibly hope to evade the troops forever, which were on his trail from every point of the compass. Two companies of the Fourth Cavalry finally contested his right of way about three miles from Dodge City, Kansas. There was some sharp skirmishing on both sides, and while a number of wounded were reported, Dull Knife was too much for the troops. He succeeded in compelling them to fall back and give him free passage—and on he went again in full flight, leading a devoted little band whose fighting warriors were showing the world what constituted the real Spartan spirit.

The Kansas-Pacific railroad was crossed without opposition, the expected check at this point failing to materialize, and the undaunted Cheyennes boldly continued on north, where the troops along the line of the Union Pacific were waiting for them.

But even here, General George Crook—probably the most successful Indian fighter the United States ever produced—

and even backed by troops from Fort Robinson and elsewhere —was fast finding out that he was battling no ordinary man, but the chief of a band of desperate Indians, whose reckless bravery and undaunted courage could but command his own admiration and respect.

And while Crook was waiting and watching, wondering where lightning would strike next, Dull Knife encountered the Nineteenth Infantry under Colonel W. H. Lewis, on Famished Woman's Fork, not far from old Fort Wallace. Here the chief again demonstrated his wonderful fighting ability and generalship in a battle which lasted two hours, in which Colonel Lewis was killed and three soldiers wounded, while Dull Knife's loss was one man killed and seventeen ponies captured by Lewis's force.

But the grim, determined chieftain never faltered! On he went, every day bringing him nearer his goal—the Canadian border.

It is possible that at about this point Dull Knife must have divided his forces, as two separate engagements were fought a few days after the battle with Lewis's troops. In one of these skirmishes, six soldiers were killed and one officer wounded. The other fight was a desperate one between some ranchmen and the Indians, in which eighteen of the settlers were killed and five badly wounded. The Indian loss was not given.

Dull Knife was indeed proving himself "a foeman worthy of his steel!" Nowhere in all the annals of Indian warfare is there another such instance of as brilliant generalship and fighting ability as was displayed by this little band of desperate warriors. The nearest approach to it is the famous retreat of Chief Joseph and his Nez Perces; but Joseph's fighting force was double that of Dull Knife's. nor was he contested by as great a body of troops as was arrayed against this redoubtable Cheyenne chieftain.

About the 4th of October, the inhabitants of the little town of Ogalalla, Nebraska, were electrified to learn that Dull

Knife's band had forded the South Platte river not over a half a mile from town, and had crossed the Union Pacific right of way!

Bold? Audacious? Nervy? Dull Knife was evidently not going into hiding to escape anything or anybody!

Major Thornburg, at Sidney, was notified by wire, and the special train at that point was brought into service. Troops were rushed to Ogalalla that afternoon, from which point they detrained to take Dull Knife's trail. Gen. Crook also ordered out five troops of the Third Cavalry from Fort Robinson to aid as a check against this uncanny fighting chief, who was fast demonstrating that a red man may possess just as many ounces of brains as his white brother—and quite often a far superior brand of fighting genius and military leadership.

And not yet satisfied with all this array of seasoned troops against Dull Knife, Crook also ordered into the field ten troops of the Seventh Cavalry—Custer's old regiment—from Fort Meade, Dakota.

But even then Dull Knife continued to advance! It began to look as though this doughty warrior would yet out-general all the great military leaders of the United States army! Who can help but admire his wonderful qualities—the genius, the skill, the leadership of such a man, even though considered by Uncle Sam as nothing but an "untutored savage!"

Major Thornburg, advancing on Dull Knife's trail, shortly found himself hopelessly lost in the great sand hills of that portion of Nebraska in which he was operating. His scouts reported that the Indians appeared to have scattered, as trails led in every direction; and Thornburg reported that it seemed like an apparently hopeless task to go further, as the traveling was terrible, and his forces were fast playing out, and that no wagon train of supplies could hope to follow him through sand more than ankle-deep. Moreover, no water was available in that section, aside from a few small alkali lakes. Without water and plenty of supplies, he could not possibly hope to overtake the Cheyenne fugitives. It appeared that Thornburg was up against a hopeless proposition.

Dull Knife himself, however, with his sub-chiefs, Wild Hog, Old Crow and Little Wolf, must have realized that the end was inevitable, and that capture was certain before many days. It later developed that the chiefs had held a council, after finding themselves corraled in the Nebraska sand hills, and it was decided that the only thing to do was to break up into small parties and each trust to "pot luck."

But before this was done, a raid was made on a trader's store at old Red Cloud Agency. Here supplies were seized, and—best of all—many fresh horses were obtained in the corral to replace their own wornout mounts.

Shortly after, it was reported that the main camp of the Cheyennes was ensconced on Crow Butte, a high and rather lonely eminence which commanded a view of the country for many miles around.

Upon receipt of this information, four troops of cavalry were dispatched to surround the location, as it was thought certain there could be no possible chance this time for the Cheyennes to break through such a cordon of troops.

But these Cheyennes were reckless, and ready to take any sort of a chance to escape their pursuers. Little Wolf led his own band and eluded the pickets posted by the cavalry, and when daylight came, the troop commander discovered to his chagrin that his bird had flown!

It developed later that at a council held between the Cheyenne chiefs, it was decided that Little Wolf should gather together the more able-bodied of the fighting strength of the band, and attempt to break through and join Sitting Bull in Canada, while Dull Knife and the others were to rest awhile, and try to reach the border by easier stages.

And, strange as it may seem, Little Wolf actually succeeded in dodging every pursuer and making junction with Sitting Bull without the further loss of a single warrior!

This left Dull Knife and the rest of the Cheyennes penned up in the Nebraska sand hills alone, with the best of the fighting strength of the band gone. But the fighting spirit of the others was by no means broken, even though they must have realized that their case was hopeless. There they were, in a veritable desert! There were no ranches in that section where they might hope to make a raid for more horses and supplies. Yet there was not, at any time, any thought of surrender!

At this juncture Dull Knife decided to send a runner through to Chief Red Cloud, the great war leader of the Sioux, who was encamped on White Clay Creek, at which point he had been placed after his surrender. Dull Knife would make an appeal for aid. The Sioux and Cheyennes had intermarried, were allied in their wars against the whites, and it was thought certain that Red Cloud would help them.

But Red Cloud could do nothing. He sent back word that his fighting days were over; that he had come to realize the power of the white man, and that Dull Knife and his followers might as well surrender one time as another. The end, he said, was inevitable. They must bow to the will of the Great Father. Red Cloud returned by the courier the sympathy of himself and his people.

"Say to Dull Knife," the chief explained, "that he had best submit to the Washington authorities. The whites are too numerous. They are like the leaves of the forest. What chance have we against so many? Our case is hopeless."

Dull Knife's disappointment was most bitter. This was indeed "the last straw." A week passed without the troops being able to contact the Cheyennes. The Indians themselves were "laying low" and resting. They were making ready for a last desperate dash.

After some days had passed, a scouting party was sent out from Fort Robinson. Capt. J. B. Johnson, the troop commander, after two days of weary riding, located a little band of the Indians with about sixty fighting warriors. It must have

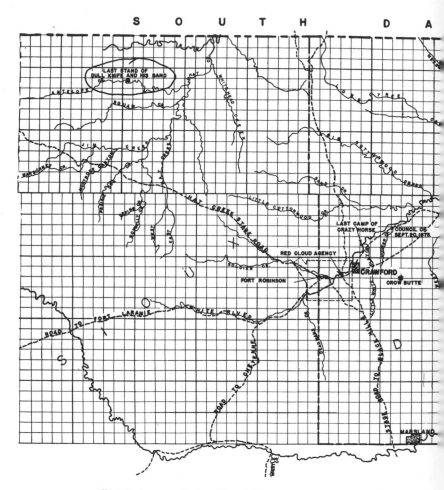

Detailed map of the Pine Ridge country in the middle '70's.

been a complete surprise for the Indians. Before they could comprehend the situation, Johnson had them completely surrounded, and a demand for their surrender was made.

Says one author, (Edgar Beecher Bronson): "In rags, nearly out of ammunition, famished and worn; with scarcely a horse left that could raise a trot; no longer able to either

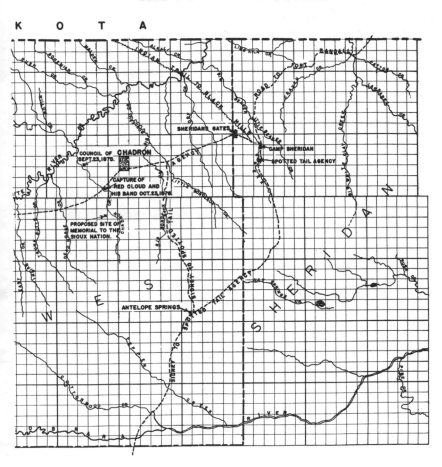

Prepared by Nebraska State Historical Society.

fight or fly; suffering from extreme cold; disheartened by Red Cloud's refusal to receive and shelter them, the splendid old war chief, Dull Knife, and his men were forced to bow to the inevitable, and surrender."

Johnson congratulated himself that he was the lucky commander who had captured the Cheyennes. With this band, comprising about 149 men, women and little children, he started back for Fort Robinson. The weather was bitter cold, and therefore no uneasiness was felt that the Cheyennes might attempt another break before the post was reached.

The first night out, the command encamped on Chadron Creek. Dull Knife and his followers were told to make themselves as comfortable as the circumstances would permit, for the night.

But instead of doing this, the Cheyennes had determined on another desperate move. They did not spend the night constructing brush tepees for their comfort; they put in the time digging rifle pits, and making ready for another skirmish when daylight came.

Dawn ushered in a strange scene. The Cheyennes had improved the time so effectually that when the troops started to round them up, preparatory to resuming the march, they were greeted with a heavy volley of rifle-fire. Brave old Dull Knife was not yet conquered!

Here was a most peculiar situation! Johnson was puzzled. He did not want to have another brush with the Cheyennes unless it was positively necessary; but the affair demanded stern action. So he sent a courier on to Fort Robinson and had a field-piece hauled out to his location. With this, the still plucky Cheyennes were shelled until it became a case of total extermination or surrender. For the sake of his women and little children, Dull Knife capitulated.

But the wily chieftain did one cunning thing before he surrendered. There were many good rifles among the warriors. These were taken apart, and the parts skilfully concealed by the squaws beneath their clothing. Only a few old and worthless guns were turned in to Johnson—and that functionary made the mistake of his life in not thoroughly searching his surrendered charges.

Then the march for Fort Robinson was resumed. The command reached the post with no further trouble from the

Cheyennes. Here Dull Knife and his people were imprisoned in an old log barracks building, which had neither bolts nor bars, and only a small guard was detailed to watch the prisoners.

Now that Dull Knife had surrendered, it was supposed that the trouble was all over. The Indian Bureau would, of course, demand that the Cheyennes be returned to the Indian Territory; but until this was positively determined, Dull Knife's band would be kept prisoners at Fort Robinson.

But the Cheyennes, after they had been imprisoned, stealthily took up a small portion of the flooring in the old barracks building, and hid the rifles underneath. It was a most fatal error for the post commander of Fort Robinson when he also failed to have Dull Knife's band searched for possible firearms, and certainly a most foolish one.

Thus matters continued, from the capture of the Cheyennes in late October, 1878, until January, 1879.

But prior to the latter date, a council was held in their prison by the Cheyennes. Several of the leading chiefs of the Sioux tribe came over to attend it. The Sioux were very anxious that Dull Knife's people be settled on the same reservation as themselves. But the fighting qualities of the Cheyennes had been so thoroughly demonstrated during the previous few months, that an alliance with the powerful Sioux nation was looked upon as an unwise procedure. Should these two nations be united, and again take to the warpath, it would mean a most bloody conflict, and probably the loss of many innocent lives.

Dull Knife's one desire at the council was that he and his people be allowed to end their days in the north, where they had always lived, instead of being returned to the Indian Territory, where there was neither game nor proper climatic conditions for these Indians. While Dull Knife presented this in the form of a *request,* it really came in the nature of a *demand.* In his concluding words the chief said:

Artist Maynard Dixon's drawing of Dull Knife protesting to the Post Commander: "Tell him if he tries to send us back, we will butcher each other with our own knives."

"Tell the Great Father that if he lets us stay here, Dull Knife's people will harm no one. Tell him if he tries to send us back, *we will butcher each other with our knives!*"

As Dull Knife stood facing the council, clad only in bits of frayed worn canvas for moccasins, and a ragged, tattered blanket about his shoulders, he must have presented a most piteous spectacle. Yet, in spite of his impoverished condition, the great chief maintained his dignity, determined to gain for his people all that was possible.

The Sioux chiefs who were present said they hoped the Great Father would allow the Cheyennes to come and live with them; that what they had, they would gladly share with their unfortunate and suffering allies.

"But," cautioned Chief Red Cloud, "you must do what the authorities direct. You cannot resist, nor can we. Listen to me, oh, my friends, and do without complaint what the Great Father orders you to do."

The council ended in bitter disappointment for the Cheyennes. The government representatives, Captains P. D. Vroom and H. W. Wessells, (the latter being then post commander at Fort Robinson) said they would do all in their power for the Cheyennes, but that final disposition of the Indians rested with the Washington authorities.

But when the matter was taken up by the Washington "higher-ups," they decided it would be unwise for the Cheyennes to be allowed to unite with the Sioux. Orders were returned to Fort Robinson that Dull Knife and his people must be sent back to the Indian Territory—the sooner the better —at least so far as Washington authority was concerned!

That was early in January, 1879. The weather was at zero, and bitter cold prevailed. These Indians had not been provided with clothing of any sort since they were captured. They were dressed in the same old worn, tattered garments in which they had been taken, and which was barely enough to cover their nakedness, to say nothing of keeping them warm and comfortable.

On January 5th, while the thermometer stood at several degrees below zero, word came from Washington to immediately prepare to march the Cheyennes back to the Indian Territory—a distance of several hundred miles. This, mind you, while there was from six to eight inches of snow on the prairie and these miserable, mistreated people were walking about with their feet practically on the ground!

Right at this point, the author is introducing a letter which Captain Wessells wrote to Col. H. W. Wheeler, late of the old Fifth Cavalry, while Col. Wheeler was a member of my family in Los Angeles. Col. Wheeler, at the author's suggestion, wrote to Captain Wessells regarding the Dull Knife tragedy, and received the following reply:

> "1832 Belmont Road
> Washington, D. C.
> Jan. 16, 1924.

"Dear Colonel:

I went to Camp Robinson, where Col. Carlton was in command, and the Cheyenne prisoners in an empty barracks building. In a few days, Col. Carlton left, and turned the post over to me. I assumed that when those Indians were captured they had been disarmed, but it was not so. They had hidden their weapons, or some of them. An order came to send them to the Indian Territory. I told them of it, and said I would do all I could to make their journey comfortable. But they said that the country where they were was their home, and they would die before they would leave it. They then barricaded the building from the inside. To prevent their escape I increased the guard around the building; but that night they broke out, using their rifles in doing so. Their fuel and food were not cut off until they had refused to surrender. *All the right was on their side!*

"Yours truly
(Signed) H. W. WESSELLS"

When Capt. Wessells received the order to return the Cheyennes to the Indian Territory, he sent for Dull Knife, Old Crow and Wild Hog. A council was held, and the Indians were made acquainted with the order. Capt. Wessells assured them that he could do nothing but obey and carry out his orders, but—as he stated in his letter—he would make them as comfortable as possible during the trip.

Then grand old Dull Knife stepped into the center of the council ring. His face fairly blazed with wrath; his voice trembled with emotion and his eyes glittered like those of a hunted wild beast brought to bay. Earnestly he spoke through the interpreter as follows:

"Dull Knife and his people want to do what the Great Father directs. We realize that we are helpless. But we are in no condition to march hundreds of miles back to the Indian Territory in such weather as this. Our old people and our little children will freeze to death. And those of us who do reach the southern country will soon fall victims to fevers that have already depleted our numbers. Hear me, my white brothers: Does the great Father desire us to die? *If so, we will die right here!* We will *not* go back to the Indian Territory, neither will we leave the building where we are confined!"

Nobody knew better than did Capt. Wessells—just as he states in his letter—that *"all the right was on the side of the Indians"*. It was a most awkward position in which he found himself! Nevertheless, his hands were tied. Orders were orders, and must be carried out *"when Washington speaks!"* The Cheyennes must go back to the Indian Territory—peaceably if they would, forcibly if they must!

But Dull Knife maintained a most defiant attitude. He refused positively to agree to the order. Wild Hog and Old Crow, grim and true-blue to their chieftain, seconded his refusal.

And then came a most cruel, inhuman and unnecessary order. Turning to the interpreter, Capt. Wessells said:

"Tell the chiefs that unless they consent to go peaceably, their food, fuel and water will be cut off until they agree to the terms which Washington authorities order."

But the chiefs remained stoically silent. They could die but once, and die they would before they would go back to the south.

Doubtless Wessells did not take their defiance seriously.

The chiefs were ordered returned to their prison. Not for an instant would any of the other Cheyennes consent to surrender. They even refused to let their little children be removed and fed, although Capt. Wessells proposed this to Dull Knife, who grimly replied that *"we will all die together!"*

And then came days of anxious waiting, while these poor, miserable, outrageously-treated wards of the United States Government sat and shivered in their icy barracks, with neither a morsel of food, a sip of water or a fire to warm themselves. Their little ones wailed and sobbed themselves to sleep; the death-songs of the warriors were daily chanted, and while the devoted little band daily weakened physically, their fighting spirit remained unconquered! *How would it end!*

Five days passed without food, water or fuel being offered the Cheyennes! Then Capt. Wessells again determined to question the chiefs. Only Wild Hog and Old Crow would deign to appear before Wessells. Dull Knife positively refused to leave his prison; in fact, his people would not allow him to leave, fearing physical violence would be done.

Grimly silent, Wild Hog and Old Crow faced the post commander.

"Are you ready to come out and go peaceably to the south?" he questioned them.

"We will die first!" was the firm, decisive answer of Wild Hog.

"Seize and iron them!" ordered the commander to the guards.

This was finally accomplished, but not before Wild Hog had managed to inflict a serious stab wound on one of the soldiers.

When the imprisoned Cheyennes discovered that their sub-chiefs were not being returned to them, great excitement at once broke out! Now indeed it would be a fight to the death!

Quickly the Indians barricaded all the windows and doors, and made ready for a desperate resistance. Their concealed weapons were brought out from underneath the flooring, their parts assembled, and the rifles were loaded, in expectation of an immediate attack.

Capt. Wessells likewise anticipated that the Cheyennes would attempt to make a break right there and then, and give battle to the troops. However, no move was made on either side. Each was waiting and watching to see what the other would do.

Another serious error was made that night by the post commander: No additional guards were posted around the old barracks building. Wessells did not believe there was any danger; but the other officers at the post were not so sure. They remained awake and alert, confidently assuring each other that "there'll be hell to pay before morning!"

Shortly after ten o'clock, when all the lights about the post had been extinguished, the Cheyennes started their last desperate dash for liberty or death. Nobody realized that they had about twenty-five rifles and plenty of ammunition in their prison!

The sentries about the building "chinned" each other on their respective beats, considering the whole affair as a joke. One sentry, noting that the Indians seemed unduly quiet, approached a window for a look inside.

"*BANG!*" went a rifle, and the sentry dropped dead. The slayer at once jumped through the window and secured the sentry's rifle. At the same instant others of the prisoners opened one of the back doors, where they encountered three more guards. These were quickly shot down by the Cheyennes!

And now the desperate little band poured forth from their prison! While the women, children and aged people started southwest through the deep snow, the fighting warriors poured a deadly fire into the ranks of the troopers who came rushing out at the first rifle-shot! Bugles blared from post quarters! Officers rushed forth, half-dressed, shouting orders, which mingled with the triumphant warwhoops of the retreating Indians.

The deadly rifle-fire from the Cheyennes served as a decided check for a brief time; but the soldiers quickly rallied, and, under their officers, started on the trail of the fleeing Indians, shooting them down like rabbits wherever and whenever the opportunity offered. No quarter was asked by the Cheyennes. In the dim moonlight, the bucks could not be told from the squaws, and the slaughter was indiscriminate. The Indians were making for the steep hills where they could not be well pursued by the cavalry, and were heading for a high divide between Soldier Creek and White River.

The Cheyennes realized that this was their last chance to give battle to their hated white foes. Encumbered with their women, little children and old, decrepit people, it was a hopeless fight! Had the bucks been alone, there would have been a different story to relate; but they would not leave their relatives and friends to again be captured. They would protect them to the last.

No more desperate defense was ever recorded in history than that gallant fight in the cold Nebraska sand-hills by these frenzied, starved, half-clad, frozen fugitives!

The fighting was severe; the slaughter terrible!

When daylight came, and the dead and wounded Indians had been gathered, the post hospital was filled with groaning, moaning humanity! And outside on the ground, piled in frozen heaps, were some thirty dead bodies—men, women and little children!

But the fighting was not yet over!

Many of the fugitives managed to escape into the hills. Not a halt did they make for seventeen miles after leaving their prison, save to stand off the troops and cover the retreat of those of their women and little children who were yet left alive.

For many days the hunt was remorselessly continued, with

daily skirmishing and some losses among the troops. From January 9th to the 21st the fighting continued, with the Cheyennes constantly retreating, but keeping themselves well in hand.

Finally the end came. It *HAD* to come! The Cheyennes were now nearly out of ammunition. They had no food; they were famished, gaunt, in rags, with frozen feet and hands! What could they do but die! *Surrender they would not!*

Some forty-odd miles from Fort Robinson the remnant of these dusky Spartans entrenched themselves in a little gully. Here they lay, awaiting the approach of the troops. Here was to be the last stand!

With the advance of the soldiers, a demand for the surrender of the Indians was made. A volley from their ranks was the reply! The troops were thereupon ordered to charge the gully. They rushed forward to its very edge, emptying their carbines into the huddled mass of humanity below, and then springing back.

This continued until all but three of the fighting warriors had been shot down. These three, shouting high their death-chant, sprang out of the gully, and with only drawn knives for weapons, charged toward the troops!

Can you imagine the scene! *Three charging three hundred!*

These three braves were of course instantly riddled with bullets as they charged!

Braver martyrs never died for a cause which was both just and right! Just as Capt. Wessells himself declared forty-five years later, when he said: *"All the right was on the side of those Indians!"*

It was indeed a charnel-house which presented itself to the horrified troopers after the slaughter had ceased!

Twenty-two dead bodies were removed from the gully. Nine, badly wounded, but alive, were carried out.

But Dull Knife himself was not at the last stand. Several nights before, he managed to elude his pursuers, and this wonderful old fighting chieftain actually reached the Canadian border and joined Sitting Bull. When the latter was brought back to the United States, in 1883, Dull Knife was with him. A few years later, when he had been returned to the Tongue River Agency, at Lame Deer, Montana, he died a natural death, bitter and defiant to the last!

Some doubt has been cast by other writers regarding the manner of the death of Dull Knife. It has been asserted that he was killed the night the Cheyennes made a break for freedom from their log barracks at Fort Robinson. That he died on the reservation, is attested by the following letter to the author, from Acting Supt. W. C. Randolph of the Tongue River Agency, under date of January 21, 1935:

> Tongue River Agency
> Lame Deer, Montana,
> January 21, 1935.

E. A. Brininstool
330 No. Poinsettia Place
Los Angeles, Cal.

Dear Sir:-

This is to acknowledge receipt of your letter of January 7th, in regard to the death of Chief Dull Knife. I have taken the matter up with the Indians here, and they advise me that he died a natural death on Rosebud Creek, on this reservation. (date not given)

> Very truly yours
> W. C. RANDOLPH
> Act. Supt.

When the real history of our Indian wars shall be written as it should be written, by those who *know,* and the wrongs and injustice to the red man truthfully told, it will be proven that no more gallant fighting spirit ever was exhibited on any battlefield, in all the world's history, than that shown by these devoted Cheyennes of Dull Knife's band in their last desperate fight for their rights.

CHAPTER VI

~

"TOBEY" RIDDLE—MODOC INDIAN
WAR HEROINE

~

DURING the latter part of February, 1920, there died
on the Klamath Indian Reservation in Southern Oregon,
a Modoc Indian woman, full of years and honor. Her
maiden name was "Wi-ne-ma," but she was better known
among her own people and the whites simply as "Tobey"
Riddle. When but a young girl she was wooed and won by a
white man named Frank Riddle, an honest, kind, temperate
and thoughtful miner. She quickly learned to speak the white
man's tongue, and in time both she and her "man" became
expert interpreters, rendering valuable service when the Indian Department held "pow-wows" with the Modoc tribe.
Frank Riddle died in 1906, honored and respected by all
who knew him.

It was during the Modoc war of 1873 that Tobey Riddle
performed her greatest service to the United States government, which resulted, some years later, in her being granted
a pension of $25 a month for the balance of her life. The
Modocs had taken the warpath—or rather had been driven
to it through the avarice, greed and unscrupulous dealings
of the white man—which has been the initial cause of every
Indian war in America.

After the first hot preliminary skirmish with the United
States troops which had been sent against them, together
with some Oregon volunteers, fifty-two Modoc warriors,

under their chief, known as "Captain Jack," (who was a full cousin of Tobey Riddle) representing the total fighting force of the tribe, with upwards of 150 women, old men and children, retreated to the "Lava Beds," a barren, inaccessible, volcanic section of country just across the northern line of California, and for several weeks defied and held at bay more than one thousand United States troops, with appalling results to the soldiers, and with but infinitesimal loss to the Indians.

After several attempts to induce the Indians to surrender, during which time several "peace talks" were indulged in, a meeting was arranged for the 11th of April, 1873, to be held midway between the camp of the troops and the stronghold of the Modocs. Both sides agreed to come to the council unarmed. Each was represented by six persons. The Commissioners went to the meeting unarmed, except one man, who carried a small Derringer pistol. The Indians, under the leadership of Captain Jack, were all armed with revolvers hidden beneath their blankets.

While the council was in progress, the Indians suddenly threw aside their blankets, grasped their hidden weapons and opened fire upon the defenseless Commissioners. Two were killed outright, two saved themselves by their fleetness of foot, and one was shot down and a Modoc brave was already scalping him, when Tobey Riddle flung herself upon the savage, fighting him with superhuman strength; then shouting that "soldiers are coming!" The Modocs thereupon fled back to their stronghold. The wounded commissioner was revived, and after several weeks of careful nursing at the hands of Tobey Riddle, recovered.

The Modoc war was the most costly to the United States of any in which it ever engaged, considering the number of opponents. And the Modocs were not subdued until after a difficulty had arisen in their own ranks, which resulted in a division of their forces, one faction finally surrendering to the soldiers, then turning about, playing traitor and assisting in trailing down their red brothers, who were finally captured. Four of the ringleaders, including Captain Jack, were hanged, and two others were imprisoned for life. During the fighting the Modocs lost but twelve warriors killed, while the total loss of white settlers and soldiers numbered 168, of whom eighty-three were killed. The cost of the war to the United States government was in excess of $500,000.

The first trouble with the Modocs started in 1853, when some Pitt River Indians waylaid and killed some settlers who were enroute to California. A few made their escape and reached Yreka, California, where they gave the alarm. Here a company of sixty-five fighting men was raised to go out and punish the hostile Pitt River savages who had attacked the emigrants. The guilty tribe was not overtaken, but the miners, in their search, came upon some of the Hot Creek Modocs. The Modocs had always lived at peace with the whites, but to the enraged miners "an Injun was an Injun," and they opened fire upon the inoffensive Modocs. Only a few escaped, while several women and children were victims of the miners' fury.

The flames had now been fanned, and for some years trouble was rife. Capt. Jack's father was at that time chief of the trible, and he counseled war against the white invaders, but the son stood firmly for peace. In 1856 occurred another disastrous affair, in which one Ben Wright, heading a company of volunteers, invited a band of nearly half a hundred Modocs to come to a feast which he had prepared for them. The Modocs were assured that the volunteers were their friends. Wright told them he was a "peacemaker." The Indians believed him. The Modocs moved their camp in close to that of the soldiers. The next morning before daybreak, the soldiers surrounded the tepees of the unsuspecting Modocs and opened fire upon them. Only five escaped.

Three years later white settlers began coming into the

country occupied by the Modocs. Captain Jack was now chief of the tribe, his father having fallen a victim to the treachery of Ben Wright's volunteers. Jack welcomed the white settlers, and there was no trouble between them and the Modocs for

Capt. Jack, Modoc Chief. From a photo taken shortly before he was hanged. Copyrighted by Major George W. Ingalls.

some time. Finally a difficulty arose between a white man named Ball and one of the Modocs, and the two became bitter enemies. Ball complained to Captain Knapp, agent at Klamath Reservation, that the Modocs were stealing cattle from the whites, as well as demanding provisions. He stated further that he "feared the Modocs were preparing for war"— when nothing of the sort was premeditated, nor were the Modocs stealing cattle and provisions, as had been alleged.

However, the government (always quick to side against the Indians) appointed Col. A. B. Meacham as a Peace Commissioner to visit Captain Jack and determine the cause of the reported trouble. After a conference, at which Frank Riddle and his Indian wife, Tobey, acted as interpreters, the Modocs were told that the government had decided to send them to the Klamath agency to make that spot their future home.

Captain Jack raised no objections to this removal. It was effected without the least trouble. But the Klamaths did not take kindly to this new state of affairs, and immediately began quarreling with their new neighbors, telling them they had no business to come there and infringe upon their territory, and stating that they (the Klamaths) owned that part of the country. They further advised the Modocs to go back to Tule Lake, their old home. Captain Jack sought the agent and asked protection from the offending Klamaths. The agent haughtily informed the chief that he "wouldn't be bothered with his complaints." The following day Captain Jack and his entire following quietly packed up and went back on the banks of Lost River to their old camping ground, where the white settlers told them "there is plenty of room for us all."

Thus matters continued harmoniously until September, 1872. Ball, the troublesome white settler, had left while the Modocs were on the Klamath Reservation. Then word was received that soldiers were coming to compel the Modocs to move back to the Klamath Reservation. Tobey Riddle rode seventy-five miles on horseback to warn her people that the troops were to be sent after them. The Modocs thereupon told the settlers about them that they expected trouble with the troops when they arrived, and advised them to take no action themselves against the Modocs, nor affiliate with the soldiers if fighting broke out. "Let the soldiers whip us if they can," advised the Modocs. They then returned to their lodges, satisfied that an understanding with their white neighbors had been effected.

The following morning, true to the report, the Modocs awoke in their tepees to find their camp surrounded by troops under Major Jackson. The latter demanded to see Captain Jack. The chief appeared and was informed that the "Great Father" at Washington had sent the soldiers there to get him and all his people and compel them to go back to the Klamath Reservation again.

Captain Jack quietly informed Major Jackson that he and his people would obey the mandate of the Great Father. The chief was then informed that before the Modocs started for the reservation, they must surrender their arms. A heated discussion followed, but Captain Jack quieted his braves and ordered them to lay down their guns. All obeyed but one Indian, who insisted upon retaining an old pistol. Lieutenant Boutelle drew his own revolver and ordered this warrior to deposit his pistol with the other surrendered arms. As Boutelle leveled his revolver, the Indian snatched out his own weapon. Both fired at the same instant. Immediately the soldiers opened a general fire upon the unarmed Modocs, who rushed for their weapons, secured many of them and returned the fire of the troops. Two dead and several wounded on each side was the result of this little skirmish.

The settlers now rushed to the assistance of the troops and a general fight ensued. The Modocs retreated to the Lava Beds. Here preparations for a most determined resistance were begun. Jack's forces were increased to fifty-two fighting men, but he was also burdened with about 150 women, old men and little children. The Lava Beds comprised a section of territory about eight miles long and four wide. They formed a perfect network of obstructions, and with their volcanic formation resembled great ocean waves "frozen solid" in great billows. Transversal crevices furnished most excellent communication whereby the Indians were enabled to pass from one ridge to another without exposing themselves in the least. Every inch of this territory was known to the Modocs. Various caves were discovered in the series of ridges which could be easily blockaded by rolling heavy stones before the entrances. It was a spot in which a handful of men could defy a hundred times their number.

In this natural fortification the Modocs rested and took life easy after their initial battle with Major Jackson's men. They kept sentinels on guard day and night, and every movement of the troops was known to them. On January 15, 1873, horsemen were seen approaching, and they were soon identified as soldiers. They were under the command of General Gillem. Gillem looked the situation over and then made preparations to advance on the Modoc stronghold on the 17th. He was instructed to "rout the Modocs." The soldiers were inclined to look upon the whole proceeding as a huge joke. The idea that half a hundred Indians would put up a fight against two or three hundred seasoned troops was well calculated to start much jesting, and many of the soldiers discussed with great gusto the "Modoc steaks" they intended to have for dinner. It was even inferred that "there won't be half enough Modocs to go around."

The morning of the 17th dawned clear and cloudless. The troops were impatient to start the drive. Not an Indian was to be seen, as the troops advanced toward the Lava Beds. It was hinted that "them Injuns have hot-footed as sure as shootin'." The officers were impatient. "We'll show you dead Indians if you'll show us live ones," they assured their scouts.

Suddenly a single shot rang out from the Modoc stronghold. An officer pitched forward to the ground, dead. This was followed by other shots from the concealed redskins, although the troopers were unable to see an Indian; but the continual crack of rifles caused great confusion among the troops. Volley after volley was poured in the direction of the Modocs. The latter knew every crack and fissure of their fortifications, and they never exposed themselves an inch. There were abundant crevices through which they could fire, and their deadly accuracy caused a panic among the soldiers.

Finally, a heavy fog blew in from Tule Lake, and this made the advance of the soldiers more precarious than ever. Men fell dead and wounded every time an advance was ordered. Thus matters continued all day, when the soldiers withdrew to their camp with their dead and wounded. It had been a most unlucky day for them. "During the whole day," records one officer who took part in the fighting, "I did not see an Indian, nor do I recall that anyone else did. The Modocs simply held us there until darkness permitted us to retreat."

When Captain Jack called his roll that night there was not even a wounded Indian among his forces. Every warrior answered to his name. War dances were indulged in within sight of the camp of the troops, and great was the confidence of the savages that they could stand off their enemies indefinitely. In the soldiers' camp everyone was busy attending to the wounded. Many of the Indians had managed to secure the weapons of the soldiers who had been killed, which were far superior to their own. They also found much ammunition scattered over the ground where the soldiers had retreated. There were no sad-hearted braves among Captain Jack's fifty-two warriors that night.

It was now very plain to General Gillem that the Modocs were not going to be subdued by ordinary methods. Troops were rushed to the Lava Beds from every available point, until there were a thousand soldiers on the ground. Before they could get into action, however, word was received from Washington instructing that a Peace Commission be formed to treat with the savages for peace.

The members of this commission were General E. R. S. Canby, Rev. E. Thomas and Colonel A. B. Meacham. Captain Jack agreed to meet the Commissioners at Fairchild's ranch on the 10th of March, 1873, and in company with several of his head fighting men, among whom were Boston Charley, Bogus Charley, Hooker Jim and Dave Rock, he met the Commissioners as agreed. Frank Riddle and his wife, Tobey, again acted as interpreters. No decision was reached at the first day's council. It was very plain to the Commissioners, however, that the Indians were not going to agree on a peace unless their wishes were, in a measure, respected regarding the land upon which they were to be placed.

Another meeting was planned for the 27th, at which it was hoped an agreement could be reached. Captain Jack asked that a reservation be set aside for his people near Hot Creek, or else near the Fairchild ranch. This was refused. Then Jack asked that the destitute and barren Lava Beds be given to his people, "as no white man would ever want to live in such a barren spot." To this the Commissioners replied that nothing could be granted "until peace was first made." Jack was insistent that "a home be given to us in this country." To this General Canby retorted, "We cannot make you that promise; you and the whites could not get along." The Commissioners told the Indians that they must come under the white man's law, and General Canby insisted that the Modocs come out from their stronghold under a flag of truce. To this Jack scornfully answered:

"Look here, Canby, when I was a boy a man named Ben Wright called forty-five of my people out under a flag of truce. How many of them do you think got away with their lives? Just seven of them. I will not come out under a flag of truce; I dare not do it.".

Nothing was gained at this council. Neither side would yield to the other. After the Commissioners had departed, the Modocs went to their stronghold and held a council of war. They were greatly wrought up over the refusal of the Commissioners to grant them a home in the country where they and their people had always lived. Black Jim, one of the warriors, made a motion that the Commissioners be killed at the next peace talk. About fifteen of the braves sided with him.

Captain Jack would not agree to anything of the sort, insisting that he would yet make the Commissioners yield to him by sticking to his point, and that he would yet get his people the land they desired for a reservation. "All I ask is that you people be patient and behave yourselves and wait," he pleaded. "I do not want to do anything rash; that will never do."

But now others of the Modocs sided with Black Jim and refused to yield to their chief. They taunted him with being "an old woman." A dozen of his warriors told him his advice was not good. "Let us take the advice of Black Jim," they urged. "We are doomed anyway. Let us fight and die like true Modocs."

Captain Jack was called a coward and a squaw, and in derision one of the warriors threw a shawl over his shoulders and a squaw's hat was forced on his head. This enraged the chief, and he declared he would show them that he was a true Modoc. It was thereupon decided—much against the advice and pleading of Captain Jack—to massacre the Commissioners at the next peace talk, and the chief was delegated to kill General Canby, while certain others were delegated to murder the other Commissioners.

For two days Captain Jack brooded over his promise to assist in the cowardly work. Then he asked that he be allowed to withdraw. "Do not hold me to this," he urged. "I ask you this for the love I hold for you all. If we go ahead with this work we are all doomed." Angrily the warriors insisted that the chief play the part he had promised.

On the 8th of April Tobey Riddle was sent by the Commissioners to Captain Jack's camp with a message that they desired to have another talk with the Indians. They wanted Jack to meet them with five of his men, unarmed, agreeing themselves to likewise attend the council without weapons. Jack sent back word that he and his men would come.

On the return of Tobey Riddle to the camp of the Commissioners, she was overtaken by William Faithful, one of the Modoc braves, who was. moreover, a cousin of Tobey.

Tobey Riddle, heroine of the Modoc war. Photo taken in 1873. Copyrighted by Major George W. Ingalls.

He warned the Modoc woman of the decision of the savages to murder the Commissioners at the next peace talk, and urged her to have them stay away. Greatly alarmed, Tobey at once sought her husband and General Canby, to whom she imparted the danger. The general at once called together the other members of the Commission, and told them of the impending peril. None would believe it. General Canby was skeptical. "What!" he exclaimed, "a mere half dozen Indians murder us right under the very noses of a thousand troops? Impossible! They cannot and dare not do it."

Said the Rev. Thomas: "God will not let them do such a dreadful thing. I trust in God to protect us."

Then Frank Riddle spoke up. "Gentlemen," he said seriously, "I have known these Modocs many years, and if they have decided to murder you Commissioners, they will do it. I know it. If you go to meet them, you will never see the sun rise in this world again. I know my wife is telling you the truth."

Colonel Meacham and L. S. Dyer, the two others of the Commission, agreed with Riddle. They had no faith in the Modocs at all, after the warning just given by Tobey Riddle.

The matter thus rested for the night. In the morning Riddle and his wife renewed their pleading with the Commissioners not to go to the meeting. With tears streaming down her face, Tobey besought them to listen to her warning, and heed the advice of her husband and herself. Soon after, Jack sent word from his stronghold that he would not be able to meet the Commissioners that day, but wished to see Tobey Riddle alone. She at once mounted her horse and rode over into the Indian camp, where Jack instructed her to tell the Commissioners to be at the peace tent, situated halfway between the Indian camp and that of the soldiers, early the following morning. "Tell them we will be there, six of us, unarmed, and nothing will happen if they talk sense to us."

To assume friendship, four of the Modoc braves accompanied Tobey back to the camp of the Commissioners, where they were invited to remain to dinner, and where, to all appearances, they were on the best terms of friendship. After the departure of the Indians, Tobey Riddle again pleaded with General Canby not to go to the meeting. "Just as sure as you go, you will all be brought back here cut to pieces," she warned.

The following morning the Commissioners once more asked Riddle if he really thought there was danger in attending the meeting. He replied with considerable emphasis. "As I told you gentlemen yesterday, you will certainly be killed if you go."

General Canby laughed, and in bantering tones he bade his brother officers goodby "in case I never return," as he picked up a box of cigars and started toward the council tent, half a mile distant, closely followed by Dr. Thomas. All of the Commissioners had been urged to secrete revolvers on their persons, and Meacham and Dyer each placed a small Derringer pistol in their pockets. But the others positively refused to go armed, for the reason that they had given their word to the Modocs to come unarmed, and they would not break their promise. Riddle and his wife, although both believed they would be massacred with the others, resolutely determined to accompany the Commissioners to act in their regular capacity as interpreters.

When the members were all assembled at the council tent, they found Captain Jack and his five braves already there. It was seen at a glance, however, that the Modocs had broken their promise about coming unarmed, as the butts of revolvers protruded from the pockets of each. The Commissioners, however, determined to face the ordeal. Those present at the council were as follows: Of the whites, General Canby, Rev. Thomas, Col. Meachan, L. S. Dyer, Frank Riddle and his wife Tobey. The Modocs were represented by Captain Jack, John Schonchin, Boston Charley, Bogus Charley, Black Jim and Hooker Jim.

After shaking hands all around, General Canby opened the box of cigars and passed them around to the Indians. The council then opened. The speechmaking lasted nearly an hour, neither side being able to arrive at a decision. The Modocs, however, grew more bold and insolent in their demands, and the Commissioners soon realized that serious trouble was imminent. At this point, Captain Jack withdrew from the council for a moment or two, but soon returned, just as General Canby arose to speak.

As he was addressing the Indians very earnestly, two Modocs not in the council suddenly appeared from behind some large rocks, each with several rifles in his arms. At this juncture Captain Jack drew his revolver, exclaiming in the Modoc tongue, "All ready!" Pointing the weapon full in Canby's face, he pulled the trigger, but the weapon failed to explode. He quickly drew the hammer back again and snapped it. There was a loud report, and the bullet struck the brave old general directly under the right eye. He reeled and started to run, but was tripped, thrown to the ground and his throat cut by Bogus Charley. At the same time Boston Charley shot Dr. Thomas, who fell to the ground, exclaiming:

"Don't shoot me again, Charley, I am a dead man!"

"Damn you," retorted Boston, mebby nex' time you b'leev what squaw tell you, eh?" He then shot the dying man again and again until life was extinct.

Meacham was also shot about the same time as the others. Sconchin did the shooting. Tobey Riddle sprang forward, and with the strength of a wild beast, struck the Indian again and again, finally knocking him down; but Sconchin arose and knocked Tobey down. He then shot Meacham seven times until he was supposed to be dead. Boston Charley then placed his foot on Meacham's neck and started to scalp him. He had already made a long cut in the wounded man's head and started to tear off his scalp, when Tobey Riddle again attacked Meacham's assailants with the ferocity of a tiger, fighting them off, at the same time screaming, "Soldiers are coming!" The Modocs at once fled to their stronghold, leaving Tobey in full possession of the field.

Both Dyer and Riddle jumped to their feet and ran at the first fire. A brave named Shacknasty Jim, who had brought some of the guns from behind the rocks, took after Riddle, emptying his rifle and six-shooter at the fleeing man without effect. Jim thereupon gave up the pursuit.

Hooker Jim took after Dyer, shooting at him several times without effect, but after a chase of about 400 yards, the Indian was outrun, and Dyer and Riddle both reached the camp of the soldiers unharmed.

Tobey Riddle was not further molested. There was not a soldier in sight coming to the rescue of the Commissioners. The brave Modoc woman examined the bodies of Canby and Thomas, finding both dead; but Meacham yet breathed. She placed her saddle blankets under him, mounted her horse and started on the run for the camp to get help. Half way there she met her husband returning with a detachment of soldiers. Meacham was yet alive. He was rushed to the hospital tent on a stretcher. His wounds, while serious, were not necessarily fatal, the surgeons said. Tobey Riddle at once insisted upon nursing him and her plea was granted. In two weeks he was able to sit up, and by the third week was sent to his home in Salem, Oregon, where he eventually recovered.

After the killing of the Commissioners there was no more fighting for three days. Then the soldiers again advanced on the Modoc stronghold. They were met by a withering fire which killed seven or eight soldiers. Not an Indian was even wounded in the three days' fighting which followed. Shells and bullet fire both were used against the Modoc stronghold without any apparent effect. Nothing could penetrate the craggy fastnesses and rocky walls which surrounded the Modocs, and it was sure death every time the soldiers charged.

This was amply demonstrated time and again. Not an Indian could the troops see. The best they could do was to watch for a puff of smoke and fire at that. The Indians now had plenty of guns and ammunition which they had secured from the dead soldiers, but provisions were running low. There were about 150 mouths to feed besides the fighting braves, and the warriors were hampered and handicapped thereby.

For some days the fighting continued, but it was soon agreed by the Indians that they could not hope to much longer continue the siege. Their women and children and the old people were in constant danger, and at last it was decided to evacuate the Lava Beds in the night. It was to be every man for himself.

The next day when the soldiers advanced, they found the stronghold deserted, save for four old blind and crippled Modocs, who were promptly shot down. While searching for the trail of the departed braves, a volley was fired at the troops from ambush which was so deadly that twenty-two soldiers were instantly killed and eighteen wounded. There were but twenty-one Indians in this attacking party, many of them now being armed with Spencer repeating rifles secured from the soldiers. Not an Indian was struck by a bullet fired by the troops.

After the battle a wounded soldier left on the field shot and killed one of the Modocs known as "Little Ike." This soldier was hunted down and shot several times by the Modocs, being left for dead on the field. He was later rescued by the troops, but died in the hospital.

Following this skirmish, the Modocs had many fights with the soldiers. Along in May, one of the Modocs named "Ellen's Man" was killed, supposedly by the soldiers. He was one of the most beloved of the warriors, and a violent quarrel broke out among the band as to the cause of his death.

This at last resulted in a division of the fighting forces of the Modocs. One faction, embracing Bogus Charley, Hooker Jim, Scarfaced Charley and Shacknasty Jim finally went to the Fairchild ranch, where General Davis—then in charge of the troops—was stationed. They told him they were tired of fighting and wanted to surrender. They also intimated that they were ready and willing to assist the troops in running down the remainder of Captain Jack's warriors. General Davis at once engaged the traitors as scouts and trailers at salaries of $100 each per month.

It was hard dodging for Captain Jack after that. However, he and his small band managed to elude the troops until June 1, 1873, when the Modoc warriors who had turned against their chief, trailed him down, and he was captured. With him at the time were his sub-chief, John Sconchin and some forty or fifty others—old men, women and children.

After the capture of Captain Jack had been effected, the prisoners were all removed to Fort Klamath, Oregon. Here the leading members of the band stood trial for murder. These were Captain Jack, John Sconchin, Boston Charley, Black Jim and Slolux. The four Modoc traitors who had assisted in the murder of General Canby and Rev. Thomas, were freed—or rather were not tried at all for complicity in the massacre, because of the fact that they had surrendered voluntarily and rendered valuable aid in running down the remnants of the band. The trial began in July and lasted nearly a month. Every Modoc Indian was placed on the stand, but they had no counsel. Frank and Tobey Riddle acted as interpreters during the entire trial, rendering invaluable service.

When Captain Jack was put on the stand he made a masterly talk. In ringing terms he scathingly denounced the treatment of his tribe at the hands of the whites and the government. Among other things he said:

"The government ought to care for my young people. See the good land and the size of the country that is taken away from me and my people. If I wanted to talk more I could tell you facts, and prove by white people that which would open your eyes about the way my people have been murdered by the whites. I will say that not one white man was ever punished for those deeds. If the white people who killed

our women and children had been tried and punished, I would not have thought so much about myself and my companions. Do we Indians stand any show for justice with you white people and your own laws? I say no! You white people can shoot any of us Indians any time you want to, whether we are at war or at peace. Can any of you tell me whenever any white man has been punished in the past for killing a Modoc in cold blood? No, you cannot tell me! I am on the edge of the grave. My life is in you people's hands. I charge the white people with wholesale murder—not only once, but many times. Think about Ben Wright—what did he do? He killed nearly fifty of my people, among them my father. Was he or any of his men ever punished? No, not one! Mind you, Ben Wright and his men were civilized white people. The other whites at Yreka made a hero of him because he murdered innocent Indians. Now here I am. I killed one man after I had been fooled by him many times, and I was forced to do the act by my own warriors. The law says, 'hang him; he is nothing but an Indian anyhow; we can kill them any time for nothing, but this one has done something, so hang him.' Why did not the white man's law say that about Ben Wright?"

When the trial ended, four of the Modocs—Captain Jack, Black Jim, Sconchin and Boston Charley—were condemned to hang. Two others—Boncho and Slolux, the Modocs who had brought the guns to the others, were sent to the penitentiary for life. Boncho died at the prison on Alcatraz Island, May 28, 1875.

The hanging of Captain Jack and his three braves took place at Fort Klamath on October 3, 1873. The balance of the tribe were sent to Quapaw Agency in the Indian Territory (now Oklahoma) where in a few years nearly all the older people died, as the climate did not agree with them there. The remnants of the Modoc tribe are now living on the

Klamath reservation in Oregon, a bill having been passed some years ago that the descendants of Captain Jack's band should be restored to the rolls of the Klamath Agency, with the privilege of removing there.

There Tobey Riddle lived, and there she died in the latter part of February, 1920. For many, many years she acted as a teacher and missionary to her own race, and was the means of pointing them to the white man's road. In 1875 she made a trip to the East, and saw for the first time the power and prestige of the white people. Tobey Riddle's son, Jeff C. Riddle, lived at Yainax, Oregon, where he raised a large family and was highly respected.

It would seem that the State of Oregon should recognize in Tobey Riddle a heroine who should become as well known in American history as Pocahontas or Sacajawea, the little Indian guide of Lewis and Clark. It was not until seventeen years after the Modoc war that Congress granted this noble Indian woman the slight pittance of $25 per month, which she received during the balance of her life, although it would seem that this estimation of her services to her country should have been recognized and rewarded at the time her valorous deed was performed; but no "back pay" was ever granted her. A monument to her memory is now the most fitting memorial that the State of Oregon could erect over her grave.

CHAPTER VII

~

THE "GHOST DANCE" TROUBLE

Causes which led to the last Indian Uprising, the killing of Sitting Bull and the Battle of Wounded Knee.

~

W HAT were the real causes which led to the last Indian outbreak in South Dakota among the Sioux, culminating in the death of the medicine man, Sitting Bull, December 15, 1890, and the massacre of the Sioux—men, women and children—December 29, 1890? Who was to blame—the Indians or the United States Government?

Doubtless the causes which led to this most unfortunate tragedy, briefly summed up, were as follows:

FIRST: Unrest among the conservative element, and the gradual breaking up and passing of the old life which the Indians loved so well.

SECOND: Continual neglect of promises made the Indians by the Government, and failure to keep its treaties.

THIRD: Hunger—cutting down the necessary supplies of rations supplied by Uncle Sam—principally the issue of beef —to a point where actual starvation faced the Sioux nation.

Doubtless this latter was the prime factor in the outbreak, when it comes right down to plain facts. The passing of the buffalo, and the killing off of the other game on which the Indian depended for his sustenance, by unprincipled and unscrupulous whites, left the Indian virtually a pauper, and dependent on the government ration; and when this also was reduced and the Indian brought face to face with actual starvation, who can blame him for fighting? Any man—red, white or any other color—will fight for his "grub."

171

When the Indian—following the Sioux war of 1876—was herded onto reservations and the freedom of the chase was exchanged for the idleness of the camp, it naturally followed that great unrest and much trouble was bound to occur. The Indian was suddenly—almost overnight, it may be said—expected to at once and without previous training, settle down to the pursuit of agriculture—a calling for which he was totally unfitted, and on land largely unsuited for such use. This was a most unreasonable and wholly mistaken idea on the part of Uncle Sam. At one stroke the Indians were reduced from a free and independent nation, to dependent wards of the government.

The Treaty of 1868, by which the Sioux were awarded certain definite boundaries for a reservation, embraced all of the present state of South Dakota, which included the Black Hills—the Indians' paradise. The discovery of gold in the Hills by Gen. Custer's expedition of 1874 brought an influx of gold-maddened prospectors and miners into a region in which, according to the Treaty of 1868, "no white man should ever set foot without the consent of the Indians." Thus, the last remaining hunting grounds of the Sioux were gobbled up by the whites. A new agreement, in 1876, clipped fully one-third of their guaranteed reservation (including the Black Hills) from the Sioux, and this naturally and rightfully led to much dissatisfaction throughout the entire Sioux nation. But "the white man wanted it," and it had to go! It was the call of "civilization," the "onward march of progress!"

The conservative element among the Sioux did not take kindly to this new order of things, and they brooded long and deeply over the injustice and unfair treatment accorded them by the government. They felt—and with good reason—that they had been tricked, robbed and cheated, and together they planned opposition to any further changes which the government might have under its hat, but which the Sioux felt that they would be unable to meet. The progressive element scorned the white man's unscrupulous and underhanded methods of doing business and scoffed at his promises— promises which they knew from long experience—and most bitter experience—meant nothing to them.

In 1889 the Sioux Reservation was yet further reduced by eleven million acres. In 1882 the government had offered the Indians eight cents an acre for certain desired territory; but the Indians refused to consider such an absurd offer.

Thus the matter hung fire until 1889, when this great reservation was reduced one-half! The conservative element among the Sioux fought most determinedly the selling of this land; but the deal was finally accomplished, and the various bands of the Sioux were eventually herded onto five small reservations.

To these wild Indians, practically fresh from the warpath, a difficult problem was now presented. The land was not fit for agriculture, yet they had to depend on what they could raise on this unsatisfactory soil. Irrigation was unknown to them; it was a case of "dry farming." Yet it was all they had left, together with their small herds of cattle and the government rations which were to be issued to them in return for the surrendered territory. Failure of crops and shrinkage of their herds meant starvation, aside from the pittance doled out by the government. And according to the best authorities, the crops of the Indians did fail; their cattle did not increase, and they were virtually driven to outbreak by starvation brought about by the reduction of their beef supply and other necessary food stuffs.

As if all this were not enough to drive the Sioux frantic and to the verge of despair, disease began to break out among them and measles, grippe and whooping cough brought about terribly fatal results. In 1889 their crops were a failure, due, according to one authority, "to the fact that the Indians had been called to the Agency in the middle of the farming season and kept there to treat with the Commissioners, going back later to find their fields torn and trampled by stock during their absence."

Who, then, can blame the Sioux for the feeling of unrest, gloom and despair, with actual starvation facing them? The wilder element among them were especially concerned about the future. What was to become of this once powerful and numerous nation?

Hopeful, yet uncertain, they awaited the dawning of another year; but the summer of 1890 was another year of crop failure, and mutterings of discontent were heard on every hand. An unexpected reduction in the government rations still further incensed the tribe, which had been repeatedly told that their rations would not be affected by their signing the treaty. "Yet," says one writer, "almost immediately Congress cut down their beef rations by two million pounds at Rosebud Agency, and one million at Pine Ridge, with less proportion at the other agencies."

The Commission which had consummated the treaty entered a most emphatic protest against this inhuman and unscrupulous reduction of the Indians' rations; but Congress dillydallied along in its usual pokey way, twiddling its thumbs and hemhawing over the matter until the Sioux were in actual open rebellion. Indeed, it was not until after the Wounded Knee trouble that Congress did finally step in and appropriate $100,000 for additional beef for the starving Sioux, whose numbers were reduced some three hundred by the inhuman massacre and slaughter at Wounded Knee.

The "Ghost Dance" of itself was NOT, as many believe, the cause for the last war with the Sioux. It was merely a symptom and expression of the real causes of dissatisfaction. Originating among the Pi-Utes of Nevada, the Sioux had heard of the doctrines and belief, which taught that the time was near when the earth was to be swept clean of the hated white men and the buffalo would return in countless millions, as in the old days, and the former state of happiness of the Indian would once more be restored to him.

The Sioux sent a delegation, in 1889, to the Ute country to investigate this new "Messiah religion." When their representatives returned and began to preach and expound the new doctrine, the infection spread rapidly, especially among the wilder and more superstitious portions of the tribe, which now grasped eagerly at this new strange belief and hope that the Indian was at last to be restored to his former state of happiness and freedom.

James McLaughlin and Dr. V. T. McGillycuddy—men who had spent long years among the Sioux as representative agents, and who knew their habits, peculiarities and customs far better than any other white men, gave it as their opinion that the new craze would doubtless increase as the time drew near for the fulfillment of the prophesy; but that when its failure was seen, the ghost-dance excitement would simply die a natural death. Dr. McGillycuddy had served as agent at Pine Ridge from 1879 to 1886, and he tersely said:

"As for the ghost dance, too much attention has been paid to it. It was only the symptom or surface indications of deep-rooted, long-existing difficulty."

In October, 1890, the agent at Pine Ridge reservation was one D. F. Royer, who had just assumed charge that month. He knew nothing whatever of the Indian character, and was very soon the laughing stock of all the Sioux at Pine Ridge. He had had no previous experience in handling Indians, lacked initiative and diplomacy in dealing with them, and was totally unfitted for such a difficult and responsible position, which demanded a man of unflinching courage and determination. It is safe to say that had such veteran Indian Agents as Dr. McGillycuddy or James McLaughlin been in charge at Pine Ridge, there would have been no Sioux outbreak and consequent slaughter of innocent Indian women and children.

Dr. V. T. McGillycuddy, the surgeon who attended Crazy Horse the night he died.

About the time that Royer assumed his duties at Pine Ridge, the Messiah or Ghost Dance craze was spreading rapidly throughout the Sioux nation, especially among the Pine Ridge element. It was earlier in the season—about June —that the ghost dance shirts (supposed to make the wearer immune to bullets) were donned for the first time at a dance held at the camp of old Chief No Water on White Clay Creek, about twenty miles northwest of Pine Ridge Agency.

A friend of the writer, George Bartlett, deputy U. S. Marshal at Pine Ridge, and who also conducted a trading store on Wounded Knee creek, and who, moreover, was well and favorably known among the Sioux, speaking their language fluently, as well as being an expert in the sign language, volunteered to visit the camp of No-Water and investigate the goings-on there. It was pointed out to him that he was taking his life in his hands, as the Sioux were by this time in no mood for interfence from any white man, no matter who it might be. However, Bartlett made the trip, witnessed the dancing, secured the information desired, and returned to Pine Ridge, without being interfered with in any manner by his Indian friends.

During the month of August, 1890, and while Agent Gallagher was yet in charge at Pine Ridge, some 2,000 of the Sioux nearly frightened him into hysterics when he appeared in their midst at the White Clay rendezvous, with several members of the Indian Police, and attempted to stop the dance there in progress. Leveling their rifles at Gallagher, the Indians told him they were ready to defend their religion with their lives, and refused point-blank to disperse. Gallagher diplomatically withdrew and the dance went on! He resigned his position a few weeks later, when Royer superseded him.

Things were rapidly approaching a crisis at Standing Rock Reservation, away to the north, where Sitting Bull was the leading "factotum." At Pine Ridge the cause had assumed proportions which caused Agent Royer much concern. In charge at Standing Rock was the veteran McLaughlin, well and favorably known among the Sioux. His twenty years experience among this tribe, coupled with his bravery and ability, enabled him to meet all the emergencies which arose with diplomacy and skill and he expressed perfect confidence in his own ability to allay the excitement and stamp out the dancing craze.

But at Pine Ridge, Agent Royer, a man described as "destitute of any of those qualities by which he could justly lay claim to the position—experience, force of character, courage and sound judgment," was now half beside himself with fear and apprehension. His ability and lack of even common sense caused him to be nick-named among the Indians "Lakota Kokipa-Kosh-kola" (Young man afraid of Indians). Hardly had he been in charge a week before trouble started. Not knowing probably what else to do, he began bombarding the Washington officials with telegrams to the effect that more than three thousand of the Indians under his charge were dancing the ghost-dance, and he suggested that the military be called at once to scatter the dancers and stop the frenzied excitement.

Royer was advised that military assistance would be provided in the event that a real crisis arrived. but that meantime he was to be cautious and diplomatic, and try by every persuasive manner possible to stop the dancing.

Gen. Nelson A. Miles, who was then on his way west, stopped off at Pine Ridge to make an investigation. He had a talk with Royer, who was yet insistent in his demand for troops. Miles listened to Royer's entreaty, but after a confab with the Indians, expressed the opinion that the craze would shortly die out. He informed the dance leaders that they must stop dancing—whereupon the Indians informed Gen. Miles that the dancing would continue!

After the departure of Miles, Royer became more alarmed than ever at the condition which affairs seemed to be assuming. On October 30th he sent a long letter to Washington in which he attempted to explain that the only way in which affairs at Pine Ridge could be properly handled was by the use of United States troops, "to the number of 600 or 700."

Getting but little or no satisfaction from this complaint, he wired Washington on November 11th that he would like to come to the capital, and "explain the situation." This permission was promptly turned down, whereupon Royer began to importune the Washington officials daily by wire that they either send troops to Pine Ridge or allow him to come to Washington and "explain."

Doubtless the Indian Department became somewhat bored at Royer's insistence, for about November 15th that Department reported the alleged condition of affairs at Pine Ridge to the Military authorities at Fort Robinson, near the town of Crawford, Nebraska. Royer also again wired that same day, stating that the Indians "were wild and crazy," and that "at least 1000 soldiers are needed."

Meantime the ghost-dancers were going right ahead with their religious ceremonies, and the excitement was spreading, but no other acts were being committed. Short Bull, one of the most indefatigable and persistent of the ghost dancers' leaders, finally declared that as the whites were interfering with their ceremonies in an unreasonable manner, he had decided to set a new and earlier date for the coming of the Messiah. He cautioned the Indians not to be afraid of anything, but to gather at a stipulated place and continue dancing, even though the troops should come out and surround them. He declared that the guns of the soldiers would be rendered harmless, and that the white race would shortly be wiped out.

In the ghost dance, those who participated and could procure the white cotton cloth to make them, wore the ghost-dance shirts. They were cut and fashioned in the prevailing Indian style. No ornament of any kind adorned them. No metal of any sort was allowed to be worn or carried in the dance, nor any sort of a weapon—not even a knife—displayed.

Finally, on November 19th, troops under the command of Gen. John R. Brooks were ordered into Dakota to assume charge of the situation and they reported at Pine Ridge Agency. This contingent was quickly augmented by other troops and in a very brief space of time, Pine Ridge bristled with infantry, cavalry, Gatling guns and all the paraphernalia of war. Eight troops of the Seventh Cavalry (Custer's old regiment) under Col. Forsyth; a battalion of the Ninth Cavalry (colored) under Major Henry; a battalion of the Fifth Artillery, under Capt. Capron, and a company of the Eighth Infantry, and eight companies of the Second Infantry, under Col. Wheaton, were soon on the ground, and on the first of December all Indian agents at the various Sioux reservations were instructed to obey and cooperate with the military authorities, and to use every possible means to suppress the threatened outbreak.

The arrival of so many troops in the field alarmed great numbers of the Sioux at Pine Ridge and the adjoining reservation on the east (Rosebud), and led by Short Bull and Kicking Bear, the two prime movers in the ghost-dance religion, many of the Indians from these two reservations fled into the rugged fastnesses of the Bad Lands, northwest of White River, and located in the extreme northwest corner of the Pine Ridge reservation.

Enroute they persuaded many of the otherwise friendly Indians to join them in flight. The agency beef herd was also "drawn on" (without Royer's permission) as a commissary and in brief space of time some 3000 of the Sioux had congregated in the Bad Lands under Short Bull and Kicking Bear, to the great alarm of the settlers and the grave concern of the military authorities, although the latter did not look upon the move as a strictly hostile one.

In justice to the soldiers, and the subsequent indiscriminate killing of some 300 Indian men, women and children, it is only fair to state that the troops were sent into the threatened district only after the agents had declared they had lost control of the Indians, were powerless to keep the peace, and that the Indians were armed and assuming a hostile attitude. However, had Pine Ridge been presided over by a man of common sense and sound judgment, there is little doubt but that the ghost dance excitement would shortly have subsided, and little, if any, trouble resulted.

Agent Royer had sent in the names of 64 Indian disturbers whom he declared should be arrested and placed where they would cause no further trouble. At all the other reservations combined, only fifteen were mentioned who should be removed.

The presence of the troops had caused a cessation of the dance near the agencies, while the wilder element had retreated into the Bad Lands, where they were simply waiting to see what was going to happen. They had created no hostile demonstrations thus far.

In the north, at Sitting Bull's camp on Grand River, the ghost dance was yet in progress. Agent McLaughlin had notified the Department that the medicine man was a disturbing element and should be arrested, but that he did not wish the troops to attempt it, feeling perfectly able, at the proper time, and with the aid of the Indian Police, to accomplish Sitting Bull's arrest, without precipitating a fight, which he felt certain would come if troops attempted to secure the wily medicine man.

Two or three dates were set for the arrest of Sitting Bull, but had to be countermanded in each instance because of interfering matters. It was also deemed advisable to withhold the arrest as late as possible after winter had fully set in, and the zero-weather had somewhat cooled the ardor of the ghost dancers.

It was at length determined to arrest Sitting Bull on December 20, at which time most of the Indians in his vicinity would be away from their camps and down at the agency drawing their rations. This would leave but a comparatively few of the Sioux in Sitting Bull's immediate neighborhood; and as the medicine man himself never came in to the agency but refused to accept the government rations, it was pretty well known that he would be at his camp with probably but a small following.

But about a week before the date set for his arrest, it was learned that Sitting Bull was making preparations to go down to Pine Ridge reservation, "as God was about to appear." He had several horses all ready for the ride, and was determined to go, whether permission was given him by Agent McLaughlin or not.

Accordingly it was decided to make the arrest at daylight on December 15, and that the Indian Police should effect the medicine man's capture. A detachment of the Eighth Cavalry under Capt. Fechet was to be within supporting distance, but were not to be called upon, save in the event of actual trouble.

Promptly at daylight, on December 15, 1890, the Indian Police, augmented by a few volunteers—43 all told—surrounded Sitting Bull's cabin. They were under the command of Lieut. Bull Head, a brave and thoroughly loyal Sioux. The medicine man was located in one of his cabins, yet asleep. He was quietly awakened.

"You are under arrest, and must go with us to the Agency," ordered Lieut. Bull Head.

"All right, I will dress and go with you," promptly replied Sitting Bull.

Giving directions to one of his wives about the clothing he desired to wear, and ordering his favorite saddle horse brought around to the cabin door, Sitting Bull, while dressing, began a volley of abuse at the police for disturbing his slumbers at such an early hour. The Police did not start any backtalk, but Bull, by his palaver, managed to gain considerable time.

Meantime, the arrival of the Indian Police had been broadcasted throughout the camp, and soon about 150 Indians had armed themselves and rushed down to Sitting Bull's cabin to see what was the matter. They entirely surrounded the small force of Indian Police, who were quietly waiting for their brother tribesmen to bring Sitting Bull outside.

In a few minutes he appeared in the doorway. Lieut. Bull Head and Sergt. Shave Head walked on each side of him with drawn revolvers, while Sergt. Red Tomahawk was directly in his rear. Just at this juncture, Crow Foot, the 17-year-old son of Sitting Bull, began taunting his father at thus tamely submitting to arrest. This so incensed Sitting Bull that he shouted out an order for his followers to rescue him.

At that instant, Catch-the-Bear, one of Sitting Bull's followers, fired at Lieut. Bull Head, the ball taking effect in his side. Bull Head immediately wheeled and shot Sitting Bull, who was also again shot by Sergt. Red Tomahawk and instantly killed.

The fight then became general and resulted in a most desperate hand-to-hand encounter of forty police against nearly 150 of the hostiles. The cavalry were ordered up at once, and the hostiles were driven off, although they were later notified by Capt. Fechet that they might return to their homes, as no further action would be taken against them, it being otherwise feared that they might join the hostiles in the Bad Lands and create yet more trouble in that section.

In this skirmish, which was fierce and determined, although lasting but a few minutes, six of the Indian Police were either killed or mortally wounded, while the hostiles lost eight killed, including Sitting Bull and his son, Crow Foot.

Late in the afternoon the Police returned to the Agency with their dead and wounded, and the body of Sitting Bull— an Indian who died defying the hated pale-faces to the end, and refusing to be reconstructed or made into an "Agency Man." Sitting Bull was 56 years old at the time of his death.

With Sitting Bull disposed of, the next dangerous element was Hump's band on the Cheyenne River Reservation. He had a following of about 400 ghost dancers and with Chief Big Foot had a camp located near the junction of Cherry Creek and the Cheyenne River.

These Indians had for several weeks been stepping out to the beat of the tom-toms in the ghost dance performance, and were considered a dangerous element. Hump was especially looked upon as a foe to be "handled with gloves" as the saying is, and it was thought that he would not surrender without a fight.

However, to the great surprise, but infinite pleasure of the Department, Hump, after being interviewed by Capt. E. P. Ewers of the Fifth Infantry, who had known the chief for many years, and had once had charge of his band, stated that he would do whatever the authorities desired.

This was indeed a most welcome piece of news. Hump at once brought in all his followers to Fort Bennett, causing no disturbance of any sort, and eventually enlisting as a scout under Capt. Ewers, rendering most valuable service in inducing the surrender of others of the hostiles.

This left Chief Big Foot as the only probable fomenter yet to be dealt with. Col. Sumner of the Eighth Cavalry was detailed to keep a watchful eye on his movements. When Big Foot learned that Col. Sumner had arrived in his vicinity, he visited his camp, and stated frankly that he was peaceable and had no intention of creating a disturbance.

These friendly overtures were continued until about the 18th or 20th of December, when Big Foot announced to Col. Sumner that he and his people were going in to the

Agency to draw their rations. After he had started, an order came to arrest Big Foot and deliver him as a prisoner at Fort Meade.

Gen. Miles was at once informed that the Indians were already on their way to the Agency, but that if the chief returned, Col. Sumner would endeavor to carry out the order; otherwise he could be arrested at the Agency just as easily.

Shortly thereafter it was reported that Big Foot had stopped at another camp on his way in to the Agency and Col. Sumner at once mounted his troop and started down to intercept him. In some manner Big Foot learned that Col. Sumner was coming, and he went out to meet the troop. He announced that he was friendly, and was ready to do whatever he was ordered. In addition to his own band, he had about forty of Sitting Bull's Indians, who had come down from Standing Rock as refugees, and who sought asylum with Big Foot's people.

When questioned as to why he had allowed the Sitting Bull Indians to come among his own followers. knowing them to be refugees, Big Foot magnanimously replied:

"These are my brothers and relatives. They have come to my people hungry, footsore and weary and almost naked. We took them in and fed them, and tried to make them comfortable. Even an Indian has a heart, and I could do no less than receive and feed them."

Truly, Big Foot, although perhaps unfamiliar with the teachings of the white man's Bible, surely was carrying out the spirit of the Master in caring for the poor and needy and feeding the hungry!

An officer was then directed to return to Big Foot's camp and bring in all the Indians to be found there. The result was that 333 of the Sioux, who went into camp as ordered. received rations, and after a quiet night, started back, escorted by the troops. No attempt was made at this time to disarm them, as they made no hostile demonstrations, but appeared perfectly friendly and amicable.

When Big Foot's band arrived in the vicinity of their own village, the chief complained to Col. Sumner that his women and children were cold and hungry, and that it would work a hardship on them to be forced away from their village at that season of the year.

"We are now at our own homes" the chief announced. "We are where the government officials have ordered us to stay. We have done nothing to justify our removal elsewhere."

However, "orders were orders," to a military man, and Col. Sumner so insisted to Big Foot, who finally sent word that he and his people would obey, and would start for the Agency the following morning.

And then, like a thunderbolt, later the same evening, the scouts came in on lathering ponies, and announced that Big Foot's band had all decamped and started southward, finally keeping on toward the Bad Lands, where the hostiles were located, but had taken only their ponies and tepee poles.

The exact cause for this sudden change of base is rather uncertain, but it is believed to have been caused by a wrong interpretation in the pow-wow between Col. Sumner's courier and Big Foot, who, it is alleged, had told the Indians that troops were coming in the morning to kill them all, in case they refused to break camp.

Other authorities hold that it was because Col. Merriam, from Fort Bennett, had been ordered to join forces with Col. Sumner in compelling the surrender of Big Foot's band. The Indians, it is alleged, became frightened at the approach of more troops and decamped in haste.

And so Big Foot was a factor again to be dealt with. The refugees in the Bad Lands finally, on December 28, 1890, broke camp and started in toward Pine Ridge Agency, being promised that if they complied with the orders of the military authorities, their rights and interests would be confidently protected.

Although this promise to "protect the rights" of the Indian was an old, a stale and a most unlikely story, the Indians accepted it for what it was worth, and started for Pine Ridge with their families, while several troops of cavalry, within supporting distance of each other, followed in their rear.

Meantime, Big Foot had continued his flight from Cheyenne River toward the Bad Lands. Orders were at once given to head off his band and arrest them if possible. A short distance west of the Bad Lands, Big Foot's band was intercepted by Col. Whitside and the Seventh Cavalry. And so once again were Custer's troops in close proximity to the same warriors who had wiped out the glory-hunting "white chief with the yellow hair," seventeen years before, along the Little Big Horn!

Noting the advance of the cavalry, Big Foot raised a flag of truce and asked for a pow-wow, which was refused by Col. Whitside, whose demand was an unconditional surrender. This was immediately given, and so captors and captives moved along together, until Wounded Knee Creek was reached, about twenty miles northeast of Pine Ridge Agency, on the evening of December 28.

Here the Indians camped for the night—the last night on earth for some 300 of them, and for some two score or more of the Seventh Cavalry. It had been the intention of Gen. Miles to send Big Foot and his followers back to their own reservation, or else remove them from the country until the ghost dance excitement had subsided.

In order to make doubly sure that the troops could handle the situation, Gen. Brooks sent Col. Forsyth to join Whitside with four additional troops of the Seventh Cavalry. These, with the scouts under Lieut. Taylor, comprised a force of eight troops of cavalry, one company of scouts and a battery of four Hotchkiss guns, a total force of 470 men.

The hostile element which had been holding forth out in the Bad Lands, were by this time nearly all encamped in and around the Agency. The two ghost dance leaders, Kicking Bear and Short Bull, had been induced, through the persuasive powers of many of the older chiefs, such as American Horse, Little Wound and others, to bring in the renegades, and these Indians had arrived at the Catholic Mission about five miles from the Agency, when the fight took place.

But Big Foot's followers must be disarmed, so agreed the military heads, before further advance toward the Agency was made.

This was a mistake!

These Indians had made no hostile demonstrations of any sort, and it is quite conclusive that when they were formed in line, and surrounded on all sides by armed troops, and then told they must surrender their guns, they immediately conceived the idea that they were first going to be disarmed, and then shot down in cold blood, right on the spot!

At any event, on the morning of December 29, 1890, the Indians were apprised of the fact that they must give up their weapons before proceeding any further. The soldiers had so placed their own tents that the camp of the Indians was surrounded on all sides. In the center of the camp was a white flag, placed there by the Indians themselves, as a peace sign, and a guarantee of their own safety. Directly in the rear of the Indian camp was a dry coulee, and on a slight eminence in the front, the Hotchkiss guns had been so mounted and trained as to completely command Big Foot's camp. The chief himself had been taken down with pneumonia and was lying in a warmed tent, supplied by Col. Forsyth.

Mutterings of discontent were heard among the Indians when soon after 8 o'clock on the morning of the 29th, they were ordered to deliver over their guns.

At the command the Indians came forward and seated

themselves on the ground, facing the troops. Still no guns were brought out. Twenty of the band were then ordered to bring out their weapons. Two guns were surrendered. More decisive mutterings were heard when the order was again repeated that their firearms must be turned over at once. Plainly the Indians were unwilling that their guns should be taken from them, and it was evident that a crisis was at hand.

A hasty consultation was held among the officers, after which many of the soldiers were ordered up to within about thirty feet of the group of sullen, silent warriors, while a detachment of troopers was ordered to search the tepees. This resulted in the discovery of about forty guns, many of which were old and obsolete and practically worthless.

During this hunt, the soldiers acted in a most indiscreet and offensive manner, overturning beds and household equipment, and driving out the inmates—to all of which the silent but maddened and aroused warriors must have taken serious objections.

During the excitement a medicine man known as Yellow Bird was circulating among the Indians, blowing on an eagle-bone whistle and speaking in the Sioux tongue, inciting the warriors to action. He declared that the soldiers had no power over them, that in the event of a fight, their bullets would not avail against the ghost-dance shirts which were worn by most of the warriors.

Came the climax swift and sudden!

A handful of dust flew into the air, hurled by Yellow Bird; and as though this were an understood signal, a young Cheyenne River brave named Black Fox suddenly slipped a Winchester rifle out from beneath his blanket and fired point blank into the ranks of the soldiers!

Like a match applied to a powder magazine was the result!

The troopers immediately responded with a volley so deadly that nearly half the warriors were killed at the first fire! So close were the contestants that their guns almost touched! Those of the Indians who remained alive, at once threw aside their blankets, displaying the hiding place of their best weapons—and the fight was on!

A most desperate hand-to-hand struggle followed! Many of the Indians had no rifles, but all carried revolvers and knives, as well as warclubs, and the conflict was bloody and at close quarters.

And now the roar of the Hotchkiss guns broke loose, and the two-pound explosive shells rained death and destruction among the women and children, who had gathered in front of the tepees, curiously watching to see what would take place, but not expecting to see what followed. As these guns threw shells at the rate of fifty per minute, and simply mowed down everything alive, the effect of this inhuman and entirely uncalled for slaughter can well be imagined.

The ground around the tepees resembled a shambles in less than two minutes, with shrieking Indian women and moaning little children, mangled and torn by the deadly missiles! In a very brief space of time scores of men, women and children, as well as two score troopers were lying either dead or writhing in agony on the ground.

There is also little doubt but that many of the soldiers were killed by the cross-fire of their comrades in this desperate engagement. The tepees were ripped and torn to shreds by the explosive shells, some catching fire and burning the helpless and wounded inmates alive.

After the first few volleys, those of the Indians who yet survived stampeded in wild disorder for the shelter of the nearby coulee, pursued by hundreds of maddened Seventh Cavalrymen, who raised their war cry of "Remember Custer!" and followed by a raking fire from the Hotchkiss guns which had been deflected so as to sweep the coulee.

Says one authority: "There can be no question but that this pursuit was simply a massacre, where fleeing women with infants in arms were shot down after resistance had ceased, and when almost every warrior was stretched dead or dying on the ground. From the fact that so many women and children were killed and that their bodies were found far from the scene of action, and as though they were shot down while in flight, it would look as though blind rage had been at work."

Who was to blame for this wanton slaughter?

Strict orders had been given that no women or children should be injured in any way, and yet those orders were unheeded. An Indian was an Indian, male or female, big or little, and "kill everything in sight" seems to have been the uppermost thought in every trooper's breast.

"This butchery," cites another authority, "was the work of infuriated soldiers whose comrades had been shot down without cause or warning." In justice to a brave regiment it must be said that a number of the men were new recruits, fresh from eastern recruiting stations, who had never before been under fire, were not yet imbued with military discipline, and were probably unable, in confusion, to distinguish between men and women by their dress."

Whatever the real cause of the affair at Wounded Knee, one thing is morally certain—the wholesale slaughter of women and children was wholly unnecessary and absolutely inexcusable. Blind rage; the desire of the Seventh Cavalry for revenge for the wiping out of Custer and his 212 troopers on the Little Big Horn, by these same Sioux, were doubtless a factor in determining the "whys" and wherefores" of the slaughter at Wounded Knee.

The actual number of the Sioux slaughtered in this one-sided engagement is variously stated at from 146 to 300. "The whole number killed on the field," states one government report, "or who later died from wounds or exposure, was probably 300."

The loss among the troopers was 31 killed and about the

same number wounded, one or two dying later. With the exception of a hospital steward and one Indian scout, all of the slain troopers belonged to the Seventh Cavalry, as did most of those who were wounded.

The only commissioned officer killed was Capt. George D. Wallace, who lost his life while searching the tepees for hidden weapons. It is said that he was shot four times through the body and struck on the head with a tomahawk, the latter wound causing his death.

The affair at Wounded Knee precipitated a stampede in the towns along the northern edge of Nebraska, and state troops were ordered out under command of Gen. L. B. Colby. They remained on duty until the last of the hostiles had surrendered, about two weeks after the Wounded Knee engagement. They took no part in the hostilities.

There were several minor engagements following that at Wounded Knee, with some small loss of life, but the winding up of the ghost dance craze, and the echoes of the guns of the Seventh Cavalry on the morning of December 29, 1890, marked the passing of the wild Indian, and lowered the curtain on the last war in which the United States has, or probably ever again will be engaged in against its red wards, now peacefully pursuing the white man's road, with but a remnant left of the old warriors who followed Red Cloud, Crazy Horse, Gall, Sitting Bull and Crow King into battle from sixty-five to seventy-five years ago.

CHAPTER VIII

THE "BUFFALO WALLOW" FIGHT OF 1874

Honors for Scout Billy Dixon

~

ONE of the most thrilling experiences, combined with desperate fighting, in the annals of frontier history, in which four enlisted soldiers and two army scouts successfully withstood for an entire day the combined attack of about 125 Kiowa and Comanche Indians, occurred on September 12, 1874, near the Washita River, in what today is Hemphill county, Texas. In 1874 this section was a howling wilderness, practically as unknown as the heart of Africa. These men were carrying dispatches from the camp of Gen. Nelson A. Miles, on McClellan Creek, to Camp Supply, Indian Territory.

In order that the reader may at the start intelligently understand the situation, I append herewith the official report of General Miles, relative to the affair:

"HEADQUARTERS INDIAN TERRITORY EXPEDITION

Camp on Washita River, Texas,
Sept. 24, 1874.

"Adjutant General, U. S. A.
(Through Office Asst. Adj. Gen.
Hdqtrs. Dept. and Mil. District of
the Missouri, and of the Army.)

"General:

I deem it but a duty to brave and heroic men and faithful soldiers, to bring to the notice of the highest military authorities, an instance of indomitable courage, skill and true heroism on the part of a detachment from this command with the request that the actors may be rewarded and their faithfulness and bravery recognized, by pensions, Medals of Honor, or in such way as may be deemed most fitting.

"On the night of the 10th inst., a party consisting of Sergt. Z. T. Woodall, Co. I; Privates Peter Rath, Co. A; John Harrington, Co. H, and George W. Smith, Co. M, Sixth Cavalry, and Scouts Amos Chapman and William Dixon, were sent as bearers of dispatches from the camp of this command on McClellan Creek to Camp Supply, I. T.

"At 6 a. m. on the 12th, when approaching the Washita River, they were met and surrounded by a band of 125 Kiowas and Comanches, who had recently left their Agency. At the first attack, all were struck, Private Smith mortally, and three others severely wounded. Although enclosed on all sides, and by overwhelming numbers, one of them succeeded, while they were under severe fire at short range, and while the others with their rifles were keeping the Indians at bay, in digging, with his knife and hands, a slight cover. After this had been secured, they placed themselves within it, the wounded walking with brave and painful effort, and Private Smith—though he had received a mortal wound—sitting upright within the trench, to conceal the crippled condition of the party from the Indians.

"From early morning until dark, out-numbered twenty-five to one, under an almost constant fire, and at such short range that they sometimes used their pistols, retaining the last charge to prevent capture and torture, this little party of five men defended their lives and the person of their dying comrade, without food, and their only drink the rainwater that collected in a pool mingled with their own blood. There is no doubt that they killed more than double their own number, besides those that were wounded. The Indians abandoned the attack on the 12th at dark.

"The exposure and distance from the command, which were necessary incidents of their duty, were such that for 26 hours from the first attack, their condition could not be known, and not until midnight of the 13th could they receive medical attention and food, exposed during this time to an incessant cold storm.

"Sergt. Woodall, Private Harrington and Scout Chapman

were seriously wounded. Private Smith died of his wounds on the morning of the 13th. Private Rath and Scout Dixon were struck, but not disabled.

"The simple recital of their deeds, and the mention of odds against which they fought—how the wounded defended the dying, and the dying aided the wounded by exposure to fresh wounds, after the power of action had gone—these alone present a scene of cool courage, heroism and self-sacrifice which duty, as well as inclination, prompts us to recognize, but which we cannot fitly honor.

"Very resp'y your obedient servant,

"NELSON A. MILES,
"Colonel and Bvt. Maj. Gen.
U.S.A. Commanding."

Two stories have been told in print of this desperate defense—one by Billy Dixon, one of the most courageous, hardy, cool and renowned army scouts of the 70's, who died in 1913—and one by Amos Chapman, also a well-known army scout and a man of reputation as an Indian fighter. But in order that Billy Dixon may receive the proper credit due him, and his honor and reputation for truthfulness and veracity may be cleared, I propose to present herewith both stories. Amos Chapman for fifty years posed as the real hero in the Buffalo Wallow fight. I offer an affidavit made by one of the four soldiers who were in the fight—Sergt. Woodall, in the form of a letter to Billy Dixon, written from Fort Wingate, N. M., in 1889. The reader must then draw his own conclusions as to who is the real hero in this thrilling engagement. Billy Dixon's account of the fight is furnished me by his wife, Mrs. Olive K. Dixon, today a well-known and brilliant newspaper woman of Miami, Texas. It is as follows:

BILLY DIXON'S STORY

The most perilous adventure of my life occurred September 12, 1874, in what was known as the 'Buffalo Wallow fight.' My escape from death was miraculous. During that

Billy Dixon, famous scout and frontiersman in 1874. Photo taken just before he died in 1912.

year I came in contact with hostile Indians as frequently as the most devoted warrior might wish, and found that it was a serious business.

On September 10, 1874, Gen. Nelson A. Miles, in command of the troops campaigning against the Indians in the Southwest, was on McClellan Creek, in the Texas Panhandle, when he ordered Amos Chapman and myself, scouts, and four enlisted men, to carry dispatches to Fort Supply. The

enlisted men were Sergt. Z. T. Woodall, Troop I; Private
Peter Rath, Troop A; Private John Harrington, Troop H,
and Private George W. Smith, Troop M, Sixth Cavalry.
When General Miles handed us the dispatches he told us
we could have all the soldiers we thought necessary for an
escort. His command was short of rations. We preferred the
smallest possible number.

Leaving camp we traveled mostly at night, resting in
secluded places during the day. War parties were moving in
every direction, and there was danger of attack at every turn.

On the second day, just as the sun was rising, we were
nearing a divide between the Washita River and Gageby
Creek. Riding to the top of a little knoll, we found ourselves
face to face with a large band of Kiowa and Comanche Indians. The Indians saw us at the same time, and circling
quickly, surrounded us. We were in a trap. We knew that
the best thing to do was to make a stand and fight for our
lives, as there would be great danger of our becoming
separated in the excitement of a running fight, after which
the Indians could the more easily kill us one by one. We also
realized that we could do better work on foot; so we dismounted and placed our horses in the care of George Smith.
In a moment or two poor Smith was shot down, and the
horses stampeded.

When Smith was shot he fell flat on his stomach, and his
gun fell from his hands, far from reach. But no Indian was
able to capture that gun. If one ventured near Smith we
never failed to bring him down. We thought Smith was dead
when he fell; but he survived until about 11 o'clock that
night.

I realized at once that I was in closer quarters than I had
ever been in my life, and I have always felt that I did some
good work that day. I was fortunate enough not to become
disabled at any stage of the fight, which left me free to do
my best under the circumstances. I received one wound—

a bullet in the calf of the leg. I was wearing a thin cashmere shirt, slightly bloused. This shirt was literally riddled with bullets. How a man could be shot at so many times at close range and not be hit, I never could understand. The Indians seemed absolutely sure of getting us—so sure, in fact, that they delayed riding us down and killing us at once—which they could easily have done, and prolonged the early stages of the fight merely to satisfy their desire to toy with an enemy, as a cat would play with a mouse before taking its life.

We saw that there was no show for us to survive on this little hillside, and decided that our best fighting ground was a small mesquite flat, several hundred yards distant. Before we undertook to shift our position, a bullet struck Amos Chapman. I was looking at him when he was shot. Amos said, "Billy, I am hit at last," and eased himself down. The fight was so hot that I did not have time to ask him how badly he was hurt. Our situation was growing more desperate every minute. I knew that something had to be done, and quickly, or else all of us, in a short time, would be dead or in the hands of the Indians, who would torture us in the most inhuman manner before taking our lives.

I could see where herds of buffalo had pawed and wallowed a depression commonly called a 'buffalo wallow,' and I ran for it at top speed. It seemed as if a bullet whizzed past me at every jump, but I got through unharmed. The wallow was about ten feet in diameter. I found that its depth, though slight, afforded some protection. I shouted to my comrades to try and come to me, which all of them, save Smith and Chapman, commenced trying to do. As each man reached the wallow, he drew his butcher knife and began digging desperately, with knife and hands, to throw up dirt around the sides. The land happened to be sandy, and we made good headway, though constantly interrupted by the necessity of firing at the Indians as they dashed within range.

Many times during that terrible day did I think that my

last moment was at hand. Once when the Indians were crowding us awfully hard, one of the boys raised up and yelled, 'No, use, boys; no use; we might as well give up!' We answered by shouting to him to lie down. At that moment a bullet struck in the soft bank near him, filling his mouth with dirt. I was so amused that I laughed, though in a sickly way, for none of us felt like laughing.

By this time, however, I had recovered from the first excitement of battle, and was perfectly cool, as were the rest of the men. We were keenly aware that the only thing to do was to sell our lives as dearly as possible. We fired deliberately, taking good aim, and were picking off an Indian at almost every round. The wounded men conducted themselves admirably, and greatly assisted in concealing our crippled condition by sitting upright, as if unhurt, after they reached the wallow. This made it impossible for the Indians to accurately guess what plight we were in. Had they known so many of us were wounded, undoubtedly they would have rode in and finished us.

After all had reached the wallow, with the exception of Chapman and Smith, all of us thinking that Smith was dead, somebody called to Chapman to come on in. We now learned for the first time that Chapman's leg was broken. He called back that he could not walk, as his left knee was shattered.

I made several efforts to reach him before I succeeded. Every time the Indians saw me start, they would fire such a volley that I was forced to retreat; until finally I made a run and got to Chapman. I told him to climb on my back, my plan being to carry him as I would a little child. Drawing both his legs in front of me and laying the broken one over the sound one, to support it, I carried him to the wallow, though not without great difficulty, as he was a larger man than myself, and his body a dead weight. It taxed my strength to carry him.

We were now all in the wallow except Smith, and we felt

that it would be foolish and useless to risk our lives in attempting to bring in his supposedly-dead body. We had not seen him move since the moment he went down. We began digging like gophers with our hands and knives to make our little wall of earth higher, and shortly had heaped up quite a little wall of dirt around us. Its protection was quickly felt, even though our danger was hardly lessened.

When I look back and recall our situation I always find myself wondering and thinking of the manner in which my wounded comrades acted—never complaining or faltering, but they fought as bravely as if a bullet had not touched them. Sometimes the Indians would ride toward us at headlong speed, with lances uplifted and poised, undoubtedly bent upon spearing us. Such moments made a man brace himself and grip his gun. Fortunately we were able to keep our heads, and to bring down or disable the leader. Such charges proved highly dangerous to the Indians, and gradually grew less frequent.

Thus, all that long September day, the Indians circled around us or dashed past, yelling and cutting up all kinds of capers. All morning we had been without water, and the wounded were sorely in need of it. In the stress and excitement of such an encounter, even a man who has not been hurt, grows painfully thirsty, and his tongue and lips are soon as dry as a whetstone. Ours was the courage of despair. We knew what would befall us if captured alive—we had seen too many naked and mangled bodies of white men who had been spreadeagled and tortured with steel and fire, to forget what our own fate would be. So we were determined to fight to the end, not unmindful of the fact that every once in a while there was another dead or wounded Indian.

About three o'clock a black cloud came up in the west, and in a short time the sky shook and blazed with thunder and lightning. Rain fell in blinding sheets, drenching us to the skin. Water gathered quickly in the buffalo wallow, and our wounded men eagerly bent forward and drank from the muddy pool. It was more than muddy—that water was red with their own blood that had flowed from their wounds, and lay clotting and dry in the hot September sun.

The storm and the rain proved our salvation. The wind had shifted to the north, and was now drearily chilling us to the bone. An Indian dislikes rain, especially a cold rain, and those Kiowas and Comanches were no exception to the rule. We could see them in groups out of rifle range, sitting on their ponies with their blankets drawn tightly around them. The plains country beats the world for quick changes in weather, and in less than an hour after the rain had fallen, the wind was bitter cold. Not a man in our crowd had a coat, and our thin shirts were scant protection. Our coats were tied behind our saddles when our horses stampeded, and were lost beyond recovery. I was heartsick over the loss of my coat, for in the inside pocket was my dearest treasure—my mother's picture, which my father had given me shortly before his death. I was never able to recover it.

The water was gathering rapidly in the wallow, and soon reached two inches, but not a man murmured. Not one thought of surrender, although the wounded were shivering as if they had the ague.

We now found that our ammunition was running low. This fact rather appalled us, as bullets—and plenty of them—were our only protection. Necessity compelled us to husband every cartridge as long as possible, and not to fire at an Indian unless we could see that he meant business, and was coming right into us.

Late in the afternoon somebody suggested that we should go out and get Smith's belt and six-shooter, as he had been shot earlier in the fight, and his belt was undoubtedly loaded with cartridges.

Rath offered to go, and soon returned with the startling information that Smith was still alive. This astonished us greatly, and caused us deep regret that we had not known it earlier in the day. Rath and I at once got ready to bring poor Smith to the buffalo wallow. By supporting the wounded man between us, he managed to walk. We could see that there was no chance for him. He was shot through the left lung, and when he breathed the wind sobbed out of his back under the left shoulder blade. Near the wallow an Indian had dropped a stout willow switch with which he had been whipping his pony. Using this switch a silk handkerchief was forced into the gaping hole in Smith's back to staunch the flow of blood, in a measure.

Night was approaching, and it looked blacker to me than any night I had ever seen. Ours was a forlorn and disheartening situation. The Indians were still all around us. The nearest relief was 75 miles away. Of the six men in the wallow, four were badly wounded, and without anything to relieve their suffering. We were cold and hungry, with nothing to eat, and without a blanket, coat or hat to protect us from the rain and the biting wind. It was impossible to rest or sleep with two inches of water in the wallow.

I remember that I threw my hat—a wide-brimmed sombrero—as far from me as I could when our horses stampeded. The hat was in my way, and further, was too good a target for the Indians to shoot at.

We were unable to get grass for bedding for the reason that the whole country had been burned over by the Indians. It was absolutely necessary, however, that the men should have some kind of bed to keep them off the cold, damp ground. Rath and I solved the problem by gathering tumbleweeds, which in that country the wind would drive for miles and miles. Many of them were bigger than a bushel basket apiece, and their sprigs so tough that the weeds had the "spring" of a wire mattress. We crushed the weeds down and lay down on them for the night, though not a man dared close his eyes in sleep.

By the time heavy darkness had fallen, every Indian had disappeared. Happily, they did not return to molest us during the night, although of course we had nothing to assure us that we would not be again attacked. There was a new moon, but so small and slender that in the clouded sky there was but little light. While there was yet a little day-light left I took the willow switch, and sitting down on the edge of our improvised little fort, I carefully cleaned every gun.

While engaged in this occupation we held a council to decide what was the best thing to do. We agreed that some-body must go for help. No journey could have been beset with greater danger. Rath and I both offered to go. In fact the task was squarely up to us, as all the other men were too badly injured. I insisted that I should go, as I knew the country, and felt confident that I could find the trail that led to Camp Supply. I was sure we were not far from the trail.

My insistence at once caused protest from the wounded. They were willing that Rath should go, but would not listen to my leaving. Once I put my hand on my gun, with the intention of going anyway, then I yielded to their wishes against my better judgment, and decided to remain through the night. The wounded men relied greatly on my skill as a marksman.

Rath, therefore, made ready for the journey, and then bidding us goodby he crawled away into the darkness. In about two hours, while we were hoping he had managed to get a good start without being detected, he returned, saying he could not locate the trail.

By this time Smith had grown much worse, and was beg-ging us, in piteous tones, to shoot him and put an end to his terrible agony. We found it necessary to watch him closely to prevent his committing suicide.

There was not a man among us who had not thought of the same melancholy fate. When the fighting was at its worst, with the Indians closing in on all sides, and when it seemed that every minute would be our last, it was only by our great coolness and marksmanship that we kept the savages from getting in among us, which would probably have compelled us to use the last shot on ourselves. At that time I was wearing my hair long and as I had quite a crop of it, I knew it would be a great temptation to the Indians to get my scalp.

Poor Smith endured his agony like a brave soldier. Our hearts ached for him, and we longed to relieve his suffering, but there was absolutely nothing that we could do for him. About 1 o'clock that night he fell asleep, and we were glad of it, for in sleep he could forget his sufferings. Later in the night one of the boys felt of him to see how he was getting along. Poor Smith! He was cold in death. Men commonly think of death as something to be shunned, but there are times when its hand falls as tenderly as the touch of a mother's, and when its coming is welcomed by those to whom hopeless suffering had brought the last bitter dregs of life. We lifted the body of our dead comrade and gently laid it outside the buffalo wallow on the mesquite grass, covering the face with a white silk handkerchief.

That was a night to try men's souls! What fate would the morrow have in store for us? It was a night that is indelibly stamped on my memory, and which time can never efface. Many a time since has its perils filled my dreams, until I awoke, startled and thrilled, with a feeling of most imminent danger. Every night the same stars are shining way out there in the lonely Panhandle country; the same winds sigh as mournfully as they did on that terrible night, and I often wonder if a single settler who passes the lonely spot knows how desperately six men once battled for their lives, where now, perhaps, plowed fields and safety, with all the comforts of civilization, are on every hand.

Like everything else the long, dreary night at length came

to an end, and the first rosy tints of dawn tinged the eastern sky, while the sun came out clear and warm. By this time all the men were willing that I should go for help. Our perilous position was such that there must be no waiting for darkness to cover my movements; it was imperative that I start immediately, and bidding them all be of good cheer I started. Daylight exposed me to many dangers from which the night shielded me. By moving cautiously at night, it was possible to avoid an enemy, and even if surprised there was a chance to escape in the darkness. But in the broad daylight the enemy could lie in hiding and sweep the country with keen eyes in every direction. On the plains—especially in the fall—when the grass was short and there was no cover, the smallest moving object could be perceived by such trained eyes as hostile Indians possessed, at an astonishing long distance. I knew I must proceed with the utmost caution, lest I fall into an ambush or be attacked in the open by superior numbers.

I had traveled scarcely more than half a mile from the wallow when I struck the plain trail leading to Camp Supply. Hurrying along as rapidly as possible, and keeping a constant lookout for Indians, I suddenly checked myself at the sight of moving objects about two miles to the northwest, which seemed to cover about an acre of ground. At first the objects did not appear to be moving, and I could not tell whether it was Indians or white men. I skulked to a growth of tall grass and lay in hiding for a brief time. My nerves, however, were too keen to endure this, so I cautiously raised myself and took another look. The outfit was moving toward me. Shortly, I was enabled to discern that it was a body of troops. Indians always traveled strung out in a line, but these were traveling abreast.

I never felt happier in all my life. I stepped out into the open and whanged away with my rifle to attract their attention. The whole command suddenly came to a halt. I fired a second shot, and presently saw two men ride out from the command toward me. When they came up, I told them my story and reported the serious condition of my comrades. The soldiers rode rapidly back to the command and reported. It proved to be a detachment under the command of Major Price, accompanying General Miles' supply train, which was on its way from Camp Supply to field headquarters.

It appeared that the same Indians we had been fighting had been holding this supply train corraled for four days near the Washita river. Major Price happened along and raised the siege. The Indians had just given up the attack on this train when we happened to run into them.

Major Price rode out where I was waiting, bringing his army surgeon with him. I described the condition of my comrades, after which the major instructed his surgeon and two soldiers to go and see what could be done for my wounded comrades. I pointed out the location, which was not more than a mile distant, and asked the surgeon if he thought he could find the place without my accompanying him, as Major Price wanted me to remain and tell him about the fight. He said he could, and they rode away.

I was describing in detail all that had happened, when I looked up and noted that the relief party was bearing too far toward the south. I fired my gun to attract their attention, and then waved it in the direction I intended they should go. By this time they were within gunshot of the wallow. Suddenly, to my utter astonishment, I saw a puff of smoke rise from the wallow, followed by the roar of a rifle— one of the men had fired at the approaching strangers, and dropped a horse ridden by one of the soldiers.

I ran forward as rapidly as possible, not knowing what the men might do next. They were soon able to recognize me, and lowered their guns. When we got to them the men said they heard shooting—the shots I had fired to attract the attention of the troops—and supposed the Indians had killed me and were coming back to renew the attack upon them. They were determined to take no chances, and not recognizing the surgeon and the two soldiers, had fired at them the minute they got within range.

Despite the sad plight of the wounded men, about all the surgeon did was to merely examine their wounds. The soldiers turned over a few bits of hardtack and some dried beef which happened to be tied behind their saddles. Major Price further refused to leave any men with us. For this he was afterward severely censured—and justly. He would not even provide us with firearms. Our own ammunition was exhausted, and the soldiers carried weapons of a different make and caliber than our own. However, they said they would let General Miles know of our condition. We were sure that help would come the instant the general heard the news.

We watched and waited until midnight of the second day after these troops had passed, before help came. A long way off in the darkness we heard the sound of a bugle. Never was there sweeter music than that to our suffering nerves! It made us swallow a big lump in our throats. Nearer and nearer came the bugle notes. We fired our guns with the few remaining cartridges we had, and soon the soldiers came riding to us out of the darkness.

As soon as the wounded could be turned over to the surgeon, we placed the dead body of our comrade in the wallow where we had fought and suffered together, and covered it with the dirt which we had ridged up with our hands and butcher knives. Then we went down on the creek, where the soldiers had built a big fire and cooked a big meal for us.

Next day the wounded were sent to Camp Supply. Amos Chapman's leg was amputated above the knee. All the men eventually recovered, and went right on with the army. Chapman could handle a gun and ride as well as ever, but had to mount his horse from the right side, Indian fashion.

When I last heard from Amos Chapman he was living at

Seiling, Oklahoma. In the early '80's, Colonel Richard Irving Dodge, U.S.A., wrote a book entitled "Our Wild Indians," in which he attempted to give a circumstantial account of the buffalo wallow fight. Sergeant Woodall was displeased with the statement of facts therein, and resented the inaccuracies.

When Colonel Dodge was writing his book, he wrote to me and asked me to send him an account of the buffalo wallow fight. I neglected to do so, and he obtained his information from other sources. If my narrative differs from that related in Colonel Dodge's book, all I can say is that I have described the fight as I saw it. In saying this, I do not wish to place myself in the attitude of censuring Colonel Dodge. However, it should be reasonably apparent that a man with a broken leg cannot carry another man on his back. In correcting this bit of border warfare history I wish to state that every one of my comrades conducted himself in the most heroic manner, bravely doing his part in every emergency.

General Miles had both the heart and the accomplishments of a soldier, and Congress voted to each of us the Medal of Honor. He was delighted when the medals came from Washington, and with his own hands pinned mine on my coat when we were in camp on Carson Creek, five or six miles west of the ruins of the original Adobe Walls.

It was always my intention to return and mark the spot where the buffalo wallow fight took place, and where Geo. Smith yet lies buried. Procrastination and the remoteness of the place have prevented this.

* * * * *

Now for the story which appears on page 631 of Colonel Dodge's well-known book, "Our Wild Indians," which was brought out in 1882:

"Heroic as was the conduct of all, that of Chapman deserves most special honor, for he received his wound while

General Nelson A. Miles.

performing a deed than which the loftiest manhood can find nothing nobler.

"The first intimation of the presence of Indians was a volley which wounded every man in the party. In an instant the Indians appeared on all sides! Dismounting and abandoning their horses, the brave band moved together for a hundred yards to a buffalo wallow. Chapman and Dixon being but slightly wounded, worked hard and fast to deepen this depression, and as soon as it was satisfactorily deep to afford some cover, it was occupied. Smith had fallen from his horse at the first fire, and was supposed to be dead. Now the supposed dead body was seen to move slightly. He was alive, though entirely disabled. Turning to his comrades, Chapman said: 'Now, boys, keep those infernal redskins off of me, and I will run down and pick up Smith and bring him back before they can get at me.'

"Laying down his rifle he sprang out of the buffalo wallow and ran with all speed to Smith and attempted to shoulder him. 'Did any of you ever try to shoulder a wounded man?' asked Chapman, in relating the story. 'Smith was not a large man—160 or 170 pounds—but I declare to you that he seemed to weigh a ton. Finally I laid down and got his chest across my back and his arms around my neck, and then got up with him. It was as much as I could do to stagger under him, for he couldn't help himself a bit. By the time I had got twenty or thirty yards, about fifteen Indians came for me at full speed on their ponies. They all knew me and yelled, 'Amos, Amos, we have got you now!' I pulled my pistol, but I couldn't hold Smith on my back with one hand, so I let him drop. The boys in the buffalo wallow opened on the Indians just at the right time, and I opened on them with my pistol. There was a tumbling of ponies and a scattering of Indians, and in a minute they were gone. I got Smith up again and made the best possible time, but before I could reach the wallow another gang came for me.

I had only one or two shots in my pistol, so I didn't stop to fight, but ran for it. When I was within twenty yards of the wallow, a little old scoundrel that I had fed fifty times, rode almost on me and fired. I fell, with Smith on top of me, *but as I didn't feel any pain,* I thought I had stepped into a hole. I jumped up, picked up Smith and got safe in the wallow. 'Amos,' said Dixon, 'you are badly hurt.' 'No, I am not,' said I. 'Why, look at your leg,' and sure enough, the leg was shot off just above the ankle joint, *and I had been walking on the bone, dragging the foot behind me, and in the excitement I never knew it, nor have I ever had any pain in my leg to this day.*"

*   *   *   *   *

I had read this account of the buffalo wallow fight as related by Amos Chapman, probably a hundred times, when a small boy—in fact, it was one of my pet stories years ago, and I always marveled at the cool courage of a man who could pack a 170-pound wounded comrade on his back, with his own leg shot off at the ankle joint!

It was not until about 1920, however, that I read Billy Dixon's version of the buffalo wallow fight. There was such a vast difference between the two stories that I immediately became interested. I wondered if Amos Chapman was "stealing Billy Dixon's thunder," or vice versa, and I determined to do a little investigating. I secured the address of Amos Chapman in Oklahoma and wrote him, calling his attention to the difference between his own story of the buffalo wallow fight and that of Billy Dixon, and asked him if his story as related in "Our Wild Indians" was really true. I never received a reply. Not knowing but what Chapman might be dead, I wrote to an attorney in the town and received a reply that the attorney could tell me anything about Amos Chapman which I might want to know. I therefore called his attention to the two stories and asked if he would query Chapman about it. I never received any further communication from the attorney, although I wrote him once or twice more.

I then communicated with Mrs. Olive Dixon at Miami, Texas, wife of the noted scout, who is at present a well-known newspaper woman of that section. She was at first loath to say anything on the subject, but I pressed the matter, insisting that for the sake of history, and the reputation of her dead husband, the actual facts should be made public. Mrs. Dixon thereupon sent me the following letter which was written by Sergeant Woodall, one of the four soldiers in the fight, from Fort Wingate, N. M., where he was then stationed, under date of January 4, 1889. This letter, it appears to me, disproves the Chapman story and proves conclusively that Billy Dixon, the intrepid scout, is the real hero of the famous buffalo wallow fight.

The reader, however, must form his own conclusions after reading Sergeant Woodall's communication.

Fort Wingate, N. M.
Jan. 4, 1889.

Friend Dixon:

Hearing that you were at Adobe Walls in the Panhandle of Texas, and as we both came near passing in our checks between the Gageby Creek and the Washita river on September 12, 1874, I thought it would not be out of place to drop you a few lines and revive old times. I hear from a man by the name of Shearer who belonged to the Fourth Cavalry, that you were there.

Do you ever see Amos, or any of the men who were with us then? I never have, and would very much like to see any of them and fight our old fights over again.

Did you read the account (in *Our Wild Indians*) where Amos carried Smith on his back, and did not know his leg was shot off until he got to the wallow? *Did you ever hear tell of such a damn lie, when he knows very well that you carried both of them there yourself?* I was surprised when I read the account in the book written by Col. Dodge. To read it you would think there was no one there but Chapman himself. The idea that a man could have his leg shot off and did not know it, makes me tired. You can bet that I came very near knowing it when I was struck, and I know it and feel it to this day, and my leg was not shot off. When I read the book I came very near contradicting it, as there were others who did just as much as Chapman, if not more. It seems that when he met Col. Dodge he took all the credit to himself. * * * Dixon, don't fail to answer this letter, because I would sooner hear from you than any man that I know of, and give me your opinion of the fight. I would have written you before, but did not know where you were. I will close this letter with my best wishes for your welfare.

From your sincere friend, and one on whom you can depend upon any and all circumstances.

(Signed)   Z. T. WOODALL,
1st Sergeant, Troop I, 6th Cavalry
Fort Wingate, N. M.

*   *   *   *   *

State of Texas,
County of Robert.

I hereby certify that I have compared the above letter (copy of a certified copy of a letter) written by Z. T. Woodall, now in possession of Mrs. Olive Dixon, of Miami, Texas, and the above copy is true and correct to the best of my knowledge and belief.

H. A. TULLEY.

Subscribed and sworn to before me as a notary public in and for Roberts County, Texas, this the 27th day of Jan. A.D. 1923.

JAS. Z. SAUL, Notary Public.

My commission expires June 1st, 1923.

*   *   *   *   *

With no other desire save to give "honor to whom honor is due," and wishing to write only the TRUE frontier history, I determined that it was high time—after a lapse of 70 years —that the reputation of Billy Dixon as the real hero of the famous buffalo wallow fight be sustained, and this noted frontiersman, who yet has hosts of friends throughout the country, who remember him with only words of praise and commendation, be placed on the pinnacle of fame where he rightfully belongs.

*   *   *   *   *

The site of the buffalo wallow fight is in Hemphill county, Texas, 22 miles south of the present town of Canadian, and 25 miles southeast of Miami, on the ranch of Charles Teas. The site was definitely located in April, 1921, by J. J. Long, of Mobeetie, Texas, who at the time of the fight, was a teamster in a wagon train hauling supplies for General Miles' army. Billy Dixon and Mr. Long became close friends, and a short time after, when Long was a mail carrier between Fort Elliott and Camp Supply, and Billy Dixon was serving as a guard or escort for the mail, their route took them over the ground on which the fight took place, and Dixon and Mr. Long would frequently halt at the site, while the former would relate certain incidents of the occurrence. Mr. Long was therefore very familiar with the lay of the land, and in 1921 had no trouble in locating the exact spot where the buffalo wallow fight occurred.

~

CHAPTER IX

NORTH'S PAWNEE SCOUTS

*How This Most Famous Battalion of Indian Allies of
the U. S. Army Was Organized, as Related by
Capt. Luther H. North to E. A. Brininstool,
1926*

~

IN THE SUMMER of 1864, Gen. Samuel R. Curtis, who
was then commander of the Department of the Missouri,
which included Kansas and Nebraska Territories, while
on his way to Fort Kearney (from which point he started
with an expedition against the hostile Indians) stopped over
at Columbus, Nebraska, and engaged a man named Mc-
Fayden, and my brother, Major Frank North, to secure the
services of seventy-five Pawnee Indians to accompany the
expedition as guides and scouts.

The Indians furnished their own mounts and equipment,
and were to have been paid $25 a month for their services.
I believe they yet have it coming to them!

McFayden and my brother went along as interpreters, both
being fluent in the Pawnee tongue. A few days after leaving
Fort Kearney, Gen. Curtis left the expedition, and with one
company of cavalry, two Pawnee Indians and my brother,
started for Fort Riley, Kans.

Enroute he talked to my brother Frank in regard to
enlisting a company of Pawnee Indians, and also suggested
calling them "The Pawnee Scouts." When Frank arrived
home from Fort Riley, the Pawnees had started on their

fall hunt, and it was some time before he could secure enough men to fill out the company.

It was in January, 1865, that they were mustered into the service, and soon after were sent to Fort Kearney, where they received their equipment and horses, and were ordered to Julesburg, thence to Fort Laramie, where they joined the Powder River Expedition under Gen. P. E. Connor, on Powder River.

The scouts found the trail of a war party of Cheyennes which had been raiding emigrant trains on the North Platte. My brother, with forty men, followed them sixty miles. They crossed Powder River seventeen times that night; but one of the Scouts traveled on foot the whole distance, and never lost the trail once.

They overtook the Cheyennes just at daybreak, attacking and killing all of them (twenty-seven in number), and got back to camp that night.

A few days later they had another skirmish, in which they killed all but one Indian. Not long after this, my brother, with five men, found the Arapahoe village on Tongue River, and Frank sent one of the Scouts to General Connor with a message, while he watched the village. Connor arrived the next morning, and charged the village, killing quite a number of the Indians, and captured eleven hundred horses and destroyed all their tepees.

Not long after, a party of the Scouts, with Frank, found Colonel Cole and his command, and they were to have made a junction with General Connor on the Little Big Horn river, but had become lost. My brother found Cole's command in a starving condition, and most of them were afoot. Frank divided what rations he had among them, and guided them to Fort Reno (formerly Fort Connor). This ended the campaign of 1865, and the Scouts were sent home, where they were mustered out of service in the spring of 1866.

In the spring of 1867, my brother recruited four companies of Pawnee Scouts, comprising fifty men to a company, and that was the real beginning of the famous "Pawnee Battalion." Frank was major of this battalion, and I was captain of one of the companies.

My company and Captain Morse's company were sent to Ogalalla, Nebraska, which was at that time the end of track of the Union Pacific Railroad. We were to guard the track-layers. The Sioux whooped down the next morning, attacked the camp and ran off some of the mules. We started after them, killed two and recovered all the mules.

A short time after, General Sherman and General Augur started on an inspection tour of the forts of the Northwest. My brother, Captain Morse and myself, with two companies of our Pawnees and two or three companies of cavalry, accompanied them.

We went up the South Platte to old Fort Morgan. A great many of the soldiers were deserting, and taking horses and arms with them. Some of the men on guard deserted one night, and after that we furnished guards (for General Sherman's tent) from our Pawnee Scouts.

From Fort Morgan we went north to Fort Laramie. Before reaching Laramie, we ran across a party of Arapahoes, who had made a raid near the fort. We gave chase, and after a run of ten miles, recovered the stock and killed a couple of the reds. We were then ordered back to the line of the railroad to guard a camp of graders at Granite Canyon, eighteen miles west of Cheyenne, Wyoming.

A short time after that, I was ordered back to the end of the track, which was then at a point about where the city of Sidney, Nebraska, is now located. The company under Capt. James Murie was sent to Plum Creek Station, where the Cheyennes, under old Chief Turkey Leg, had wrecked a train and killed all the crew.

A day or so after Murie arrived at that point, the Indians returned and my brother and Captain Murie, with forty men,

Major Frank North, organizer and commander of the famous "Pawnee Scouts," with his wife.

crossed the river and attacked them, killing seventeen and capturing thirty-five head of stock, and one squaw and a boy.

Two or three weeks later, at a meeting of General Sherman, General Harney, General Augur and others representing the Government, together with Chief Spotted Tail and several others of the Sioux chiefs, and Turkey Leg for the Cheyennes, with my brother, all were in the tent where the council was being held, and Turkey Leg, who knew Frank, had the interpreter ask him if he had some prisoners.

On being told that he had a woman and a boy, Turkey Leg said the woman was his wife, and that he had some white prisoners which he would exchange for her. He sent out to his camp on Medicine Creek, and brought in two girls and three boys. My brother took the woman and the boy up from Plum Creek, and the exchange was made in the old railroad eating-house at North Platte, Nebraska.

In the fall I made another trip from the end of track, which was then at Pine Bluffs, to Fort Laramie, and back to Fort Kearney, where the three other companies had preceded me, and there we were all mustered out about the first of January.

Early in the spring of 1868, two more companies of Pawnee Scouts were enlisted. They were placed at different points along the railroad, twenty-five to a place, and small scouting parties of eight or ten were kept patrolling the railroad. Lieut. Billy Harvey, who was stationed at Wood River, ran across a war party north of that point one day, and after chasing them several miles, overtook and killed three of them.

My brother and Capt. Morse, with one company, were scouting on Muddy Creek with seven men, when they were surrounded by a large body of Sioux. They got into a washout, and fought their enemies off for six hours, killing fifteen Indians.

That year I did not serve with the scouts. They had one

other battle that fall at Roscoe, just east of Ogalalla, where they drove off a band of Sioux who were trying to tear up the track.

They were mustered out in the fall, and in February, 1869, two other companies were enlisted. I was with them, and we went to Fort McPherson, where the horses of the Scouts had been wintering. As soon as we could get ready, I was started for the Republican River to join Major Noyes, who had already gone.

My brother returned to the Pawnee Reservation to enlist another company. When I got to the Republican I met Major Noyes, who was on his way back to the post. He had run out of rations. He had expected to find plenty of buffalo, but had not seen a single animal. I divided my rations with Noyes.

The following morning we started on the return trip in a snowstorm. Before we had gone five miles a raging blizzard developed, and it grew very cold. We faced it for 25 miles to Frenchman Creek. I did not know where Major Noyes was. The cavalry horses were in much better condition than our own mounts, and had traveled so much faster that their trail had blown full of snow, and we could not follow them.

When I thought we must be getting near to Frenchman Creek, one of my men rode up beside me, and said that he thought he could locate a canyon that had timber in it. As the snow was blowing fiercely, so that it was impossible to see ten feet ahead, I thought he was crazy, but ordered him to go ahead and lead on. He took the lead, and soon brought us to a canyon where we had good shelter.

Here the men cut some poles, and taking the covers off their wagons, soon built me a tepee, and in half an hour we had a good fire inside, and were as comfortable as was possible, with ears, noses and hands frozen.

The following morning was bright and clear, but very cold. When I got to the Frenchman Fork, I found Major Noyes in camp. There was no shelter where they had camped, and no wood available. The men were nearly all more or less frozen, and over fifty horses and some of the mules were frozen to death. The river was frozen over, and as my Scouts were the only ones not suffering severely, we had to chop a channel across. I then had them fasten ropes to the wagons, and put twenty men to each wagon. They walked on the ice on each side of the channel, and helped pull the wagons across.

We were three days in reaching Fort McPherson. The Scouts were sent to North Platte, and we remained in camp until April, and were then ordered back to McPherson. General Eugene A. Carr, with the Fifth Cavalry, had come from the south, with Buffalo Bill Cody as guide and scout.

We left McPherson in June and went south to the Republican, and down it one or two days' march. One evening seven Indians dashed into camp, killed two men who were herding the mules, and stampeded them. The Scouts were camped just across the river. We caught our horses, jumped on them bareback, and were across the river before the Indians were out of sight.

As soon as the redskins saw that we were overtaking them, they abandoned the mules. We chased them for perhaps ten miles, killing two of the rascals; the others got away. We arrived back at camp about midnight.

The next day we went south. We scouted over as far as the Solomon River, followed it up one day, and then back to Prairie Dog Creek, where my brother met us with the third company of Scouts, and took command of the battalion. We then crossed to the Republican, and followed it up till near its headwaters.

While out with a scouting party, I discovered a Cheyenne camp. This was on the 7th of July. I reported to General Carr, who was twenty-five miles down the river. We took up the trail where I had seen the camp, and on the 11th overtook them at Summit Springs, Colorado. We surprised the Indians in camp, and killed Tall Bull, the chief, and a lot of his warriors, captured four women, thirteen children, six hundred horses and a hundred and twenty mules. They had two white women in their camp as prisoners.

After going into Fort Sedgwick, where we drew rations and forage, we started south. The expedition was under the command of Colonel Royal. We found the trail of the Cheyennes, and followed down the Frenchman, then back north, crossed the Platte just west of Ogalalla, and on north into the sand hills of Nebraska. At the head of the Loup River we ran out of rations, and came back to Fort Mc-Pherson, where we were mustered out. That was in 1870. There were two companies of Scouts. My company was stationed at Plum Creek Station, about two or three miles east of the present city of Lexington.

In September, General Carr made a campaign to the Republican and took my company. We found one small war party, but after pursuing them several miles, we lost the trail. On the return to McPherson the Scouts were again mustered out.

Four years later the Pawnees were removed from their reservation in Nebraska to the Indian Territory, and in 1876, soon after the Custer fight, Gen. Sheridan sent Frank and myself down to recruit one hundred more of the Pawnee. We brought them by rail from Coffeyville, Kansas, to Sidney, Nebraska, where they were mustered into the service, and drew horses, arms and equipment.

We were then ordered to Fort Robinson, Nebraska, where we joined General MacKenzie. We made a night ride down to Chadron Creek, and captured Red Cloud and his band, and brought them to Fort Robinson. We took Red Cloud's horses (seven hundred and twenty head) to Fort Laramie, and turned them over to the quartermaster.

Then we went on the winter campaign with General Crook

Capt. Luther H. North, at age 17, as a Captain in the famous "North's Pawnee Scouts."

into the Powder River country. We were with MacKenzie when he fought the Cheyennes under Dull Knife, on a branch of the Powder River, in the Big Horn mountains. After this battle, we came with General Crook's command to Fort Laramie. We were ordered to Sidney, Nebraska, where we were mustered out of the service for the last time.

* * * * *

On all our campaigns it was the Pawnee Scouts who were always first to find Indian signs. They were always sent ahead to do the trailing. They located every war party and every Indian village which we captured, with the single exception of Dull Knife's village in the Big Horn mountains, which was located by the Arapahoe scouts.

While scouting south of the Republican River, with ten men, we were "jumped" by a war party of about one hundred and fifty hostiles. We were mounted, and I told the men we would run for the creek, about a mile distant, where we would dismount and put up a fight. We were armed with Spencer carbines, a seven-shot weapon.

When within half a mile of the creek, my horse jumped on some ice, slipped and fell. I struck on my head, and was knocked unconscious. The boys stopped and dismounted, while nine of them, with their horses, formed a ring around me, the remaining man picked me up. When I came to, the Indians were all around us, but the Pawnees met them, with such fierce resistance that they scattered and fell back to a safe distance. As soon as I could ride, we moved slowly to the creek, where we stood the hostiles off until night, when they gave it up, and rode away to the south.

* * * * *

In regard to that battle of Summit Springs, Frank's diary gives the number of troops engaged as two hundred of the Fifth Cavalry, with Gen. Carr in command, and forty of our Pawnee Scouts with Frank, Capt. Cushing and myself.

Soon after leaving camp the morning of July 11th, 1869, the trail we were following split up, one trail leading to the northeast, a second almost due north, and the third to the northwest. Gen. Carr divided his command into three columns, he taking command of the column that went northwest. He had about 200 cavalry and ten of our Pawnees with him.

Frank, Cushing and I, with 35 of our Scouts, followed the middle trail that went north. Col. Royal, with about 200 cavalrymen, and a few of our scouts, and Cody (Buffalo Bill) followed the trail to the northeast.

After separating, we traveled at as brisk a pace as the horses could stand, for about three hours, when we were overtaken by one of our Scouts who had gone with Gen.

Carr, who said that they had discovered the Indian village, and that we were to join his command as soon as possible.

We followed him at a gallop for about seven miles, when we joined Carr's command. He had dismounted them behind a ridge of sand hills. He told Frank that he had sent a courier to Col. Royal, but as he had heard nothing from him, he said it would be best to attack the village at once, before the Indians had a chance to break camp and scatter into the sandhills.

He waited for perhaps ten minutes for our Indians to unsaddle horses. (They always went into battle bareback if possible.) Then the charge was sounded. The village was about three miles away, and was out of sight from us, but the Indian ponies were in sight on the hills near the village.

Our men, riding bareback, made much better time than the cavalry, and we were perhaps three hundred yards ahead of the troops. As we came over a low hill at the lower end of the village, the Indians met us there, and halted us for a few minutes; we only had forty men.

Then the cavalry came charging on, and turning to the left, galloped up the line of tepees to the Springs, about a half mile above, where they halted and began firing into the village. From this time on, we saw but little of the troops as we crossed the little stream, and went into the lower end of the village.

It was about 2 o'clock, and very hot. About the first tepee we came to was Tall Bull's, though of course none of us knew it at the time. The fighting here was pretty brisk, and as we came to the tepee, Capt. Cushing discovered a one-gallon keg of water near it. He dismounted and took a drink. Frank then asked him for the keg, and as he handed it to him (Frank was on his horse), a white woman crawled out of the tepee, and, screaming and crying, caught Frank around his knees.

This woman was a Mrs. Weichel, whom the Indians had

captured in Kansas in the spring of 1869. She could not speak English, and was so terror-stricken that it was hard to pacify her. She was shot through the fleshy part of her breast by an Indian (probably Tall Bull) as she was in his lodge.

Capt. Luther H. North, in later years. His death occurred in Columbus, Nebraska, April, 1935.

About this time, a saddled Indian horse trotted out in sight just above us, and as my own horse was pretty well exhausted, I ran to catch this stray animal. In passing over a low sandhill, I saw a woman lying on the ground, and on getting nearer, saw that she also was a white woman. It was Mrs. Alderdice, who had been captured at the same time with Mrs. Weichel, in Kansas. She had been tomahawked, and was dead.

After returning to where Frank and Cushing were, we left a guard with Mrs. Weichel, and continued across the lower end of the village. The Indians were running away as fast as they could catch horses, but quite a few warriors who hadn't caught horses, were falling back on foot, and twenty of them ran into a ravine or wash-out that extended back into the hills for nearly a quarter of a mile.

We saw one Indian on horseback enter the washout. He was riding a yellow gelding. When we were within a hundred yards of the mouth of this ravine, this yellow horse trotted out, and after staggering around, fell over and died.

When we rode up the hill that the ravine was in, Frank and I happened to be riding side by side. The ravine was nearer than we thought, and an Indian had climbed up the side where the dirt had washed down, making a sort of steps. He stuck his gun over the bank and took a shot at Frank, who dropped off his horse so suddenly that I thought he was hit. He landed on his feet, handed me his reins, and said, "Ride away, and he will stick his head up."

I turned and started away on a gallop, but had only made a few jumps when Frank fired. I rode back and asked "if he got him." He said, "Yes." Just then an Indian girl about 12 years old, and a squaw, climbed out of the ravine where the Indian had been hiding. They came to us, and signed to have mercy. Frank signed to them to go over where we had left Mrs. Weichel, and stay there until we came back, which they did.

Some of our boys had joined us, and we walked over to the ravine and saw the Indian whom Frank had shot. He was lying on his back, and was shot in the center of his forehead. We didn't go down into the ravine, but followed up the bank on foot. Up at the head of this blow-out the banks were perpendicular, and about fifteen feet high. There were 13 warriors there.

We would slip up as near the edge as possible, stick our

guns over, blaze away and jump back, throw in another shell and repeat it. At about my second attempt I guess I was a little slow, and as I stuck my head over, an arrow met me. It hit me just in the eyebrow, cutting to the bone, and glancing off. It felt like I had been hit with a club, and turned me half way around, and I would have fallen over the bank if one of my boys had not caught me by the arm and dragged me back. It made me sick for a few minutes, but Frank bound it up with his handkerchief, after disposing of the Indians in the ravine, and I want to tell you right now, there wasn't a single white soldier there except Frank, Cushing and myself.

The white soldiers under Gen. Carr, Lieut. Mason, Lieut. Hayes (and I think two other officers) were taking care of the upper end of the Indian village, and they did a good job of it.

We all joined in the chase through the sand hills, and in the evening, about 6 o'clock, returned to the village, where we went into camp. Then came a terrific thunder-storm and after that came Royal's column, who had Buffalo Bill with them.

The next day we pulled out for Fort Sedgwick, but before we left the battlefield Lieut. Mason came to our camp. He had a beautiful eagle-feather head-dress, and the band that fitted around the forehead was decorated with two small buffalo horns. He asked Frank if this might not have been Tall Bull's war-bonnet. That was one of the stories that was started about the killing of Tall Bull. No one knew that he had been killed until we got to Fort Sedgwick. When Leon Pallada came to our camp I sent one of my men to bring the woman we had captured at the ravine. As she came toward the tent, Pallada said, "I know that woman; she is Tall Bull's wife." I then asked him to ask the woman who killed Tall Bull. She turned and pointed to Frank, and said that the Indian that Frank shot at in the ravine was Tall

Bull; that he rode a yellow horse into the ravine, and told the woman that when the soldiers came, she should surrender to them; that he was going to die. Then he shot the yellow horse in the belly, and turned it loose. That was the horse we saw die.

That very day, Col. E. C. Judson (Ned Buntline) came to our camp with a proposal to write Frank up. Frank was just ready to start to Omaha with Gen. Augur. He laughed at Judson (who was pretty well filled with booze), and took him to Cody's camp and introduced them.

Judson lost no time in telegraphing the New York Herald (I think it was), about Cody shooting Tall Bull off his horse, and capturing the horse; but the only Indian that Cody ever shot off a horse was in his Wild West show!

* * * * *

One time I said to Frank, "Why don't you write the true story of the killing of Tall Bull?" and he replied, "What difference does it make who killed him? I am not in the show business."

CHAPTER X

~

CALIFORNIA JOE

One of the Greatest Scouts and Guides of the Ola Frontier, in Custer's Time

~

CALIFORNIA JOE! What a wealth of romance, adventure, mystery, humor and pathos is wrapped up in his well-remembered name!

What stirring tales of the old frontier could be related around a blazing campfire, if, among the hosts of great frontier characters who have "cashed in" and passed to their reward in the happy hunting grounds of Oblivion, old California Joe could step into the firelight, with his stubby briarwood pipe ablaze, and recount some of the stirring adventures through which he passed; or if Capt. Jack Crawford, the famous "poet-scout," could arise and, amid the crackle of the embers, recite his well-known poem, "California Joe!"

There seems to be little doubt that California Joe was known far and wide as one of the best and most reliable of that army of keen-eyed frontiersmen acting in the capacity of scouts and guides during the Indian campaigns of the late '60's and early '70's. His one fault, according to the best authorities, was over-indulgence in liquor—sometimes at the very moment when his services were in greatest demand. Yet, in spite of this shortcoming, California Joe's name is bound to go down in the history of the West as a plainsman, guide and scout of great distinction, and well deserving of a high place on the scroll of fame.

Moses E. Milner was California Joe's real name. He is said to have been born in Stanford, Ky., May 8th, 1829, the descendant of a family which emigrated from Yorkshire, England, early in the eighteenth century and settled in West Virginia, later removing to Kentucky, where Moses E. Milner was born.

Apparently conditions in Kentucky did not suit the elder Milner, or else the love of adventure and the desire to "seek pastures anew" lured him to Missouri. Likewise there must have been something about Missouri which young "Mose" Milner did not like, as at the age of fourteen he ran away from home, remaining away two years. Just how he engaged those two years we are not informed, as there appears to be nothing to record his wanderings until he attained his majority.

Arriving at manhood's estate, Moses Milner fell in love with a pretty little Tennessee girl named Nancy Emma Watts, and although she was but thirteen years of age, Cupid got in his work and the couple were married. History next records that the youthful couple, on the day following their marriage, packed their belongings and joined an emigrant train bound for the California gold fields.

A story is told to the effect that while this wagon train was enroute to the Pacific coast, it was attacked by Ute Indians. No details are given, save that young Milner was taken captive, bound to a stake, and the savages were engaged in torturing him, when his lusty yells brought a band of trappers to his rescue, and the Indians fled, leaving their captive in welcome hands.

When young Milner arrived in California he at once entered the "diggings" near Sutter's Fort, and for the ensuing two years worked steadily as a miner, with what success we are not informed, but probably with the usual run of miner's luck—"rich today and poor tomorrow." At the end of two years he removed to Oregon, where he operated a packtrain service from Benton county to the various gold mines in the northern part of that state.

At thirty years of age, we find Milner in charge of a packtrain to Walla Walla, Washington, and from there to the gold

"California Joe," Custer's favorite scout in 1868.

diggings in the Oro Fino district. Here the idea of building a toll road entered Milner's head, and he constructed such a road from the gold mines to Mount Idaho, an enterprise which must have drawn great patronage, as it is said to have netted him $60,000 in the ensuing two years. Whether Joe salted down this nest-egg or "spent it in riotous living," is not on record.

"But," you ask, "how did Milner acquire the title of 'California Joe'?" It came about in this manner:

When Milner first appeared in Virginia City, Montana, he was accosted by several persons, who, noting that he was a stranger, began quizzing him. Probably Milner did not take kindly to this sort of an interview, as, when asked "Where from and whither bound?" he replied: "I'm from California, where most of the gold is, and my name is Joe. That's enough for you to know."

"All right," was the answer, "we'll just call you 'California Joe,' then." And "California Joe" it was, from that time until his death. Indeed, but few persons ever knew what Joe's real name was, as he never mentioned it. Even Custer did not know it, and apparently was not sufficiently curious to ask, as he states in his own biography, "No other name than California Joe seemed necessary."

Doubtless Joe hung around Virginia City for the next two or three years, although nothing of special importance regarding his movements is noted until 1862, when he won considerable notoriety by killing a camp bully under the following circumstances:

The fellow had been running things with a high hand in Virginia City, and without opposition. Joe had been doing some market hunting, using a valuable dog in his quest for game. One night in Harry Pearson's saloon the bully swaggered in and became abusive. Joe's dog came sniffing about his heels, and he landed a hard and cruel kick against the animal's rib.

This was long before the advent of that one-time popular song, "You Gotta Quit Kickin' My Dawg Around," but nevertheless it stirred the ire of California Joe. Walking up to the bully, Joe looked him in the eye and exclaimed:

"You flannel-mouthed blankety-blank, I hev bin wantin' a good excuse to kill you fer a long time now, and I've got it right here. If you ain't armed, you better go git yer gun, for I'm a goin' to kill you afore mornin'."

The bully lost no time in vacating the saloon, in company

with several friends. As they went out, Harry Pearson remarked:

"Joe, if you'll kill that fellow I'll make you a present of two gallons of the best whiskey in the place."

The proposition must have struck Joe as quite agreeable to him, as he left the saloon and hurried to his cabin, presently reappearing with a double-barrel shotgun loaded with buckshot.

One of his friends queried, "Are you a-goin' up to his cabin?"

"You bet I am," retorted Joe, "right now!"

"All right, I'll go with you."

The two men started for the bully's cabin. As they drew near, a bright light from the fireplace made the interior of the cabin visible. When within hailing distance, Joe shouted:

"Come out o' thar, you blankety-blank cusses!"

The door opened and all the occupants filed out, except the bully. Joe went to the door and peered about. His pal likewise was attempting to locate the bully by looking under Joe's arm, which was resting against the door casing.

Suddenly a gun roared from within. A charge of buckshot struck the casing, ripping slivers from it. One of the buckshot struck Joe's friend in the throat. Joe himself was untouched, and throwing his weapon forward he "cut loose," getting his man at the first fire.

"Well?" inquired Pearson, as the two re-entered the saloon.

"Let's see that two gallons of whiskey," was Joe's response. And as it was set on the bar, he continued:

"I won't charge you but one gallon, and I reckon as them other cusses are likely to be lookin' fer trouble, we might as well git ready to accommodate 'em."

But no trouble occurred, and California Joe was told the following morning that the friends of the bully were glad their hard-boiled companion had been shot.

Just how California Joe came to engage himself to the

Seventh Cavalry as a scout under General Custer, we are not told. But in the late '60's we find him one of that army of professional guides and scouts who were attached to Custer's command. The selection of a leader to head these men was a question requiring considerable forethought and serious consideration, as none of the officers appeared acquainted with the merits or demerits of any particular scout. The selection, therefore, had to be somewhat at random, and Custer cast about for the best man to fill the position.

"There was one among their number," says Custer, in his own personal memoirs, "whose appearance would have attracted the notice of any casual observer. He was a man about forty years of age—perhaps older; over six feet in height, and possessing a well-proportioned frame. His head was covered with a luxuriant crop of long, almost-black, hair, strongly inclined to curl, and so long as to fall carelessly over his shoulders. His face—at least so much of it as was not concealed by the long, waving brown beard and mustache, was full of intelligence and pleasant to look upon. His eye was undoubtedly handsome, black and lustrous, with an expression of kindness and mildness combined. On his head was generally to be seen, whether asleep or awake, a huge sombrero or black slouch hat. A soldier's overcoat, with its large circular cape, a pair of trousers with the legs tucked in long boots, usually constituted the make-up of the man whom I selected as chief scout. He was known by the euphonious title of 'California Joe.' No other name seems ever to have been given him, and no other name ever seemed necessary. His military armament consisted of a long, breech-loading Springfield rifle, from which he seemed inseparable, and a revolver and hunting knife, both the latter being carried in the waist-belt. His mount completed his equipment for the field, being, instead of a horse, a finely-formed mule, in whose speed and endurance Joe had every confidence.

"California Joe was an inveterate smoker, and was rarely

seen without his stubby, dingy-looking briarwood pipe in full blast. The endurance of his smoking powers was only surpassed by his loquacity. His pipe frequently became exhausted and required refilling, but California Joe never seemed to lack for material or disposition to carry on a conversation, principally composed of personal adventures among the Indians, episodes in mining life or experience in overland journeys, before the days of steam engines and palace cars rendered a trip across the plains a comparatively uneventful one. It was evident, from the scraps of conversation volunteered from time to time, that there was but little of the Western country, from the Pacific to the Missouri river, with which California Joe was not intimately acquainted. He had lived in Oregon years before, and had become acquainted from time to time with most of the officers who had served on the plains or on the Pacific coast. I once inquired if he had ever seen General Sheridan.

" 'What! Gin'rul Shuriden? Why, bless my soul, I knowed Shuriden way up in Oregon more'n fifteen year ago, an' he was only a secunt lootenant of infantry. He was quartermaster of the foot, or sumthin' of that sort, an' I had the contract of furnishin' wood to the post, an' would yer believe it— I had a kind of a sneakin' notion then that he'd hurt sumbuddy if they'd ever turn him loose. Lord, but ain't he ol' lightnin'!"

"Such was the character of the man whom, upon a short acquaintance, I decided to appoint as chief of scouts. This thrust of professional greatness, as the sequel will prove, was more than California Joe aspired to—or was, perhaps, equal to."

Having appointed California Joe to such an important position, Custer took great pains to inform him what was expected of him and the men under his command. Joe likewise appeared somewhat skeptical of Custer's ability as an Indian fighter, or what sort of a soldier he was—Custer being only 29 years of age at that time—and the following conversation ensued between them:

"See hyar, Gin'rul, in order that we have no misunder-standin', I'd jest like to ask yer a few questions."

"All right, Joe, what is it?"

"Air you an amb'lance man er a hoss man?"

Custer smiled. "Just what do you mean by that?" he queried.

"I mean, do you b'leeve in ketchin' Injuns in amb'lances er on hoss back?"

"Well, Joe," laughed Custer, "I believe in catching Indians wherever we can find them, whether they are found in am-bulances or on horseback."

Joe looked perplexed. "But, Gin'rul, that ain't what I'm a-drivin' at," he argued. "S'posen you wuz arter Injuns an' reely wanted to hev a tussel with 'em; would you start arter 'em on hossback, er would you climb into an amb'lance an' be hauled arter 'em—that 'ere's the p'int I'm a-headin' fer?"

"Well," replied Custer, striving hard to restrain an impulse to burst out laughing, "I should prefer the method on horse-back, provided I really desired to catch the Indians; but if I wished them to catch me, I would adopt the ambulance method of attack."

"Now you've hit the nail squar' on the head, Gin'rul," exclaimed Joe. "I've bin with 'em on the Plains whar' they started out arter the Injuns on wheels, jest as if they wuz a-goin' to a town funeral in the States—an' they stood 'bout as much chance of ketchin' 'em as a six-mule team would of ketchin' a pack of thievin' ki-o-tees—jist as much!"

Having relieved his mind thus, California Joe took his place at the head of the column, accompanying the detach-ment which, in his opinion, seemed to have the best chance of encountering the savages.

This was just prior to the battle of the Washita, in Novem-ber, 1868, and while Custer was endeavoring to locate the village of Black Kettle, the celebrated Cheyenne chief (which, by the way, he attacked and destroyed while that chief, and others, were encamped along the Washita River under the protection of Gen. W. B. Hazen, not being hostile at that time—in fact, Black Kettle, according to the testimony of old army officers and interpreters, was never considered a hostile chief, and personally was never known to go on the warpath against the whites, although he was unable to restrain many of his young men from so doing).

The command started out in the darkness of night, and after proceeding for some distance, it was deemed advisable to know something of the numbers and exact position of the Indians. Custer therefore decided to send a party of picked men under the guidance of California Joe, to crawl up on the supposed position of the savages and learn what they could.

But while Custer was selecting the proper men to accompany California Joe on this dangerous mission, and trying vainly to locate his chief of scouts, there came a rifle shot, accompanied by terrific screams and howls, and who should come charging forward out of the darkness, striking right and left with his long-barreled musket, but California Joe, as drunk as a "biled owl," under the imagination that he was charging an Indian camp!

There was no way of stopping him or of quieting him, and orders were therefore given to bind Joe hand and foot to the back of his faithful mule and convey him to the tender mercies of a guard, as a prisoner, for such misconduct.

Right there California Joe's career as "chief of scouts" for Custer ended, although he continued with the expedition, and did most valiant work at the proper time.

The Cheyenne village was located on the Washita River, and the entire camp surrounded in the dead of night. The attack was to be at dawn, and there was a long, cold wait while the troops were reaching their various positions. During this enforced delay, Custer strolled to the camp of the scouts, where California Joe and his pals were engaged in low but earnest conversation.

Custer inquired what their opinion was in regard to the prospects for a real fight.

California Joe snorted.

"Fight!" he exclaimed. "I ain't nary doubt concernin' that part uv the bizness; but what I'm tryin' to figger out is whether we'll run agin more'n we bargained fer."

"Then you think, Joe," continued Custer, "that the Indians will not run away?"

"Run away? How in thunder kin Injins er ennybuddy else run away when we'll hev 'em clean surrounded afore daylight?"

"But supposing that we get the village surrounded all right —do you think we can hold our own against the Indians?"

"That 'ere's the very p'int," argued Joe, scratching his bushy head in perplexity. "If we jump these here Injins at daylight we're a-goin' to do one o' two things—we're either goin' to make a spoon er sp'ile a horn—that 'ere is my candid jedgment sure, an' if them injins don't hear nothin' ov us till we open up on 'em at daylight, they'll be the most powerful 'stonished redskins that's been in these 'ere parts lately. An' if we git the bulge on 'em, an' keep a-puttin' it to 'em sort o' lively-like, we'll sure sweep the platter."

And so the "battle" of the Washita was fought, with California Joe in the thick of the fray. Custer reports him as moving about in a most independent and promiscuous manner, now here, now there, according to where the fight raged fiercest.

While the fray was at its height, California Joe came galloping up to Custer and reported that a large herd of ponies was to be seen near at hand, and requested authority and some assistance to bring them in. The proper authority was given him, and Custer had forgotten all about the inci-

dent, when, in the course of half an hour, in came tearing
a herd of about three hundred Indian ponies, driven by a
couple of squaws, with California Joe bringing up the rear,
mounted on his favorite mule and swinging his lariat about
his head as a whip, to urge the "drags" in the herd forward.
Joe had captured the two squaws while endeavoring to secure the ponies, and had wisely made use of the women to
help bring the herd in.

After the capture of the Indian village, and while Custer
was wisely retreating to avoid another serious engagement
with several hundred Indian allies who were encamped some
miles further down the Washita, and who had promptly
rallied to the defense of their tribesmen, the leader of the
Seventh Cavalry was desirous of sending a message to General Phil Sheridan, who was at Camp Supply, detailing the
outcome of the fight.

Calling California Joe to his side, Custer informed him
that he had been selected as the bearer of the message, and
that he was at liberty to name the number of men he desired
to accompany him as an escort and guard, as it was a most
perilous mission which Joe was about to undertake.

However, California Joe was not in the least perturbed
or worried about it. The greater the chance for a scrap, the
more eager Joe would doubtless have been to get into it.
Custer had expected that Joe would select at least ten or
twelve men for an escort, as very few persons would have
cared to undertake such a perilous ride through a country
swarming with savages, without at least several times that
number of soldiers for an escort.

California Joe quietly remarked that he would talk the
matter over with his "pard." He disappeared for a few moments, and presently rejoined Custer.

"I've bin a-talkin' this 'ere matter over with my pardner,"
he volunteered, "an' him an' me concludes that ez safe an'
sure a way thar' is, is fer me an' him to take a few extry

ca'tridges an' strike out together the minnit it gits dark. We don't want any more men along, becuz in a case o' this kind thar's likely to be more dodgin' an' runnin' than fightin,' an' two men kin do better'n twenty; they can't be seen half ez fur, an' won't leave much of a trail fer the Injins to find. If we git away from here by dark, we'll be so fur away by daylight that no Injins is a-goin' to bother us. Wal, I'm goin' back to the boys an' see if I kin borry a leetle tobacker, so whenever you git them dockiments ready, jist send yer orderly to me, an' me an' my pardner'll be ready."

Custer thereupon penned his report to General Sheridan and had finished it when California Joe appeared and re-marked:

"Wal, I hope an' trust yer won't hev enny skrimmages whilst I'm away, 'cuz I'd hate mightily now to miss enny-thing of the sort, seein' I've stuck to yer this fur."

Joe and Corbin then took their departure as Custer shook hands heartily with both men and wished them good luck and a safe journey. The troops, by easy marches, gradually drew near to Camp Supply, and Custer was uneasily wonder-ing whether his two couriers had gotten through safely. Two or three days had elapsed since their departure.

While the general and some of his staff were riding in ad-vance of the troops, the attention of the party was directed to three horsemen who were riding slowly along near a fringe of timber. Custer was at a loss to determine who they might be. The three horsemen evidently discovered Custer's party, as they at once turned their mounts and dis-appeared into the timber, doubtless taking them for an enemy.

Custer's field glasses at once were leveled toward the spot, and just as the last horseman disappeared into the timber, the joyful discovery was made that it was none other than California Joe mounted on his raw-boned mule. Custer at once put spurs to his horse and dashed forward toward the horsemen, who presently rode cautiously out of the timber for another look at the approaching party. Custer swung his hat, and Joe appeared to recognize him, as he stuck the spurs into his long-legged mule and was soon grasping his chief by the hand.

"I counted on it bein' you when I fust ketched sight ov yer," he exclaimed heartily, "but I wasn't takin' any chances on it bein' Injins, an' conclooded that this 'ere timber would be the best place to make a stand in case I war mistaken. We war a-gittin' ready to sling lead into yer in case it turned out to be Injins. Wal, I'm powerful glad to see yer again, that's dead sure. How be ye, ennyway?"

Joe then related that Corbin and himself had made the trip in safety, and that General Sheridan, after complimenting them, had fed them well and then started them back, in company with one other scout, to meet Custer and deliver a package of letters and orders.

Such were some of the incidents in which California Joe figured while scouting for Custer in 1868.

* * * * *

An old friend of California Joe, in the person of G. W. Stokes, of New York City, has given some interesting sidelights on the character of the famous frontiersman. He states that California Joe was doubtless engaged in placer mining on or near Woolsey's Flat, California, some of the time between 1863 and 1868, because Jim Woolsey and Joe met in Deadwood in 1876 where Stokes heard them discussing the matter.

"I heard them talking about some of their experiences," said Mr. Stokes, "as I was in Deadwood at that time. I know that Joe and Dick King came to Cheyenne from up Pioche, Nevada way in November, 1875. Maybe they met there, for I think Joe went into the Black Hills with Custer from Fort Abraham Lincoln, near Bismarck, in 1874. We went into the Hills together from there. Custer had a blue greyhound which he had presented to California Joe. Our party was composed of California Joe, Dick King and my party of four, and eight other teams, for self-protection from the Indians, which were bad at that time. We were all 'holed in' about six miles from Fort Laramie, waiting for the squadron of the Third Cavalry to come back with the last batch of gold miners they had rounded up at French Creek stockade (not Custer City).

"We lit out for the Black Hills as soon as the troops and the prisoners had passed our hiding place. Joe had two pack horses, his saddle horse, his greyhound, and was accompanied by a young man named Benson, a youth of twenty or thereabout. Joe had his bedding and some grub on Dick King's four-horse wagon.

"When we reached the stockade we found five or six miners with some gold dust, but no grub except venison. They had succeeded in dodging the soldiers. Joe and Dick, Benson and our four partners left the others and went over the divide to Spring Creek, where Prof. Jenny's exploring party had found more gold than on French Creek. We all took up 300-foot claims and had them recorded. Joe and Dick went two miles down the creek from our claims, near the mouth of what we called Palmer's Gulch. We washed out about one thousand penny-weight of coarse gold that winter, but Joe, Dick and Benson didn't get to bedrock, and some time early in the spring, went over to Bear Butte creek.

"I next saw Joe in June of '76. He and a man named Wood were prospecting for quartz. They had some drill steel and dynamite, and had found a ledge of white quartz on Deadwood Creek, opposite the rich Father De Smet ledge. Neither of them understood the use of dynamite, so they asked me to join them. On our way through Gayville, where gold was first mined on Deadwood we saw Bill Gay unsaddling his horse. Bill called Joe aside. They were well acquainted. They conversed in a low tone for a few minutes, while Wood and I squatted in the shade of Al Gay's store.

"When Joe returned he informed us that Bill had told him that Custer, he of the long hair, had been wiped out with his whole command. Bill was a squaw-man—had an Indian wife and two kids at Spotted Tail agency. He had been down to take them some supplies and money, and on his return had met an Indian runner—a relative of Bill's squaw—then on his way to report to Spotted Tail and Red Cloud of the Custer disaster on the Little Big Horn. Three days later the news was confirmed by the Cheyenne mail stage.

"We fired a shot or two into the quartz vein, but the ore yielded less than $2 a ton on assay. I bought an interest in Claim No. 10, on Deadwood Creek, and never saw Joe Milner again. I think he left the hills with Gen. Crook's command in September, 1876, and perhaps went as a scout on the successful rounding up of that wonderful fighter, Crazy Horse."

During California Joe's residence in the Black Hills country, he met and became quite a pal of Capt. Jack Crawford, known the country over as the "Poet-Scout." Capt. Jack was an intimate friend of the writer many years ago, and we corresponded quite regularly. At that time he was on the lecture platform reading his poems and giving entertainments at Chautauquas and on Y. M. C. A. courses. Capt. Jack passed away at his home in New York City, February 28, 1917, of pneumonia. A treasured volume in the writer's library is an autographed copy of Capt. Jack's poems, presented in 1909.

Captain Jack has the following to say about California Joe:

"About the middle of April, 1876, I received a note from California Joe, who then had a fine ranch on Rapid Creek, and was trying to induce newcomers to settle there and build a town. I was then at Deadwood. Joe's letter was written in lead pencil, and barring his bad spelling, ran as follows:

" 'Rapid, April 10, 1876.

" 'My Dear Jack:

" 'If you can be spared from Custer, come over and bring Jule and Frank Smith with you. The reds have been raising merry old hell, and after wounding our herder and a miner named Sherwood, got away with eight head of stock —my old Bally with the rest. There are only ten of us here all told, and I think if you can come with the two boys, we can lay for them at the lower falls and gobble them the next time. Answer by bearer if you can't come. And send me fifty rounds of cartridges for the Sharps (big 50). Hoping this will find you with your top-knot still waving, I remain as ever,

" 'Your pal,
" 'Joe.'

"I immediately saw Major Wynkoop, commanding the Rangers, and got his permission to leave, and arrived at Rapid Creek the following night, with four comrades. After two days and nights watching at the lower falls, Jules Seminole, one of my scouts (a Cheyenne), came in at dusk, and informed us that there were between twenty and thirty Indians encamped at Box Elder, about twenty miles away, and that they were coming from the direction of the Big Cheyenne, and would probably move to Rapid during the night.

"About three o'clock next morning Joe went up to his cabin and there started a big log fire; also two or three other fires in other cabins. These cabins were over a mile from where we were in ambush, while our horses were all picketed a quarter of a mile down the creek, which was narrow at its point of entrance from the prairie, but widened into a beautiful river half a mile up.

"Just as day was breaking, one of the Indians was discovered by Frank Smith wading up the creek. Frank reported to Joe and I, and Joe remarked, 'Let him go; he will

soon signal the others to follow.' In fifteen minutes more the
shrill bark of a coyote proved Joe's judgment to be correct.
Twenty-three well-armed Indians—all Sioux—rode up along

Capt. Jack Crawford, the famous poet-scout.

the willow bank in Indian file. There were seventeen of us—
Bob Swearingen and Ned Baker, two old miners. having
joined us the night before. We had six men on one side of
the creek near an opening which we believed the Indians

would break for on receiving our fire from the opposite side.
"We took aim as best we could in the gray of the morning,
and fired nearly together. Then, before they could recover,
we gave them another volley, and leaving our cover, followed on foot those who did not stay with us. We were disappointed in their taking the opening, but the boys were
in fair range and did good work, killing one, wounding two
and unhorsing three others, who took to the woods. We got
fifteen ponies. Our first fire never touched a horsehair, but
emptied several saddles. Out of the twenty-three Indians,
fifteen escaped. Joe killed three himself with his big Sharps
rifle, the last one being nearly five hundred yards away when
he fired from a rest off Frank Smith's shoulder. Joe had a
piece taken out of his left thigh; Franklin was wounded in
the left arm, and the writer slightly scratched near the guard
of the right arm. Nobody was seriously hurt, and we had
eight scalps to crown our victory."

In the spring of 1875, California Joe happened to wander
into Fort Laramie, where his well-known reputation was such
that he was engaged as chief scout and guide for Professor
Jenney's Black Hills exploring expedition, sent out by the
government to confirm Custer's report of the previous year
(1874) of gold being found in that region. The expedition
kept Joe in the field until it was disbanded that autumn.

It was late in 1875 or early in 1876 that General Custer
saw Joe in Bismarck, Dakota, and asked him to go with the
expedition which the government was to send out in the
spring of 1876, in charge of General Terry, to round up the
bands of hostile Sioux under Sitting Bull and Crazy Horse.
These Indians were supposed to be encamped somewhere in
the Yellowstone country—just where, nobody knew. Custer
was just leaving for Washington, where he had been called
as a witness in the notorious Belknap case. He advised Joe
that he would probably return in about four weeks. Failing
to appear for some time after the expected date, Joe guided

a party to the Black Hills, where he remained until after Terry's expedition, with Custer and the Seventh Cavalry, had departed for the Yellowstone country. Doubtless Joe thus escaped the terrible fate which overtook Custer and five companies of his regiment in June, a few short weeks later.

During the fall of 1875, California Joe was at Red Cloud Agency, in Northwestern Nebraska, from which point he wrote a letter to his sons, then living in Oregon, which reads as follows, capitalized and punctuated just as California Joe wrote it:

"Nov. 1, 1875.

"Red Cloud Agency, Neb.

"Dear sons i received your Kind letter yistidy and was glad to hear from you all i returned from the Black Hills 10 days ago after having a six months travel through the prettyes country that i have seen for many days it would take me a month to discribe it to you so i give you the outlines in short as for gold there is good wages from 5 to 25 dollars per day by good work the mining destrict is 40 miles long by 20 wide (it is) placer diggings there is some quartz but not developed as yet for a stock country the world cant beat it some of the creeks (is the best) for rances (ranches) I ever seen timber & water splendid if you all want (to) start in a new country this is about your last chance i wish (you) was all here any (way) in (the) spring there will be a grand rush the country is not treated for yet so the government is trying to keep the miners out but the (y) keep going and the soldiers keep brin(g)ing the (m) back the indians talk fight but it (is) all talk there is three companies of soldiers stationed in the Black Hills to keep miners out it is 100 miles from here there is 30 soldiers start from here tomorrow and i am going with them i want to make some new locations because i know all the country and where the best pay is in my opinion that the first man gets on the ground in the spring will hold it as you say that (you) want to come out i would be more than glad to see you all you Charley and Eugene augt to come for this is a better country to mak money in than Oregon but wait until i rite again i will rite in time for you to come and tell you how to come if the Indians dont get me on this trip i (saw) five thousand indians yestidy drawing their rations the happyest days i see after deer with my pony dog and gun direct Fort Laramie, W. T. to California Jo.

"Your affectionate Father

"M E MILNER."

General Custer had lost track of his old friend Joe after the last meeting at Bismarck, but upon the publication of his first and only book, entitled "My Life on the Plains," Custer, in almost the last paragraph in the volume, again refers to his former old scout as follows:

"A few words in regard to one other character with whom the reader of these sketches has been made acquainted. California Joe accompanied my command to Fort Hays, Kansas, on the Kansas-Pacific railroad, where the troops were partially disbanded and sent to different stations. California Joe had never seen a railroad or a locomotive, and here determined to improve his first opportunity in these respects, and to take a trip on the cars to Leavenworth, distant about four hundred miles.

"A few days afterward, an officer of my command, happening to be called to Leavenworth, thought he recognized a familiar face and form in front of the leading hotel in that city. A closer scrutiny showed that the party recognized was none other than California Joe. But how changed! Under the manipulations of the barber, and through the aid of the proprietor of a gentlemen's furnishing store, the long, curly locks and hair of California Joe, both of which had avoided contact with comb, brush or razor for many years, had undergone a complete metamorphosis. His hair and beard were neatly trimmed and combed, while his figure—a very commanding one—had discarded the rough suit of the frontiersman, and was now adorned by the latest efforts of fashion. If the reader imagines, however, that these changes were in keeping with the taste of California Joe, the impression is wholly incorrect. He had effected them simply for a sensation. The following day he took the cars for the West, satisfied with the faint glimpse of civilization which he had had.

"As I soon left that portion of the plains in which these scenes are laid, I saw no more of California Joe; but I often wondered what had become of my loquacious friend. whose droll sayings and quaint remarks had often served to relieve the tedium of the march or to enliven a group about the campfire. I had begun, after a few years had passed without trace or tidings of Joe, to fear that he had perhaps gone to that happy hunting ground to which he had no doubt sent more than one dusky warrior, when a few weeks ago I was most agreeably surprised to receive indubitable evidence that California Joe was still in the land of the living, but exactly where, I could not determine, as his letter was simply dated 'Sierra Nevada Mountains, California.' Now, as this range of mountains extends through the entire length and embraces a considerable portion of the State of California, Joe's address could not be definitely determined. But as his letter is so characteristic of the man, I here introduce it as the valedictory of California Joe:

" 'Sierra Nevade Mountains, Calafornia
" 'March 16, 1874.

" 'Dear General after my respects to you and Lady i thought that i tell you that i am still on top of land yit i hev been in the rocky mountain the most of the time sence i last seen you but i got on the railroad and started west and the first thing i new i landed in san Francisco so i could not go any further except goen by water and salt water at that so i turned back and headed for the mountains once more resolved never to go railroading no more i drifted up with the tide to sacramento city and i landed my boat so i took up through town they say thare is 20 thousand people living thar but it looks to me like 100 thousand counten chinamen and all i cant describe my wilfish feeling but i think that i look just like i did when we was chasing Buffalo on the cimarone so i struck up through town and i come to a large fine building crowded with people so i bulged in to see what

was going on and when i got in to the counsil house i took
a look around at the crowd and i seen the most of them had
bald heads so i thought to myself i struck it now they are
indian peace commissioners so i look to see if i would know
any of them but not one so after while the smartes lookin
one got up and set gentlemen i interduce a bill to have
speckle mounten trout and fish eggs imported to calafornia
to be put in the american bear and yuba rivers—those rivers
is so muddy that a tadpole could not live in them caused by
mining—did ennybuddy ever hear of speckle trout living
in muddy water and the next thing was the game law and
that was very near as bad as the Fish for they aint no game
in the country as big as a mawking bird i herd some fellow
behind me ask how long is the legislaturs been in session
then i dropt to myself it wuzent indian peace commissioners
after all so i slid out took acrost to chinatown and they smelt
like a kiowa camp in august with plenty buffalo meat around
—it was getten late so no place to go not got a red cent so
i happen to think of an old friend back of town and i knowed
25 years ago so i lit out and sure enough he was thar just
as i left him 25 years ago baching so i got a few seads i
going to plant in a few days and give my respects to the 7th
calvery and except the same yoursley

" 'CALIFORNIA JOE.' "

We now come to the last days of this droll, quaint, rough-
and-ready, devil-may-care character of the old frontier.
California Joe made many strong friends in his last days.
Chief among these was Dr. V. T. McGillicuddy, formerly
one of the best-known Indian agents that ever acted as a
guard for Uncle Sam's red wards—a man of unflinching
courage, thoroughly familiar with the Indian character, and
a fighter for the red man in seeing that he got every ounce
of rations promised by the government. Writing in 1922 to
the author, Dr. McGillicuddy says:

"California Joe and I became closely acquainted in the
spring of 1875, when he joined the Black Hills expedition
at Fort Laramie as chief scout and guide. He was by nature
a scout, and thoroughly reliable. He stood over six feet two;

had long, reddish hair and whiskers; spare build, but athletic; indulged in liquor occasionally, but was never quarrelsome, and was one of the best-known scouts of his day. He served with the expedition until we disbanded in the fall at Fort Laramie.

"In the spring of 1876 he joined the expedition sent out to round up the hostiles under Sitting Bull, serving under the command of General Crook. He rendered good service to the end of the campaign, which resulted in the so-called Custer massacre, in which expedition I was surgeon of the Second and Third Cavalry.

"Early in October, 1876, the expedition broke up at Fort Robinson, in the far northwest corner of Nebraska, and the troops were distributed to various winter quarters. A new expedition was organized under General Mackenzie of the Fourth Cavalry, to push into the Big Horn country and round up scattered bands of Northern Cheyennes and Sioux, who were still active in that section, and California Joe was selected as chief scout.

"There was employed in the post butcher shop at Fort Robinson a man named Newcomb or Neukem, with whom Joe had had some trouble. But the day before the expedition was to leave, the two met at the post trader's, where they had a few drinks and apparently became good friends. About 5 p. m. California Joe was standing on the banks of the White River with some comrades, when suddenly Newcomb appeared at the corner of the quartermaster's corral, and without warning shot Joe through the back with a Winchester. Joe died instantly. Newcomb was thrown into the guardhouse, and I had the remains of the old scout carried to the post hospital, where I made an autopsy on my old friend.

"When Mackenzie's expedition marched past the hospital next morning, California Joe was resting in his coffin in front of the hospital, with the flag draped over him. I found memoranda in his clothing that he was Moses Milner of

Kentucky, and I placed a red cedar headboard with the inscription, 'Moses Milner of Kentucky (California Joe), murdered October, 1876,' over his grave on the banks of the White River.

"As the law required, we notified the authorities of the nearest organized county (Holt) 33 miles away, in Eastern Nebraska, of the affair. Four days elapsing, and no one appearing, we were obliged to turn Newcomb loose, and rigid army discipline prevented his just lynching, and he is now living at Gardiner, Montana, as a hunting guide. Thus ended the life of the most reliable scout of the northwest."

Captain Luther H. North, of Columbus, Nebraska, brother of Major Frank North, organizer and commander of the famous "North's Pawnee Scouts," and himself a lieutenant in that organization during its entire enlistment, has sent the writer the following interesting letter regarding California Joe:

"Columbus, Nebr., March 30, 1925.
"My Dear Mr. Brininstool:
"Your letter just came, and I will tell you what little I know about California Joe.

"I thought when I wrote to an Eastern magazine several years ago, that I was the last man to talk to California Joe before he was murdered, but perhaps not.

"When we got to Fort Robinson, after capturing Red Cloud, we camped on the creek about a mile below the fort, and Joe came down to see my brother (I never had seen Joe before). He ate supper with us, and soon after went back up to the fort, saying he would come back in the morning.

"Just after he left, my brother got orders to send some men with the horses that we had taken from Red Cloud, to Fort Laramie. Frank took twenty men and started at once, about 8 o'clock. I think there were 722 head of ponies, and before noon the next day he had them at Laramie, ninety miles from Robinson. I was to come on the next day with the rest of the men.

"When I was breaking camp the next morning, Joe came

down. He was on foot. I told him about Frank having gone, and as soon as we got loaded up, we started. I bade Joe goodby, and he started back for the fort.

"There was a company of infantry that had started for Laramie that morning ahead of me, and one of the lieutenants had stayed behind for some reason. When I had gone about ten miles, this officer overtook me and rode with me for some distance. He said:

" 'There was a killing at the fort this morning. California Joe was shot.'

"I replied, 'Why, he was at my camp when I left.'

"The officer replied, 'Well, some fellow shot him in the back when he was on his way to the fort.'

"This was the only time I ever saw California Joe. As I remember him he was a man over six feet tall and powerfully built; had black hair, turning gray, and a heavy growth of beard all over his face. He was dressed in an ordinary civilian suit of clothes, and my impression is that he wore a cloth cap, but am not sure. He was not very talkative.

"When Frank introduced us, he grinned and said:

" 'The major thinks so much of me that he used to come and see me every day.'

"It seems that the year before (1875) or maybe the spring of 1876, Joe started to guide a party of miners into the Black Hills, and the troops stopped them at Fort Laramie. There were several other parties which were stopped there. They camped along the Platte River, waiting for the government to conclude a treaty with the Indians to allow them to proceed. Frank was chief of scouts, guide and interpreter, at the time, at Fort D. A. Russell, and he was sent to Laramie, and every day was sent out to patrol the river and see that none of them crossed. That was what Joe meant by saying that 'the major thinks so much of me that he used to come and see me very day.' "

California Joe's experience in California consisted principally of mining around Sutter's Fort, in the Marshall diggings, until 1852. After that, he went to Oregon, where he took up 640 acres of land in Benton county, twelve miles west of Corvallis, near Wren Station. This ranch is known today as the "old Milner place." Here four of California

Joe's sons were born—Edgar A., October 1, 1853; George, February 17, 1855; Charley, February 18, 1857, and Eugene, March 17, 1859.

While in Oregon, Joe ran a pack train from Benton county to the mines in Southern Oregon. He made three trips in all, then in 1857 went back to Missouri and Kentucky, returning with his wife's sister. Joe acquired a valuable Kentucky mare while in that country, which he took along on the return trip to Oregon. This animal became quite famous as a race horse, and Joe pitted the animal against all competitors and always won, save once.

On the occasion of losing a race, it appears that at Corvallis, the animal was "salted." When Joe discovered the trick that had been perpetrated against him, he promptly belted on his old six-shooter, hunted up the man and shot him.

The year 1860 found California Joe at Walla Walla, Washington. After a brief sojourn there, he went to Northern Idaho, where a new diggings promised good returns. It is claimed that Joe founded the town of Mount Idaho and cut a toll road into the new diggings. After remaining there two years, and cleaning up some $60,000.00, Joe sold out in order that he might go to the Montana gold mines.

A rather uncalled-for killing alleged to have been done by Joe occurred during his stay at Mount Idaho. It is stated that a stranger rode up to Joe's shack one evening, and that Joe fed his animal and kept the man all night, and the following morning the stranger left without offering to settle. Joe took after him, and report has it, shot the man off his horse. The wound was mortal. Joe asked why the man had left without paying his bill. The answer was, "I was broke." Joe replied, "I never turned anybody away that was broke. You should have reported your condition to me." The story goes that the stranger died a few minutes later and that Joe buried him where he fell.

After Joe's arrival in Montana, he filed on a couple of

claims not very far from Virginia City. Building a small shack he worked in the diggings for a time, going to Virginia City for supplies as needed.

Returning to his claim one day after one of these trips, he was surprised to see three men on his claim. Joe rode up to the cabin, which was at the edge of a small creek, and observed that the rifles of the men were stacked against the cabin. The spokesman of the claim-jumpers had a pistol in his belt, the other two having no small arms. Joe had his rifle strapped on the side of his mule, but carried two pistols in his belt.

Joe ordered the men off his claim, saying it belonged to him. Hot words followed, and finally Joe pulled his two guns and starting shooting. Two of the claim-jumpers were killed at the first shots, but the third man escaped by running.

Joe worked this claim for about six months and then left the county, as the so-called Vigilantes were hot after him for the killing of the claim-jumpers.

In Wyoming, Joe became acquainted with Jim Bridger, the famous plainsman, and they became very good friends. In 1865 Joe went to New Mexico and did some mining; he also guided various hunting parties in Arizona. In New Mexico, Joe and his partner were camped alone one night, when they heard a noise among their horses, which were hobbled. Grabbing his rifle, Joe walked quietly out where the animals were snorting and prancing about. Two horse thieves were attempting to run the horses away. Joe shot and killed one of the men, and catching his own horse, he took after the other man, but he escaped, although compelled to abandon the stolen animals, which Joe recovered.

During a short residence in Texas, drifting about, Joe acted as guide for a small party of emigrants. After being paid for his services, he came to a small frontier town noted for its gambling dens. Joe became pretty well intoxicated and lost all his money in one of the games. The winner was sober at the time, and took advantage of Joe's condition by cheating him in the game. The following morning some of Joe's friends made him acquainted with the circumstances. Wild with rage, Joe walked into the back door of the saloon, and approached the man who had cheated him. The gambler took to his heels, but before he could get across the street, Joe's gun was belching lead and the gambler dropped in his tracks. Turning to the crowd which had gathered, Joe quietly remarked, "I am California Joe, and if that man I just shot has got any friends, let them step to the front and I'll just have it out with 'em right here." Nobody spoke, and Joe became a great favorite during his stay in that vicinity.

In the spring of 1873 Joe went to Pioche, Nevada, with a man named Wilson. They filed on a claim about 40 miles from Pioche, and started a cattle ranch to supply the mines with beef. My uncle, George Milner, and my grandmother went down there to see him. On the Fourth of July that year a shooting match was held, open to everybody at a fee of $50. Joe won the entire stakes of $600, outshooting them all. My grandmother was a witness at this shooting match, as was my Uncle George. Joe was known as the best all-around shot on the plains. Buffalo Bill, who knew Joe well, once told me that California Joe beat any man with a gun that he ever saw.

Acting as guide for a party of sixty men who went from Pioche, Nevada, down into New Mexico, California Joe told my uncles that before they reached their destination, the Apaches were so bad that twenty of the original sixty men were killed.

Joe landed in Wyoming in the early spring of 1874, forming a partnership with a man in Laramie City. The partner got drunk one day, and sold a team of Joe's horses, after which he made ready to leave the country. A friend of Joe's came to Laramie City and told him about it. Joe went down to the camp and found his partner sitting on a box in the tent. As Joe appeared, the fellow opened fire on him, shooting three times and missing. Joe then whipped out his own gun and shot the man through the shoulder, but spared his life.

A couple of months later, Joe was passing through a canyon alone, when suddenly he was fired upon from both sides. Joe dropped to his knees and crawled out of range, running down the canyon and then doubling back and approaching the place where he had been fired on. Here he saw three men together, watching for his appearance, one of the trio being the same fellow whose life he had shortly spared. Joe opened fire and shot the coward dead. The other two men got away. Joe afterward learned that these three men were laying for him in revenge for the shooting of the partner at Laramie City.

Joe is said to have founded Circle City, South Dakota, and named the town, plotting it on his 160 acres. The Deadwood gold excitement, however, spoiled his plans for a permanent settlement.

William F. Hooker, one time editor of the Erie Railroad Magazine, New York City, a friend of the writer, sends the following interesting communication, which was given Mr. Hooker by one of his old Black Hills friends:

"I was in Rapid City in February, 1878, when a big young husky came into the hotel, approached the bar and asked for a drink. Cranky Tom, an old-time steamboat bartender, was on watch, and when the stranger said, 'I am the man who killed California Joe,' I saw Tom's hand drop down on the mixing board where lay his gun. Securing the weapon, he then told the stranger what he thought of a cur who would shoot a man in the back. I expected to see the stranger draw, but just then two other men came in from the hotel office, and he took a look at us boys standing there with our guns on, then whirled about and slid out the front door.

"The news soon spread around town, and the livery-stable

man said the stranger told him he was going up on the Yellowstone, and then headed due north.

"Some time afterward a man brought in the report that this stranger had been killed by some friend of old Joe's up in the Big Bend country, and I saw him there about the time you were here in 1921, and the cowboys who worked under him told me he had, for years, been foreman for a big cattle company; but since those large cattle companies have gone out of the business, I surmise that he settled on some land and probably is now running a small herd for himself."

At the time of his death, California Joe was 47 years, 5 months and 21 days old. His body lies in grave No. 14, in the post cemetery at Fort Robinson, Nebr.

CHAPTER XI

~

THE PONY EXPRESS

*How William H. Russell "Made History" in the Mail
Service of the United States*

~

THE most unique and romantic mail service ever attempted in the United States—or any other country—was the famous "Pony Express," operating between St. Joseph, Mo., and Sacramento, Cal., for a period of eighteen months only during 1860-'61. It was looked upon at the time as one of the most stupendous undertakings of the age.

The "Pony Express" began operations April 3, 1860, and the service was of the utmost benefit to the Pacific Coast, furnishing news from the far East to the leading San Francisco dailies in eight to ten days, which was at least two weeks in advance of the Overland mail coach, and nearly three weeks ahead of the Pacific Mail Company's steamers.

The service proved to be a complete success in every way except financially, for the enthusiastic projector sunk over $100,000 in the enterprise, while his two nervy partners also lost their fortunes.

The man who started this great innovation was William H. Russell of the pioneer freighting firm of Russell, Majors & Waddell. The idea was really born in the brain of Senator William Gwin of California, so that the Golden State can therefore claim the honor of originating the scheme.

During the winter of 1859, Mr. Russell happened to be

in Washington on business, and he there met and became acquainted with Senator Gwin. The senator was very anxious to establish a line of more rapid communication between California and the distant East, and he broached the matter to Mr. Russell of starting a pony express mail line across the continent. It required considerable urging on the part of Senator Gwin to induce Mr. Russell to undertake such an experiment, but the latter finally consented, providing he could also induce his two partners, Majors and Waddell, to join him.

A consultation was held at Fort Leavenworth between the three partners. Majors and Waddell, after the object of the enterprise was explained, did not enthuse over the proposition. They declared it could not be made to pay expenses. Mr. Russell, however, stated that he had practically given his word to Senator Gwin that he would undertake to start the enterprise, feeling confident that Majors and Waddell would fall in line and cooperate.

The two partners, therefore, were finally won over and decided to back Russell with their money and influence. While the latter was really the "power behind the throne," the great firm of Russell, Majors and Waddell were the backbone of the enterprise.

Few frontier activities can in any way be compared to the Pony Express, looking at it in the light of a matter of great public importance. No similar undertaking of such magnitude had ever been attempted in America, and so quietly and systematically was it worked up that in a little over four months after the subject was first broached, the entire line was fully equipped and in successful operation.

When the three partners had fully decided to try out the experiment, Russell bought at different points in the West, five hundred of the best and fleetest horses he could find—steeds noted for their endurance and ability to make the fastest possible time between stations.

It cost an enormous sum of money to stock and keep the Pony Express in operation. One hundred and ninety stations were established, in addition to acquiring the use of many of the Overland Stage stations for housing their horses. Nearly 200 men were employed as station keepers to look carefully after the stock and keep the horses in the pink of condition for their fast runs. The riders—of whom there were eighty—were all young men—wiry, nervy, used to life on the frontier and filled with the spirit of adventure. No youth was employed to ride the Pony Express who weighed in excess of 135 pounds, and one of them, "Little Yank," is said to have tipped the scales at less than 100 pounds. The only arms allowed to be carried were revolver and knife—no rifle, for the riders were not expected to stop and give battle to Indians or outlaws, but to depend upon the speed of the animal they rode to carry them beyond danger of close personal contact with any enemy. Most of the grain used by the Pony Express animals between St. Joseph and Salt Lake City had to be transported from Missouri and Iowa, across the plains and over the Rocky Mountains, at a freight cost of from ten to twenty-five cents per pound.

The line of the Pony Express was 1,980 miles in length. Of the eighty daring riders, forty were in the saddle at Sacramento, going east, and forty similarly mounted at St. Joseph, going west. For every twenty-four hours an average distance of 250 miles must be covered, the riders being in the saddle day and night, in all kinds of weather, rain or shine, never stopping, except to change mounts, until the end of their run was reached, the runs often covering from 75 to 100 miles if it developed that a station had been attacked by Indians and burned, the stock run off and the keepers killed, which often occurred. Two minutes only were allowed at stations to transfer saddle and mail pouch to a fresh mount; but so expert did the riders become that this change was usually made in from ten to fifteen seconds. Over some portions of

the route, twenty miles an hour was the speed maintained—
a remarkable feat for horseback travel.

The route covered was over all kinds of country. There
were ravines, gullies, creeks and rivers to cross; mountain
torrents to be forded; parched stretches of sand and alkali to
cover; weird and rugged canyons to traverse and high and
difficult passes in the Rocky Mountains and the Sierra Nevada to cross, where deep snows were encountered. A considerable portion of this distance, it must be remembered,
was through hostile Indian country on the Plains, swarming
with warlike tribes, all eager for the scalps of these daring
riders, but seldom able to overtake them, owning to the
fleetness of the horses used on the Pony Express. Other portions of the journey were often swept by terrific hail, sleet
and wind storms.

The total weight of the mail carried by the Pony Express
rider was limited to twenty pounds. The cost of carrying a
letter through to the Pacific Coast was, at first, $5 for each
half ounce, though this was shortly reduced to $1 per half
ounce. All the letters were required to be written on a special grade of tissue paper. These were wrapped in oiled silk
as additional protection against the weather. It was necessary that each letter and message transmitted by the Pony
Express should be enclosed in a ten-cent government en-
velope. In addition, there were affixed the regular government stamps. Some of these letters cost as much as $27.50
to transport. This was an expensive luxury, but to the wide-
awake business man on the Pacific Coast, time was money,
and expense not counted. Needless to say, there were no
"flapperized" love missives carried by the Pony Express at
these extravagant tolls!

About two months after the establishment of the line,
several tribes of Indians in the Northwest—the Bannocks,
Piutes and Shoshones—had gone on one of their periodic
outbreaks west of Salt Lake City, and the Pony Express

route for a long distance was thus interrupted. While on the warpath the Indians burned a number of the company's stations, ran off considerable stock and committed other depredations which crippled the line, in addition to murdering several of the station keepers.

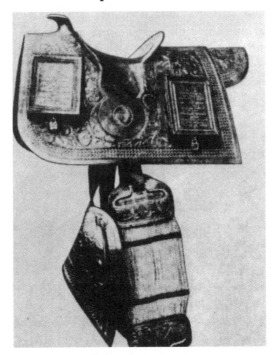

"Pony Express" saddle used in 1860 by W. A. Cates, one of the riders.

This disastrous raid forced the company to suspend operations for a few trips. Many thought this would be the last of the Pony Express—and doubtless it would have been with any other men behind it but the plucky and resolute firm of Russell, Majors & Waddell. These enterprising men knew no such word as "fail," and determined to keep the line in operation, regardless of the consequences. Volunteers were raised, the outbreak put down, stations rebuilt and restocked and the line was soon again in operation. But the trouble and delay incurred necessitated an expenditure of over $75,000.

Originally a few of the stations along the route of the Pony Express were twenty-five miles apart, but shortly these were reduced to from ten to fifteen miles. Each rider was supposed to ride three animals in succession, traversing three stations, and to go at least 33 1/3 miles. Quite often, however, it would be necessary for one rider to cover as many as five stations, due to Indian depredations.

The saddle, bridle and pouch used by the rider weighed but thirteen pounds, not including the contents of the pouch; so that the total weight carried by each horse, including the rider, was from 150 to 175 pounds.

When a station was reached—it mattered not what hour of the day or night—the substitute rider would invariably be at his post, ready to grab the precious mail pouch, leap into the saddle and be off like the wind. In all their trips across the continent made by the riders of the Pony Express, and the 650,000 miles covered by them during its existence, only one mail was lost, and that was a comparatively unimportant one.

The first trip was begun on April 3, 1860, starting simultaneously from St. Joseph, Mo., then the western terminus of railway communication, and Sacramento, Cal. The St. Joseph rider was Johnny Frey, mounted on a jet-black steed, while Harry Roff, on a snow-white charger, left from Sacramento.

Roff rode out of Sacramento on the dead run, making the first twenty miles, with two changes of horses, in fifty-nine minutes. Then seconds only were lost by him in changing mounts and he finished his run to Placerville, where another rider carried the mail to the next waiting man. Roff rode fifty-five miles all told, making his entire run in two hours and forty-five minutes, notwithstanding he had a number of hills to climb.

The jet-black animal ridden by Johnny Frey was watched by one of the largest crowds of anxious spectators that ever assembled on the banks of the Missouri River. Frey was 20 years of age and weighed 125 pounds. He rode to Seneca from St. Joe, a distance of eighty miles, at an average speed of twelve and one-half miles per hour—a most remarkable horseback feat—in addition to making his change of mount.

The first Pony Express to reach Salt Lake City was from the west, which arrived in the Mormon metropolis on the 7th of April, having left Sacramento on the night of the 3d. The first pony out of St. Joe arrived in the City of the Saints on the evening of the 9th. For the first time in all history, Utah was brought within six days' communication with the Missouri River, and within seven days of the nation's capital. For years before that important event, Salt Lake residents had been accustomed to receive news from six weeks to three months old.

The Civil War broke out about a year after the starting of the Pony Express. Never was news more anxiously awaited than on the Pacific Coast when hostilities were raging between the North and the South. The first tidings of the firing on Fort Sumter reached San Francisco in eight days and fourteen hours. From that time on, a bonus was given by California business men to the Pony Express Company to be distributed among the riders for carrying the war news as fast as possible. The sum of $300 was collected for the riders for bringing a bundle of Chicago newspapers containing the news of the battle of Antietam, a day earlier than usual.

A number of important events were connected with the history of the Pony Express, perhaps the greatest being the news of the election of Abraham Lincoln, in November, 1860. This information was brought through from the east in eight days.

The quickest time on record made by the Pony Express was in March, 1861, when President Lincoln's inaugural address was carried through from St. Joe to Sacramento, a total distance of 1,980 miles, in seven days and seventeen hours—a most extraordinary feat, and calling for wonderful tests of endurance on the part of the wiry Pony Express riders. On another occasion an important dispatch was carried from St. Joe to Denver, a distance of 675 miles, in sixty-nine hours, the last ten miles being covered in thirty-one minutes.

Among the important documents carried from St. Joe by the first Pony Express rider, was a brief message of congratulation from President Buchanan to the governor of California. The few words were transmitted by wire from the executive mansion at Washington to St. Joe by wire, where they were taken off by the operator, transferred to the pouch of the Pony Express rider and rushed westward.

In California there were many people who seriously doubted the success of the Pony Express. The newspaper editors of San Francisco were among the first in their belief that it could never be made a success because of the dangers to be encountered from Indians. To use their own language, it "was simply inviting slaughter upon all the foolish young men who had been engaged as riders."

The pay of the riders was from $125 to $150 a month and board, depending upon the dangerous character of the country they had to traverse.

The operations of the Pony Express covered a period of only eighteen months, as stated. Two months before it ceased doing business the Daily Overland Stage was in operation. Four months later came the Pacific Telegraph—in comparison with which the Pony Express was as an ox-train pitted against the present day racing automobile.

The expenses of the Pony Express during the eighteen months of its existence were, approximately, as follows:

Equipping the line $100,000
Maintenance 480,000
Nevada Indian War 75,000
Miscellaneous 45,000
                                   ————————
    Total $700,000

The total receipts did not exceed $500,000, leaving a net loss of $200,000.

A volume could be written of the thrilling adventures and hairbreadth escapes of many of the riders of the Pony Express, whose lives were continually in danger through the Indian country. Probably the most daring of these young men was Robert Haslam, known as "Pony Bob," who died some years ago in Chicago. His territory was through Nevada, and on one occasion he made the longest run ever covered by a single rider in the history of the organization, making 380 miles without sleep or rest, due to the fact that the intervening stations had been attacked and burnt by Indians and the keepers and riders killed. Some of the distance on Haslam's route had to be traversed at a pace of twenty-five miles an hour.

With the coming of the Pacific Telegraph, the usefulness of the Pony Express ended, and the enterprise was at once discontinued. While it was a costly undertaking, it demonstrated—at an enormous cost—what could be done by Western Americans of enterprise and determination.

CHAPTER XII

~

"LITTLE BAT"

A distinguished Frontier Scout, another unrecognized
hero of the old West

~

AMONG the many frontiersmen who rendered distinguished service during the Indian campaign of 1876 and the Ghost Dance outbreak of 1890, none won a higher place for efficiency, in the estimation of leading army officers, than Baptiste Garnier, known all over the middle West and around old Fort Laramie and Fort Robinson, as "Little Bat." Not that he was by any means small of stature, for he was of most powerful physique, but to distinguish him from another skillful army scout, Baptiste Pourier, known as "Big Bat." The two men were not related in any way.

Little Bat was a great favorite with General George Crook, the noted Indian fighter. Crook was himself a most skillful hunter of big game, and he did not consider any of his hunting parties complete unless Little Bat accompanied it, because Bat was second to none in that particular line.

Little Bat's father was a Frenchman, while his mother was a Sioux Indian. Bat was born in 1854. At a very tender age his father was killed by an Arapahoe Indian. His mother died soon after, and Bat was raised in the family of E. W. Whitcomb until he attained the age of 15 years, or about 1869, when he seems to have been shunted about, living with various families and people until the winter of 1871-'72, when he went to live in the family of John

Hunton at his ranch on the Chugwater, twenty-seven miles southwest of Old Fort Laramie, Wyoming. The Hunton ranch continued to be Little Bat's home until about 1880. He married a daughter of a Frenchman named Mousseau. The mother of Mousseau's daughter was a Sioux woman. He had three half-brothers—full blooded Indians, and one sister, also a full-blood.

During Little Bat's residence on the Hunton ranch, he became a most expert cow hand, being above the average. As a hunter his skill was marvelous, while as a trailer he was known far and wide. Never was an Indian born who could follow the trail of a lost animal with the assurance of finding it with such unerring accuracy as was displayed by Little Bat.

One strong feature stood out above all others—his wonderful "bump of locality." Land him blindfolded in a strange country, and he would go as straight to his camp, in daylight or darkness, as a needle of a compass points to the north.

In a letter written to the author by Mr. Hunton, he gives some interesting data regarding Little Bat. "While he lived with me," writes Mr. Hunton, "he did any and all work I required of him. In 1876 he was with Generals Wesley Merritt and George Crook on expeditions covering a period of about nine months. In 1877 he was my companion most of the time in the Fort Fetterman and McKinney country. He then took sub-contracts and put in wood and hay on my contracts at Fort Fetterman. He was located for a short time on Muddy Creek—near where the present oil fields are located. After 1880 I saw but little of him, as he was then living at or near Fort Robinson, Nebraska, where he was in the employ of the government.

"In 1890 he came here (Fort Laramie) with a Mr. Taylor and a detachment of soldiers, while dismantling the post, preparatory to its abandonment. His duty here was that of a courier to carry dispatches to Bordeaux and Fort Robinson, as the telegraph and telephone lines had both been taken down.

"It was while here in 1890 that he heard of the death of General Crook, which was, he told me, 'the hardest thing that ever happened to me'. That was the only time I ever

Baptiste Garnier—"Little Bat," a scout in the Sioux Ghost Dance "War".

saw Little Bat shed a tear. We had our last hunt together at that time. We left here after breakfast, and long before night were back, each with a large blacktail buck. I did not see Bat again until 1892, when I was at his home at Fort Robinson, where we had quite a visit. He gave a bow and some arrows to me, together with a fine Indian pipe, which he had picked up on the Wounded Knee battlefield.

"I never saw him again after that visit."

When General Crook organized his 1876 campaign against

the Sioux Indians, Frank Grouard and Little Bat were chosen as the principal guides, scouts and couriers. At the end of the campaign, General Crook filed in the War Department a recommendation that both Grouard and Little Bat, because of their valuable services through the campaign, be given government positions to the end of their lives, Grouard at $150 a month and Little Bat at $100, which was done. Little Bat remained at Fort Robinson, and was there at the time of his death, which occurred soon after the troops of the old Ninth Cavalry were ordered from Fort Robinson to Cuba, during the Spanish-American war.

In November, 1882, General Crook with members of a hunting party had been camped on Salt Creek for several days. Not finding game as plentiful as had been expected, the party planned to move over to the head of the Dry Cheyenne.

Little Bat instructed the men in charge of the teams to "follow a blind game trail over a strip of bad lands to a deep washout, to cross that and keep along the divide to the bed of a dry creek, then follow that down to a point of rocks and strike for a lone pine tree on the side of a steep bluff, where camp was to be made."

General Crook and Bat cut across country to look for bear sign, and at dark were at the designated camping ground; but the teams had not shown up, and the general became uneasy. The fact was, the men got lost, and Bat was questioned as to their non-appearance.

"You bet them drivers lose their heads," he commented. "I go find them and fetch them all in, mebby near daylight."

About midnight, while General Crook and his friends were toasting their shins over the campfire, and wondering if Bat could "make good," they heard the rattle of wagon wheels, and in came the lost outfit, led by Little Bat. The harness boss remarked, as they unharnessed the teams, "That feller Bat he got eyes just like a cat. He see at night just as well as daytime."

Little Bat was thoroughly honest. He could be trusted with any property, and his promises could always be relied on. What he pretended to know, he knew, and his knowledge was not to be questioned. If Bat were asked, "Can we do it?" and he said "yes," then the matter could safely be left in his hands, for he was sure to accomplish it.

Bat has been known to go out on the trail of a bear with General Crook, when the trail was so difficult to see that the animal's soft foot made no impression on the hard ground, yet this remarkable hunter would follow the bear's trail over that sort of country for miles, his only clue being the occasional turning over of a bit of dirt or a pebble. His trailing instinct was marvelous and absolutely unerring.

On one occasion, while one of Bat's friends was at Casper, Wyoming, preparing for a hunt with General Brooke, Bat was asked, "Is there any elk left in the Casper mountains?" To which he replied, "I guess not. I was up there awhile ago. I saw seventeen and killed them all."

One of Little Bat's most intimate friends was Capt. James H. Cook, whose ranch was in Sioux county, Nebraska. Captain Cook was an intimate friend of the author, to whom he gave the following interesting information about Little Bat:

"We were close friends from 1876 to the day of Bat's murder at Fort Robinson. He was well thought of by all the officers and men who were ever associated with him. He was good-natured and even-tempered at all times. He was considered by Gen. Crook as one of the best big-game hunters in the Rocky Mountain section.

"During the years that Little Bat and I were such close friends, I never knew him to have a quarrel with anyone. He was murdered by a scoundrel named Jim Haguewood, in Crawford, Nebraska, near Fort Robinson, Haguewood was a barkeeper in a saloon run by a man named Dietrick. Haguewood had been having some family trouble, and had been drinking heavily at the time he murdered my friend Bat.

Capt. J. H. Cook on horse.

"Little Bat went into the saloon and drank a glass of beer with an acquaintance. He was unarmed, and was wearing a heavy buffalo overcoat. While chatting casually, Haguewood, who had served them their drinks, asked, in an insulting manner, 'Who pays for these drinks?' Bat replied, 'I will when I get ready.'

"Even at that moment he was unbuttoning his overcoat to get out his pocketbook. Haguewood grabbed a revolver lying handy under the bar, and shouted, 'You are ready right now!'

"Bat saw the move, and knew the man meant to shoot, and he crouched in front of the bar to avoid the attack. Haguewood leaned over and shot Bat in the neck, the bullet ranging downward through the center of his body. Several civilians witnessed the shooting.

"Little Bat immediately ran out into the street, evidently intending to get to his horse. He staggered across the street and fell helpless. Someone notified his wife at Fort Robinson. Bat was carried into a room nearby, where he died in the arms of his devoted wife a couple of hours later. He would see nobody but his wife, and seemed to be able to converse only in the Sioux tongue. He told her, when dying, that he thought Haguewood was his friend, and he could not understand why a friend should shoot him.

"Bat had no hatred in his heart except for the Indian who had killed his father, and he certainly met an undeserved death. At that time all his army friends were, for the most part, in Cuba. A man named Freeman, who had resided at Fort Robinson since the post was established, and myself, were about the only close friends Bat seemed to have in Northwestern Nebraska when the trial of Haguewood was held. He was acquitted of the charge of murder, or manslaughter, which had been preferred against him. There were some people in Crawford who seemed to consider that Bat was 'only an Indian' who had merely been 'killed by a white man.'

"The services rendered by Little Bat as scout and interpreter for the United States Army, even as late as the Wounded Knee campaign during the winter of 1890-91, should, I think, entitle him to be honored by old army friends and his many other American admirers in a more fitting manner than by the simple little marker which stands at the head of his grave in the Fort Robinson cemetery. On this is inscribed merely his name, and underneath is chiseled just one word—'Employe.'

"When that unfortunate affair known as the battle of Wounded Knee took place, near Pine Ridge Agency, South Dakota, December 29, 1890—which was perhaps the last clash that will ever occur between United States troops and American Indians, Little Bat was present. After Chief

Big Foot's band of Sioux had been surrounded by the soldiers, and orders had been given to search their lodges for
firearms, Little Bat was sent to interpret for the soldiers
detailed for that purpose.

"Bat was to inform the Indian women what the soldiers
had been ordered to do, and to explain to them that they
should not be harmed. After he had so informed them, and
while a portion of the lodges were being examined, the
fatal shot was fired which precipitated the battle.

"In a second death reigned on all sides. The Hotchkiss
rapid-fire guns which had been trained on the Indian camp,
opened their deadly fire, and Indian women and children
who had just been informed that 'no harm should come
to them,' were slaughtered by the score.

"Some of the soldiers who were with Little Bat, engaged
in searching the tepees, were killed. Bat had no weapon with
him at the time, as he thought by going unarmed he would
be better able to demonstrate to the Indians that there was
no danger. When the firing began, Bat's clothing was pierced
by bullets in many places, and his escape from death was
miraculous.

"He attempted to reach the tent where he had left his
weapons. He found it burned. A dead Indian was lying inside
it, and beneath his body was Bat's Winchester rifle, with
the stock half burned away. His saddle had been riddled
with bullets.

"I met Bat soon after the fight, and he told me he witnessed sights during the slaughter of those poor Indian
women and little children which would never be effaced
from his memory.

"Little Bat had a family consisting of his wife, one son
and six daughters, who lived at Pine Ridge reservation. Bat
was a man possessed of more than ordinary intelligence.
During his later years he spent a great deal of time at my
ranch home, twenty miles from Fort Robinson, so that I
had ample time to know him as well as anyone ever did.

"Although he possessed no school training, he had certain remarkable qualties which made him distinctive. His honesty and fearlessness were never questioned. His skill as a hunter, and his knowledge of the Sioux language and their customs and manners, made his services to the government invaluable during the Indian troubles of 1876 and later.

"He was not a 'long-haired man of the Plains' who had more hair than brains. He was a most modest and unassuming character of the frontier. His home and family, and the simple life of the Western pioneer, were what he most desired, and his name will be associated with the history of the West, and go down to posterity, as one of its greatest sons, so long as time shall endure."

On his way home from the Custer semi-centennial celebration in June, 1926, the author made it a point to stop at Fort Robinson, Nebraska, and visit the post cemetery where "Little Bat" is sleeping his "last long rest." A most shocking condition of affairs was revealed. In this cemetery lie the remains of many time-honored frontier characters and army officers, their wives and children. And yet the place was, on the occasion of the visit of the author, so overrun with weeds and underbrush that it was only with the greatest difficulty a person could open the squeaking gates and force one's way through the tangled, neglected burying ground. Indeed, it would appear that no work of any sort had been done to keep the post cemetery free of weeds and underbrush, which were from four to six feet high, and in many cases completely obliterating the headstones.

CHAPTER XIII

~

THE STORY OF FORT PEASE

*How an Historic Spot in Montana was made
Famous by, Adventurous Traders and Wolfers*

~

ONE of the most interesting historical spots among the many in the State of Montana is what is known as "Pease Bottoms" or "Fort Pease." Contrary to what might be the general expectation, Fort Pease was not a military post, but a trading and trapping station. The history of the luckless expedition, which was formed by a party of Bozeman adventures, for trading and trafficking among the Indians, is one of the most thrilling in the annals of the Western frontier. "Fort Pease" was located on the Yellowstone River, about three miles from the spot where the Big Horn River empties into the Yellowstone.

The leader of this band of venturesome traders, trappers and "wolfers" was Major F. D. Pease, formerly Indian Agent at Old Crow Agency on Mission Creek. Assisting in the formation of the expedition was Zed Daniels, a one-time post sutler at Fort Ellis. The balance of the party, thirty in number, was, with one exception, composed of old frontiersmen, skilled in Indian campaigning, and eager for whatever of sport or adventure might come their way. The single exception was a "tenderfoot" Frenchman, who had but recently come to Bozeman from the provinces of the Northwest. He was entirely unused to Indian warfare, but was a skilled cook, and it was thought he would make an excellent

281

addition as a general utility man. The party was to share and share alike in whatever of profit or danger might overtake it.

It was late in the summer of 1875 that the party was formed, and September saw them on their way. No trouble with the Indians was anticipated, as they were inclined to be friendly at that particular time in the section of country expected to be visited, and eager to "make swap" with their white brothers.

The actual purpose of the trip was with the thought (from news that had been circulated) that a new army post was to be established down on the Yellowstone, which would induce considerable steamboat travel, which would bring all kinds of adventurers and possible settlers into the territory, and a brisk trade in goods of all kinds might be expected, which could be exchanged for furs or cash, as the occasion required.

It may be well at this point to state that the expedition was doomed to disappointment as regards the establishment of a new fort at the expected point on the Yellowstone; neither did any steamboat travel materialize.

The entire party was well armed, and had plenty of ammunition for a prolonged stay. All were mounted, and their goods for barter were loaded on pack-mules, which also carried the camping outfits and supplies. There were many noted men among that band of adventurous spirits, notably the well-known McCormack brothers, Paul and John, both celebrated frontiersmen who had served as scouts and guides in previous Indian campaigns. There was also "Muggins" Taylor, who became famous as a scout under Col. John Gibbon in the Sioux campaign of 1876. Another prominent member was the famous X. Biedler, celebrated as a prominent vigilante in the days of Montana's early mining history of the '60's, and perhaps the best-known "old-timer" in the entire state.

Arriving at the Yellowstone, about where the city of Livingstone is now located, a halt was made for a few days to construct boats to take certain of the party down stream, while the others were to travel along the banks with the mules and horses of the party. All were to unite some distance down the river, wherever a suitable permanent camping site could be located.

The spot where the men embarked was known as Benson's Landing. Before the party got away, however, a courier arrived from Bozeman with urgent news for Major Pease which required his immediate return to conclude some government business. He remained with the outfit, however, until the boats were finished and the party ready to start out on what proved to be a decidedly adventurous career.

Nothing of any particular consequence occurred during the trip down the Yellowstone. Reaching a point about three miles above where the Big Horn River empties into the Yellowstone, an admirable spot for a permanent camp was located on a high bluff, which rose some fifty or sixty feet above the surrounding country, which commanded a distant view in every direction.

Here several log buildings were erected, enclosed by a formidable stockade, utilizing a space about two hundred feet square. The buildings and the stockade were loopholed on every side, commanding the interior as well as the exterior of the "fort." The place was christened "Fort Pease" in honor of the founder of the expedition, and the spot itself has ever since been known as "Pease Bottoms."

For two or three months matters went along without any trouble from the Indians, who, during the building of the stockaded post, had appeared quite friendly, and had opened barter with the whites, exchanging gladly their peltries for the goods of the traders. Indeed one lot of furs had been sent back to Bozeman and fresh goods packed in.

In trapping, the men were also expert. Wolves were

numerous, and they were captured by the usual method employed—poisoning the bait with strychnine. This was a method which the Indians did not take kindly to, as occasionally their own dogs located some of the poisoned meat. However, there was no open hostility for some time.

But bad luck was to follow. On the last trip down the river one of the boats capsized, and with it went eighteen of the rifles of the party and a quantity of ammunition. When a "count of noses" was taken it was discovered that there were but fourteen rifles left among the thirty-one men. However, there was nothing to do but make the best of a bad situation. Winter was setting in, and it was too late to return to the settlements for a supply of arms and ammunition to replace the lost stock.

Under these circumstances it behooved the party to "get a move on" and lay in a plentiful supply of firewood against the severe winter which would soon be upon them. It was thought there were sufficient provisions to last until spring, and as game was plentiful, the meat question was thought to be easily solved.

But early in December the Indians began to get troublesome. They were restless and inclined to resent the intrusion of the white men into their hunting country, and particularly their use of strychnine in their trapping methods. Some few depredations had already been committed, but nobody looked for a general outbreak among the Indians before spring, as they were inclined to prefer the shelter of their warm tepees during the severe winter weather, to the hardships of the warpath, as the traders well knew.

They were not to be caught napping, however, and took no chances. They had done guard duty regularly, keeping an open eye for hostile Indians; but the untutored "tenderfoot" Frenchman hastened the outbreak. Being detailed for guard duty, he was instructed to be extremely cautious about firing on anything that looked suspicious until he was really assured of danger, as several of the more friendly of the Sioux would often straggle up to the stockade to "make swap" in the evening, and it was not desired to start trouble by firing on them.

The Frenchman had been on duty a few hours one night when the report of his rifle echoed through the stockade. This was followed by a rousing volley, which apparently came from all sides of the stockade, and the Sioux war-whoop aroused the entire party. Following the volley the thoroughly-frightened Frenchman was rushing about, shouting that "Indians had fired on him." The condition of his clothes bore this out, as two bullet holes were found through his coat, and one through his hat.

Almost immediately galloping hoofbeats bore out the fact that the Indians had stampeded the livestock of the traders. It was a clear moonlight night, and objects at some distance were distinguishable, and the frightened horses and mules could be seen running down the valley, followed by the whooping redskins.

It was deemed unwise to venture outside the stockade until daylight. When the Frenchman was questioned as to the cause of his firing, he said that he had seen an Indian skulking on the river bank; that he had challenged and received no reply and had fired. He declared that the redskin fell, and that almost immediately the sagebrush became alive with the Sioux, who had fired the volley at him.

Such was the Frenchman's story, but the others declared that he should not have fired without some hostile act on the part of the redskin, none of which had seemed apparent, although it looked as though the Sioux were attempting to surround the stockade.

At daylight several of the men ventured out, fully armed against a surprise attack. An investigation was made at the spot where the sentry reported having seen and fired at the Indian. Blood was found, and apparently the Frenchman had hit the mark and possibly killed his man, in the event of which, immediate war would doubtless be declared against the traders.

Their worst fears were soon realized. Shortly thereafter an Indian approached the stockade, making overtures of peace and asking for a parley. Paul McCormack was selected to meet him. After a short pow-wow he returned with bad news. He said that "Frenchy" had shot and killed an Indian known as "Long Face," one of the best of the more friendly of the Sioux, and that after the firing the entire party of redskins had rushed the stables and run off the riding stock of the whites with the exception of three animals.

"We're up against it," soberly announced McCormack. "The Indians demand that we give up the man who fired the shot. Of course we are not going to do that, and they don't get him unless they rush us and break over the stockade; but it was a mighty foolish move putting 'Frenchy' on guard last night. We should have known better than to depend upon a tenderfoot in an emergency."

While McCormack's conclusions were agreed to by the others—that the Frenchman should not be turned over to the Indians—the balance of his remarks were received with emphatic nods of the head. McCormack then went out and gave the Indian their ultimatum, whereupon the savage trotted away and McCormack returned to the stockade.

It was a rather desperate situation—thirty-one men with but fourteen guns among them, and a none-too-plentiful supply of ammunition, and just what the outcome would be was problematical.

Several days passed, with the traders constantly on their guard, but no signs of Indians were seen. A week, two weeks went by, and still no acts of hostility. Soon food began to run short, in spite of the fact that the men had been living on half rations ever since the trouble. There was game in plenty all about them, but none had dared to venture out after it.

But the time came when this chance had to be taken, and one morning, after a week of unusual quiet, Paul Mc-Cormack was selected to make the attempt to kill some game. It was decided that the French tenderfoot should accompany him. The pair succeeded in dodging the Indians and went into the hills about three miles from the stockade, where they shot three antelope and an elk. They loaded as much of the meat as possible on their horses and "cached" the rest, then started down a coulee for the stockade.

While passing a thick fringe of sagebrush, the two were fired upon. The Frenchman fell from his horse dead, and McCormack received severe flesh wounds. His horse became unmanageable and thoroughly frightened by the gunfire, and McCormack had all he could do to stick to the saddle, but he managed to open fire on his foes, as his frantic horse plunged hither and yon, one minute headed toward the stockade and the next toward the Indians. The horse had also received several wounds, which rendered the frenzied animal uncontrollable.

The sounds of battle reached the ears of the men at the stockade, and McCormack's brother, John, "Muggins" Taylor and Zed Daniels led a party of the frontiersmen on the run toward the battleground. One volley and the Indians fled, and McCormack's horse dropped dead as the rescuers arrived.

"Back to the stockade, boys," he shouted, "or the red devils will make short work of us!" The retreat was none too soon, for the Sioux quickly recovered from their fright and appeared in hordes. The men made a mad run for the stockade, and had just reached the doors when a shower of bullets rained upon them, killing one of the men named Jack Cowles, who was shot through the back. Pulling him through the gates, the frontiersmen made ready for a desperate defense.

The first thing to do was to attend to the wounds of

Paul McCormack, none of which were dangerous. Although the expected assault on the garrison did not materialize, watch was maintained. It is stated on reliable authority that when Paul McCormack awoke the next morning his dark hair had turned snow-white from the terrifying, nerve-wracking experience he had undergone the previous afternoon.

As the party was yet without fresh meat, two of the men, "Muggins" Taylor and another known simply as "Dave," determined to go out late that night and reach the "cache" which McCormack had made of the antelope and elk meat. None of the others attempted to dissuade them from the trip, as the meat was an absolute and immediate necessity. It was simply a case of being starved out or of all of the party making a dash through the Indian lines as a last resort. Taylor and Dave were confident they could go and return without being discovered.

Shortly after one o'clock in the morning the two men set out on foot, after being furnished with directions to the "cache" by McCormack. Those behind listened intently for some time, expecting to hear the crack of rifles which would indicate the discovery of the two daring men, and the stockade gates were kept in position to be opened quickly in the event that they had to "make a run" for shelter.

Carefully feeling their way, Taylor and Dave succeeded in reaching and locating the cached meat without being discovered or encountering a single Indian, although their campfires could be seen along the river bank. Three hours after leaving the stockade, the men were back, dragging between them the supply of meat, greatly to the relief of their comrades.

But this small quantity could last but a short time, and in two or three days the situation was as bad as ever. John McCormack, after a consultation with the others, determined to try and get through the closely-infested lines of the hostiles and reach the nearest settlement, Billings, and bring back a rescue party. It was a decidedly risky proposition, but all within the stockade knew that if the trip could be made by anyone, John McCormack was the man to do it, because of his knowledge of the country and his experience as a scout. The attempt was to be made that night. He did not ask nor desire that anyone accompany him, arguing that if two men could go out and bring in that meat from the "cache," one man should be able to slip through the Indian cordon.

An incident occurred during the afternoon which was the talk of the frontier for years afterward. "Muggins" Taylor made a long-distance shot at an Indian which was little short of miraculous, and while he always modestly claimed that "it was jest a fluke shot," and that "it couldn't be done agin on a thousand trials," the others argued that his marksmanship had more to do with it than anything else.

Taylor was armed with a Colt repeating rifle which had been given to him by a party of wealthy Eastern sportsmen whom he had guided through Yellowstone Park on a hunting expedition a few years before. Taylor was very proud of the beautiful weapon, and had tested its shooting qualities on more than one occasion on both Indians and dangerous big game.

For several successive days an Indian had appeared on an eminence at a considerable distance from the stockade, where he had gone through mocking antics and derisive gestures. Considering doubtless that he was well out of rifle range he had grown bolder with his insolent gesticulations and insulting signs. Nearly every man in the party had taken a shot at the defiant redskin, without "potting" him. Either their guns were not of the long-range type or their aim was poor.

On this particular afternoon, "Muggins" Taylor had announced his intention of "givin' that there Injun a lettle dose from ol' Betsy," in case he again appeared. His patience was rewarded about sunset, when the Indian, wearing a beautiful feathered head-dress, showed himself and again began his mocking antics. Now was Taylor's opportunity!

Rushing to one of the portholes, where he could get a careful rest, Taylor "drew down" on the defiant figure. "Crr-rack! W-h-a-m!" and as a cloud of smoke breezed away from the muzzle of his rifle, the interested watchers saw the Indian reel unsteadily and dizzily. Several within the stockade had field glasses trained on the distant redskin, and noted that he sank to the ground. As the body remained there until

Artist Bolenbaugh's sketch of Muggins Taylor firing at a defiant Indian outside the stockade.

"The Indian reeled dizzily and sank to the ground"—from the story of
Muggins Taylor.

dark at least, it was always supposed that Taylor had made
a "good" Indian. Doubtless his red companions were unwilling to come within range of such a marksman.

Shortly after midnight, McCormack announced that he
was ready for the start. With a small quantity of food, his
rifle and plenty of ammunition, but on foot, he slipped out
through the stockade gates and stealthily began creeping
through the sagebrush toward the river. His objective was
Billings, from which place word was to be sent to the commanding officer of Fort Ellis to send out a relief party to the
beleaguered "wolfers." McCormack reached the river un-
observed, crossed on the ice and began the long journey
to Billings.

The trip was made in safety, and Gen. Alfred Terry was
notified of the desperate plight of the party at Pease Bottoms.
He ordered Major Brisbin, at Fort Ellis, to take four troops
of the Second Cavalry and make a forced march to their
relief. Brisbin, accompanied by McCormack as guide, left
Fort Ellis February 22d, and made the march of over two

hundred miles down the Yellowstone, crossing the river several times en route on the ice, and reached the worn-out "wolfers" within a week after leaving the post. Needless to say, the arrival of the relief party was hailed with delight, although, prior to their arrival, the Indians had grown weary of the stubborn defense put up by the stockaded men and retired from the vicinity, applauding the courage of the garrison and asserting that they had "had enough" and were ready to quit, and that they might stay there as long as they wished so far as the Indians were concerned.

Several skirmishes had taken place during the absence of McCormack, and the garrison was reduced to twenty-eight fighting men. The few remaining members were only too well pleased to take advantage of the opportunity of getting away from the unwelcome spot. The fort was abandoned in March, and the colors were left flying. It was the intention of the party to leave the buildings entire, but the story goes that a discontented member of the expedition set fire to one of them, which was burned, but without injury to the balance of the buildings or the stockade itself.

For years old "Fort Pease" was a noted landmark in that section of the country, until decay and the passing of years obliterated what was left of it, marking one of the most historic and thrilling episodes within the borders of Montana.

CHAPTER XIV

~

AN UNEQUAL DUEL

A True Story of Northern Cheyenne Indian Fanaticism

~

"THEN you don't think, Lieutenant, that young Boyle accidently shot himself?"

"No, Major, I don't. It looks to me like Indian work. No white man would have taken the pains to conceal his body in the place we found it, either."

"But what could the Indians have against Boyle? He has always treated them well; besides, he wasn't scalped or mutilated."

"I know, Major. He was shot in the back of the head; it wouldn't have been possible for Boyle to have done it himself. My scouts found the spot where he'd been murdered —presumably from ambush—and his body dragged down into that deep ravine where we located it. Besides, there were moccasin tracks about. No white renegade did that job. I think it was the work of some of these young Cheyenne bucks who thought it would be smart to count coup on a white man; and as Boyle was alone, they figured they could get away with it undetected. I think I'm on the right trail, and I don't believe it will be long before we run down the murderers." Lieutenant Robertson nodded significantly to Major Carroll.

It was a puzzling case. Boyle, a young rancher whose homestead claim was about three miles from the camp of

293

the First U. S. Cavalry, under command of Major Carroll, along Lame Deer Creek, Montana, had been missing for several days. He had gone on a hunting trip and failed to return. His absence had been reported to Major Carroll, who had ordered out a searching party. Boyle's body had been located in a deep and remote ravine, by Lieutenant Robertson's Indian scouts. It was at first surmised that Boyle had fallen, his gun accidentally discharged, and that his death, therefore, was due to his own carelessness.

But the keen-eyed scouts in Robertson's command had pointed out certain tell-tale signs—moccasin tracks along the ridge at the head of the ravine; blood on the leaves, evidences of a struggle, or of a body having been dragged along the ridge and then flung into the ravine. Several empty cartridge shells had been found in a clump of brush about fifty feet from the blood-spattered leaves.

"No white man—Injuns!" grunted Lone Wolf, one of Robertson's trailers.

For several days no fresh clue was obtained. Then one afternoon two members of the Indian Police trotted up to the Agent's office.

"Head Swift and Young Mule gone—five, six days," they reported.

Here at last was a clue!

Head Swift and Young Mule were Cheyenne youths about eighteen years of age. Both were well known on the reservation—and none too favorably. Indolent, restless, they spent their time principally roaming the hills, and were looked upon as a disturbing element among the young Indians on the reserve.

The sudden disappearance was at once reported to Major Carroll. These two young braves belonged to the Northern Cheyennes, a part of old Dull Knife's band, which had made such a masterful retreat after the Fort Robinson outbreak twelve or thirteen years previously. These Indians had since remained in comparative quiet, until about 1886, when they became restive, and gave signs of discontent, rendering necessary the establishing of an annual camp of regular army troops in their vicinity.

It was early in September, 1890, that young Boyle's body had been found. It was several days later that the Indian Police reported Head Swift and Young Mule to have taken to the hills.

The young bucks were suspected of hiding out for some good reason, and a scouting party had been made up to run them down and bring them in for an interview.

"But we've scoured the hills high and low, Major," reported Lieutenant Robertson, "and we can't find hide nor hair of them; they're laying low."

"Keep right after them, and bring them in at all hazards," was Major Carroll's order.

Twenty-four hours later, old Brave Wolf, a warrior of many battles, trotted in to the Agency and dismounted at the office. He asked to see the Agent at once.

"Head Swift and Young Mule no surrender," he indicated through the interpreter. "They kill man—no come in— want heap fight!"

And then followed a most astounding and seemingly unbelievable confession. The two Cheyenne boys had sneaked in to the Indian camp under cover of darkness and told their parents the whole story, admitting the murder of Boyle. They realized that their lives would be the forfeit if they surrendered. Therefore, they would never give themselves up, but would die fighting.

"Fight all the troops," declared old Brave Wolf. "Tell sojer chief bring heap men."

To Major Carroll hastened the Agent with the amazing proposal.

"WHAT!" exclaimed Major Carroll in undisguised astonishment, "those two boys challenge me to a duel with all my command—is that what you mean?"

And Brave Wolf nodded emphatically. "All," he said, "Injun boys heap brave; no surrender; fight all, or say they raid Agency; kill heap white people."

It seemed preposterous—positively ridiculous, that these two rash Indian boys should thus defiantly challenge three troops of seasoned cavalrymen to a duel to the death!

"Why, that's a joke!" exclaimed Major Carroll. "It would be useless for me to order out my command on any such fool's errand. They'd never show up. Where are those boys now? I'll send out a dozen men to bring them in."

One of the older of the white scouts with Carroll's command shook his head.

"Dunno 'bout that, Major," he mused. "These 'ere young Injuns gits plenty of fanatical notions in their fool heads sometimes; and if they told Brave Wolf that they're ready to fight your troops to the death, I reck'n you won't be dissi'pinted, as fur as they are concerned."

Old Brave Wolf gravely nodded assent. "They come," he soberly announced, "No stay 'way if so'jers come now; they fight—heap brave."

"Well!" declared the astonished cavalry leader, "I guess if that's really the case, and they mean business we can accommodate 'em. Orderly, have 'boots and saddles' sounded at once. Lieutenant Robertson, you will have a sufficient guard deployed about the Agency at once, in case of trouble, while we are accommodating these young Indian fools."

Following this command, there was a scurrying of troopers, a saddling of horses and a jingling of accoutrements, as the men, laughingly, and with much banter, made ready to start.

During the previous few days' excitement, the entire Cheyenne village had been gathered by the Agent and placed in camp about the Agency, the better to watch their actions, and prevent any possible disturbance. Excitement had been tense, and it now looked as though a climax was at hand.

"Prepare to mount—mount!" came the order, when the troopers had assembled.

And then, led by old Brave Wolf, the troopers under Major Carroll, with Lieutenants Robertson and Pitcher, started on their strange mission of death.

Among the command it was looked upon as a great joke, as Major Carroll had said. That two Indian boys would have the nerve to attack three troops of cavalry in open combat, was unbelievable! It was the concensus of opinion that the trip would be nothing but a "fool's errand."

"Two agin three hundred!" snorted Trooper Calahan to Trooper McCarthy. Both veterans shook their heads in unbelief.

A half mile from the Agency, at a sign from Brave Wolf, Major Carroll gave the command "HALT!" This was the spot, said Brave Wolf, which the young Cheyenne bucks had chosen for their battleground. Here was to be enacted the strangest drama ever performed upon the stage of frontier life.

The road at this point ran through a narrow valley, flanked by rock-crowned hills, covered with a forest of low pine, forming an amphitheater. No more spectacular spot could have been chosen.

Here the troops were posted—some mounted, others dismounted. Excitement was at fever heat. Upon the hills surrounding the valley had gathered the entire population of the Cheyenne village, the bucks taking position close in upon the hills, and the women and children where they would not be endangered by rifle-fire, yet could watch the two Cheyenne boys die like true warriors.

It was an ideal autumn afternoon. Nature was at her loveliest, in colors of gold and brown. The haze of Indian summer was in the air. Peace and quiet were in the scene.

Across the valley was heard the death-chant of the squaws. The stage was set, and it only lacked the two actors to step forth and play their respective parts.

"Where can they be?" was the eager query which ran

through the command as keen eyes watched various vantage points.

Major Carroll and Lieutenant Robertson were scanning the distant clumps of timber through their field glasses. "I don't believe they'll ever show up!" declared the former, closing his glasses with an impatient snap.

"Well, Major—*there they are!*" suddenly exclaimed Lieutenant Robertson, pointing toward two figures on horseback which had glided phantom-like from the darkened background of pines. "It looks like they mean business, after all!"

Glasses were again leveled, and it was seen that the two Cheyenne youths were fully armed and decorated in war costume. To the ears of the astonished troopers was borne the echoes of the Cheyenne death-song, solemnly taken up and echoed by the distant Cheyenne women.

The plumed war bonnets of the youthful fanatics nodded in the breeze, while nickeled ornament on wrist and arm, the gaily-decorated regalia and the glint of rifle-barrel, flashed in the sunlight.

Exclamations of excitement ran through the entire command! The troopers watched the young braves urge their ponies toward the top of one of the highest and steepest ridges, down which there was an open space to make a charge. All their actions could be easily watched and noted by their tribesmen; every detail observed.

Reaching the very pinnacle of the ridge, the young Cheyennes suddenly wheeled their ponies, and for an instant sat gazing down the lane of death. Then the warwhoop echoed from the ridge—and then—

"HERE THEY COME!" was the cry.

And come they did, with fanatical fury! Down the slope with Winchesters loaded, magazines filled and cartridge belts sagging with lead. It was a sight the like of which had never before been seen upon the American frontier!

"HOLD YOUR FIRE!" came the orders from troop commanders. "Not yet, men!" Excited troopers thrust carbines forward, and triggers clicked as hammers were raised.

Down the steep hillside headed the two Cheyennes directly for a line of troopers which had just been led up the southern crest of the valley by Lieutenant Pitcher. Ponies straining every nerve; moccasined feet drumming at heaving flanks; rifles streaming leaden death—and over all, the Cheyenne death chant!

Dismounted, the troopers waited the command to fire, the horse-holders in the rear. When the fire-order came, carbines belched forth a roaring blast! Others in reserve crashed out! The pony of the foremost brave stumbled—regained its feet—again pitched forward, hurling its rider through the air!

Apparently unharmed, his companion continued to ride straight into the jaws of death, right at Pitcher's command, firing rapidly. But apparently his aim was high, as no trooper was struck by a bullet. Fifty carbines and revolvers roared in return, and yet, in some miraculous manner, the daring young warrior escaped death until he had actually penetrated the line of troopers! There, both pony and rider crumpled under the leaden hail!

"Look out for the other Indian!" came the warning cry.

The dismounted Cheyenne, flung to the ground when his pony went down, had meantime regained his feet and turned down the valley in the direction of the Agency. Volley after volley saluted him, and he returned the fire as rapidly as he could work the lever of his Winchester. Bullets rained around him, kicking up the dust and ricocheting off into space like angry bees! Finally, seemingly badly wounded, the youthful warrior limped painfully into a dry wash to make a stand to the death. In his wake streamed excited troopers, firing volley after volley!

"We crawled through the brush toward him," recounted Lieutenant Robertson, in his official report, "not aware that he was yet dead, and suddenly stumbled upon his body. I was startled, awe-struck, by the weird beauty of the picture he made, as he lay in his vivid color of costume and painted face, his red blood crimsoning the yellow of the autumn leaves upon which he lay."

~

CHAPTER XV

BENT'S OLD FORT

A Noted Old Outpost of Early Days of the West

~

OF ALL the noted outposts of civilization on the old
frontier of the West, none, perhaps, was of greater
importance, or has a more interesting history, than Bent's
Old Fort, located on the Arkansas River, in 1832, near
the mouth of the Purgatorie Creek, in the present state of
Colorado. It became a noted trading spot, from its erection
to the day it was purposely destroyed by exploding the
powder magazine, by William Bent, in person, in 1852.

The Bent brothers, George, William, Charles and Robert,
began the erection of the fort in 1828. Prior to this date, the
Bents had occupied a stockade above the present site of
Pueblo, Colorado, for a couple of years, later moving down
the Arkansas River and erecting a second stockade, which
they occupied while building their very pretentious adobe
structure, which was destined to become famous all over
the Western frontier as "Bent's Old Fort."

Four years were occupied by the Bents in the erection
of their post. There was some discussion among the brothers
as to the material they should use in its construction. Charles
Bent was greatly in favor of an adobe fort. Logs, he con-
tended, were not fireproof, but adobes were, and the use
of the latter material would render the fort impregnable
against Indian fire-arrows, or any other inflammable mate-

rial. Further, an adobe structure would be cooler in summer and warmer in winter.

The arguments of Charles Bent finally won out, and he thereupon made a trip down into the lower country—probably to Santa Fe or Taos—and engaged a number of expert Mexican adobe-workers to go up to the site of the proposed fort, and there make the adobe bricks and lay the walls.

In the manufacture of these adobes, a considerable quantity of wool was mixed with the clay, which, it was agreed, would greatly lengthen the life of the adobes.

It is related by Kit Carson that at one time more than one hundred and fifty expert Mexican adobe makers were at work on the walls.

In the erection of this noted old outpost, the Bents had the assistance and counsel of Ceran St. Vrain, an Indian trader, whose name will always be indelibly linked with the history of Bent's Old Fort and the Southwest.

During its construction, smallpox broke out among the Mexicans, and it was stated that William Bent, Kit Carson, Ceran St. Vrain and others among the white population became infected, and were badly pock-marked in consequence. During this epidemic, work on the fort ceased, but after the infection had run its course, more Mexicans were engaged and the work resumed. Kit Carson worked for the Bents a couple of years, most of the time as post hunter.

Bent's Fort was five hundred miles from the nearest settlement of any sort—a veritable "jumping-off place." Its dimensions were: one hundred and eighty feet long, one hundred and thirty-five feet wide, the walls fifteen feet high and four feet thick. It was a most impregnable structure when completed.

Bastions, or round towers, occupied the southeast and northwest corners. These towers were about ten feet in diameter inside, and contained loop-holes for cannon and rifle fire. As defense against any possible attack, or attempt to scale the high walls of the fort, the second-story walls were hung with numerous sabers and lances, pistols and muskets.

Two heavy swinging doors, made of thick planks, and covered with sheet-iron, opened from the east wall. A watch-tower was built over the main gate, with windows opening from all sides. Within, at all times, were certain members of the garrison, who constantly maintained a vigilant lookout through a large spyglass or telescope, mounted on a tripod which could be swung in any direction, and sweep the country. This watch-tower was furnished with a bed and other conveniences.

In a little belfry over the watch tower hung the fort bell, which was always sounded for meals.

The west end of the fort contained a second-story room, in which a billiard table and bar were placed—the latter being especially well patronized.

Stores, warehouses and living rooms of the fort were arranged around the walls, and opened into the patio or court. In the center of the court was a brass cannon of six-pounder dimensions, and several light field-pieces, which had been brought out from St. Louis. These were used to intimidate the Indians if they became "contankerous" in their trading operations. The brass cannon eventually burst from a too-heavy powder charge, fired as a salute to General Kearney, when his army passed the fort in 1846. Later, a large iron cannon was purchased in Santa Fe, and placed just outside the large gate of the fort, being often fired when noted Indian chieftains came to trade.

An immense horse corral outside the main walls, and on the west side of the fort, was enclosed by eight-foot walls. The tops of these walls were thickly planted with cactus, which soon grew to such proportions that ample protection was afforded against any possible attempt to scale the walls and stampede the herd within. The walls of this corral were three feet thick at the top.

The Bents, with an eye for "all the comforts of civiliza-tion," built a large icehouse of adobe, not far from the river bank, which, in the winter time, was filled with ice cut from the near-by stream. Thus, during the summer months, the fort occupants were able to serve cooling drinks. The ice house also served as a splendid receptacle for all the fresh meat, in the shape of buffalo-tongues, saddles of venison and other game. The ice house is said to have been a favorite resort on hot summer days for the small children about the post, who would steal inside to cool off.

George and Robert Bent did not spend as much time at the fort as did their two brothers, William and Charles. The two former are said to have not taken to frontier life very energetically, but to have put in much of their time at Santa Fe and Taos, "where there was something doing."

In 1839, a traveler from Peoria, Illinois, named Farnham, visited at Bent's Old Fort. He describes two of the Bent brothers "and one other man" (probably St. Vrain) as being dressed in the costume of the early-day trapper, wearing buckskin hunting shirts and leggings, elaborately fringed and beaded, and decorated with beautiful designs in dyed por-cupine quills, with moccasins similarly adorned.

Farnham "wondered at the novel manners and customs I saw; at the grave bourgeois, the clerks and traders, who, in time of leisure, sat cross-legged under a shady bower, smoking long-stemmed Indian pipes, which they deliberately passed from hand to hand, until smoked out. I marveled at the dried buffalo meat; at the bread made from unbolted wheaten meal, with no sweets or condiments."

Here at Bent's Old Fort were gathered (so it seemed) people from the ends of the earth—old trappers whose faces were seamed and leathery from long exposure to the snows of winter and the burning heat of summer. Farnham wond-ered at the Indians, some of whom were clad like their white companions, but who retained the silence and reserve of the race. There were Mexican servants, hardly more civilized than the Indians. All these latter were seated on the ground, around a huge dish of dried meat, which constituted their only food.

Farnham likewise noted, "The prairie-men who narrated their adventures in the north, west and south, and among the mountains, while others, less given to conversation, nodded or grunted their assent or comment. The talk was about the buffalo, and where they would be; of the dangers from hostile tribes; of past fights, where men had been wounded or killed, and of attacks by Indians on hunters and traders who were passing through the country."

Likewise, Farnham noted, "with interest the opening of the gates of the fort each morning; the cautious sliding in and out of Indians, whose tepees stood in array just outside the fort, till the whole area inside was filled with people, strange people, with long, hanging black locks, and dark, flashing, watchful eyes; the traders and clerks busy at various vocations; the patrols walking the battlements with loaded muskets; the guards in the bastions standing by the carronades with burning matches. Then, when the sun had set, I noted the Indians retiring again to their tepees to talk over the newly-purchased blankets and beads, and to sing and drink and dance; and finally, the night sentinel on the walls, treading his weary watch away."

For the most part, Bent's Old Fort was in charge of William Bent, from the day it was completed, in 1832, until its destruction, twenty years later. He was in full charge of the Indian trading, being more intimately acquainted with the various tribes that visited the post. Moreover, he was recognized by the Indians as fair, honest and just in all his dealings with them, being absolutely fearless in his conduct; and he thus won and held the respect and confidence of the tribes. William Bent is said to have been the very first permanent white settler in what is now Colorado.

Charles Bent seems to have taken a more active part in the Santa Fe and Taos trade, although well liked and respected by both trappers and Indians of the upper Arkansas country; but he preferred to let the Indian trade be in the hands of the other partners. Traders, bull-whackers and the rough teamsters spoke of Charles Bent in the highest terms, and among them he was as well liked as was his brother William among the Indians and trappers.

Charles Bent was very often chosen to act as captain to various caravans enroute to Santa Fe with wagons loaded with rich stores of goods, which he invariably guided safely through the hostile Indian country. Often these caravans sold out their stocks and returned to the States with as much as $100,000 in Mexican silver dollars.

* * * * *

Life at Bent's Old Fort was unquestionably and undeniably pleasant and profitable. Special duties were assigned the various employes. Certain ones, noted for their expert marksmanship, always were on guard duty, maintaining a watchful eye on all who came and went. There were clerks, storekeepers and mechanics who kept the accounts and who worked on the books. Other employes exercised special oversight on the livestock, herded and cared for the horses, mules and oxen, lest they be stampeded and run off by marauding redskins.

None the less important were the employes whose duty it was to load and accompany the wagon-trains which hauled the bales of valuable furs back to the States, and returned with cargoes of new goods for the fort. The long trip of these wagon-trains—between 500 and 600 miles—was wholly devoid of any sign of civilization, there not being a shack or dwelling of any sort between Bent's fort and the frontier of Missouri; but the men who accompanied the trains were inured to all sorts of hardships and discomforts, as well as all lack of outside companionship, and the trail was as easily read by these keen-eyed frontiersmen as is a crowded street to a city dweller.

From ten to fifteen miles a day was the average rate of travel, the wagon-boss so timing his marches that the night camp would, when possible, be made where there was wood, water and good grazing for the stock.

From twenty to thirty wagons constituted a "train" from Bent's fort to the markets of Missouri. Two hunters accompanied the train, their sole duty being to start out in quest of game as soon as camp was broken in the morning. Wild animal life was abundant, and plenty of fresh meat was always in evidence.

Another class of men about the old fort were those who were keen on the trade—expert judges of furs and skins. These would visit the Indian camps at a distance, and dicker for the peltries which the Indians took by trap or weapon.

*   *   *   *   *

Taken altogether, Bent's Fort was a lively place in its palmiest days, the population averaging about one hundred employes. Summertime was the "slack season," the wagon-trains being then enroute to St. Louis or Westport with the valuable peltries. The volume of business conducted at Bent's Old Fort at the height of its popularity as a trading-post was only excelled by the American Fur Company, headed by John Jacob Astor.

In the main, the employes were Americans—such as the traders, clerks, expert mechanics and artisans; but among the hunters and trappers many nationalities were represented. Needless to say, most of the men at the fort, irrespective of race or color, had taken Indian wives, and in consequence the "mixture" among the progeny was very pronounced.

With the wagon-trains started on their long haul, life at Bent's Old Fort during the summer months was quite devoid of excitement, with the exception of an occasional Indian scare. However, the Indians soon recognized that this was

the one spot in all that vast section where they could replenish their supplies of ammunition; consequently, they
were cautious about making raids. White hunters, also, frequently stopped to obtain supplies, as did the overland emigrants. Yet, in spite of the occasional roving war parties
of savages, throughout the warm months, the number of
employes at the post was much less than during the winter
season. Nevertheless, "constant watchfulness" was always
maintained. The fort closed early in the day against all out-
siders, and the vigilance of those on guard never relaxed.

*   *   *   *   *

But when the winter season had advanced, then Bent's
Old Fort was a bee-hive of activity. Traders were constantly
going to the Indian camps and returning with bales of furs;
hunters and trappers from the plains and mountains, with
buxom Indian wives and a full complement of the "small
fry," rode in to outfit for their spring trapping expeditions,
and to exchange greetings with old friends and "compadres."
Everybody was made welcome. Amusements in the shape of
dances and games made the walls of the old fort ring with
good-natured hilarity, participated in by buckskin-clad trappers, swarthy "breeds" and loungers about the post. Teamsters and laborers would engage in various card games in
their quarters by the light of tallow "dips," and candy-pulling
parties were a source of amusement among the younger element.

*   *   *   *   *

Thus the years passed profitably and happily until the
great Pacific Coast "gold rush" began, when the business at
Bent's post began to suffer a decline. The Indian trade was
falling off; the beaver were becoming noticeably scarcer, and
the operation of such an extensive business became too
expensive to profitably continue it.

About this time, the United States Government was beginning to establish military posts along the frontier for the

protection of west-bound "pilgrims"; and with the usual
sharp eye to the reduction of expenses, Uncle Sam began
casting about for the purchase of trading posts already
established, which could be used as military quarters, in
sections of the country convenient for the protection of the
overland people.

The promoters of Bent's Old Fort came to the conclusion
that here was a good chance to "unload" before the bottom
dropped out completely. Negotiations with the Government
for the purchase of the Bent property were opened. There
is no record that William Bent placed any special price on
the value of the property, but evidently his price did not
come within the range of Uncle Sam's pocketbook at the
time, as the Government finally refused to purchase the Bent
property.

That was a black eye for William Bent, who evidently
had power of attorney to dispose of the property. He had,
on many occasions, given special favor to the troops which
the Government sent into the Southwest. He had cared for
their sick and infirm, placing the entire fort at their dis-
posal as a hospital base and supply depot, and he rightly
felt that he was being unjustly treated, and in modern par-
lance, being "played for a sucker."

Therefore, seeing that further dickering with the Government was out of the question, and resolving not to be drawn
into an unfair deal, Bent decided to destroy that old fort,
and move to some other locality.

* * * * *

For exactly twenty years this famous old frontier trading
post had been the most prominent spot in the entire Southwest. It was in the autumn of 1852—over 100 years ago—
when, saddened by the memories of the Past, and the injustice of the Government in refusing him a fair price for
the property—and further disheartened over the loss of two
of his brothers and his wife, Bent loaded all his worldly

possessions upon twenty wagons and conducted them five miles down the river and camped for the night.

That it was a sleepless night for the old trader there can be no doubt. Early the following morning he rode away up the river alone to the old fort, now silent and tenantless. He went to the powder magazine, whose contents he had purposely left intact, opened a sufficient quantity of kegs of powder to guarantee the explosion of the contents of the entire magazine, and then, with his own hands, set the old fort on fire, and, from a safe distance watched the flames consume that historic old land mark.

When the flames reached the powder magazine, there was a most tremendous explosion! Timbers and showers of adobe went skyward, and the flames soon reduced everything to ashes. Those in charge of the wagon-train, five miles down the river, heard the detonation, which echoed for miles up and down the stream!

* * * * *

Such was the untimely end of Bent's Old Fort. William Bent built other trading posts in later years; but none of them ever developed the volume of business which had been transacted at his famous old post on the Arkansas.

CHAPTER XVI

~

JIM BRIDGER, GREATEST OF
PLAINSMEN

Had Many Imitators, but No Peers; Founded Fort Bridger.

~

IN THE years between 1825 and 1870, the West harbored a class of men of a caliber, courage, determination, pluck, fortitude and bravery, whose like has never since been seen. These were the trail-blazers—the men, who, with rifle and pack; wandered far from the confines of civilization into an entirely unknown and uninhabited wilderness. With no knowledge of the country into which they ventured, save what they learned from the Indian tribes infesting the same, they fared forth in their quest for adventure—and fur— and there was plenty of both to be had at that early day.

These men were hardy, bold, fearless and self-reliant— men "with the bark on," if you please. They were familiar with every phase of the rough, out-of-door life they had chosen. No obstacle was too great for them to surmount; no stream too dangerous for them to cross; no mountain too steep for them to scale; no section of country too wild for them to penetrate its depths. In fact, the wilder and more dangerous the country, the more eager they were to venture into it, with the spirit of adventure leading them on.

Among these hardy, self-reliant plainsmen and mountaineers was one who stood unrivaled. And yet, he was the most modest, quietest, most unassuming frontiersman of his time. His name was James Bridger, or, as he was more affectionately and familiarly called, "old Jim Bridger." The name and fame of this greatest of plainsmen will go down in the history of the West, and he will be revered and honored long after the lesser lights of frontier history are forgotten.

Just as there is "only one Niagara," so there was only one Jim Bridger. Born in Richmond, Virginia, March 17, 1804, he soon left that part of the country with his parents, who emigrated to St. Louis when the boy Jim was but eight years of age. There were three children in the family. The mother died in 1816, and the father the following year. Jim Bridger's brother also passed away at an early age, leaving him with the care of a younger sister; and for a boy of thirteen, this was no small task.

Bridger shortly thereafter started in to learn the blacksmith trade, at which he worked until the adventurous spirit locked up in his bosom asserted itself, and in 1822 he joined a band of trappers under command of Gen. William H. Ashley, who were bound for the Rocky Mountains and the fur-bearing sections thereof.

Here Bridger found himself in his element at last, and he took to the rough life of a trapper with a zeal and earnestness which soon attracted the attention of his older and more experienced companions, all of whom predicted that young Jim Bridger would, some day, become renowned as a trapper and rifle-shot.

The Ashley party was under the direct command of Andrew Henry, and on their way into the fur-bearing country they encountered one misfortune after another. One of their boats, loaded with goods intended for barter with the Indians, was upset enroute up the Missouri River, entailing a loss of some $10,000. Their horses were stolen, and the party so badly crippled that they were compelled to halt near the mouth of the Yellowstone and "fort up" for the winter. In this wilderness they hunted and trapped, making extensive explorations into the surrounding country, until the spring of 1823.

During the ensuing seven years, Jim Bridger underwent the usual rigorous life of a frontiersman, developing into a

Jim Bridger, greatest of plainsmen, scouts and guides, between 1825-1868.

keen, shrewd, courageous character, an unerring rifle-shot, and a trapper of wonderful renown. He developed into an Indian fighter whose name quickly spread through the camps of the Blackfeet—then the most war-like of the Rocky Mountain tribes, as a "holy terror." It is to be greatly regretted that there is so little actually known of Bridger's wanderings in this period, as he had but little education, and could neither read nor write in those early days, and therefore kept no account of his meanderings.

It was during this period of his wanderings—probably about 1824 or '25 that Bridger first saw Great Salt Lake, being, so far as is known, the first white man to gaze upon that vast body of water. He thought—noting that the water was salt—that he had discovered an arm of the Pacific Ocean; but upon making a tour of observation, it was discovered that the body of water had no outlet.

In 1830 Bridger had become so proficient in his calling. and was considered so competent by the Rocky Mountain Fur Company, that he was sent with two hundred men on a side scout for fur into the Big Horn Basin country. The party crossed the Yellowstone River and went north to about the present site of Great Falls, Montana. It is claimed that it was on this trip that Bridger first saw the wonders of the present Yellowstone National Park.

Bridger was so impressed by this strange spot that when he began to relate the beauties and almost-supernatural features of it, he was not believed. His stories of boiling hot water spouting hundreds of feet into the air; of boiling pools of water within a few feet of pools of ice-cold water, and all the other wonderful natural features, which are today one of our greatest tourist attractions, were not believed by his companions, and "Jim Bridger's lies," as they were dubbed, were soon the talk in every trappers' camp.

All this so angered Bridger that, in disgust, he began to invent "real whoppers." He declared that one day, while out elk hunting he saw a fine specimen feeding but a couple of hundred yards away. Being out of meat, he drew up his rifle, took careful aim and fired. To his astonishment, the animal did not move nor pay any attention to the discharge of his rifle. Unable to account for such poor shooting, Jim took more careful aim, and fired again. Still the elk remained undisturbed.

Bridger thereupon started on a run toward the animal, when, to his astonishment, he plunged "slap-dab" against a solid mass of clear transparent glass, hundreds of feet in height; and it developed that he had been shooting at the elk on the opposite side of this glass mountain several miles distant, instead of the few hundred feet which he supposed was the actual distance! Today this formation is known as "Obsidian Cliff."

Another of Bridger's wild-eyed yarns was his "sure 'nuff idee" as to why ice-cold water dropped into a pool where it instantly became boiling hot. He declared it was due to the friction produced by the rapid descent of the stream over the rocks!

Bridger tried to have the wonders of the Yellowstone exploited, but could get no Eastern newspaper to take any stock in his "wild-eyed yarns." It is said that the editor of the *Kansas City Journal* stated editorially, in 1879, that Bridger had told him of these wonders fully thirty years before, and that he had really prepared an article for publication, but finally decided against it, fearing the ridicule to which he would be subjected if he printed any of "Jim Bridger's lies."

In spite of the fact that Bridger talked about this wonderful region to everyone whom he met, he was simply laughed at, called "just a little bit off," and unmercifully ridiculed; nor was it until nearly 1870 that any specific exploration was made to determine the accuracy of Bridger's report— all of which was found to be literally true. Bridger had described it as a place "where hell literally bubbled up." And such indeed IS the Yellowstone Park section of today!

Today it is well known that park visitors can catch trout in an ice-cold stream, and, without moving from their tracks, can swing the fish about into a boiling pool. This was one of the stories which Bridger had declared so vehemently as an actual fact. Yet he was mocked and derided, and branded a liar of the first water!

One of the great natural wonders along the Sweetwater

River is the famous "Independence Rock," a vast formation lying in a perfectly open country. Just how this great rock —nearly a mile in circumference and about one hundred feet in height—came to be placed there, is best told by Bridger:

"That'ere rock, when I fust come into this country, was jest a pebble on t'other side of the Sweetwater, which I picked up one day and threw over to this side, and the soil is so derned prolific that it grew into this 'ere rock!"

In one of Bridger's Indian battles in the Blackfoot country, he was wounded in the back with an arrow, the iron point of which remained firmly imbedded in the flesh for nearly three years. It was finally removed by Dr. Marcus Whitman, the noted Oregon missionary, at that time enroute to his station near the present city of Walla Walla, who fell in with Bridger's party at the annual "rendezvous" of the trappers in 1835 at Pierre's Hole. No anesthetic was administered during the operation, and speedy relief was afforded from the extraction of the iron arrow-point, which was nearly three inches in length.

The historic Fort Bridger, located on Black's Fork of the Green River, was erected by Bridger in 1843, and this point became a most noted one during the year of overland travel to the Pacific Coast states. The old Mormon Trail was close by, and the North and South Platte routes met near Fort Bridger, hence the place became well known. Here Bridger's skill as a blacksmith—which had long layed dormant—came into play. He opened a shop, supply store and trading post, and as the overland travel was heavy, he soon had more work on hand than he could possibly attend to. Most of the emigrants were fairly well supplied with money, and of course had to buy provisions and supplies and have their animals re-shod and wagons looked over about the time they reached Bridger's post.

As these transactions were mostly for cash, Bridger soon

acquired considerable money, and he did a lively business, although he doubtless did not spend all his time at the post, as history records that he made various trapping excursions into the mountains from time to time. However, Fort Bridger soon came to be looked upon as a veritable "oasis in the desert," and Bridger certainly exercised good judgment in locating his post at such a favorable spot.

By 1857, however, overland travel had dropped off considerably from what it had been in previous years, and Bridger leased his property to the United States Government for the sum of $600 per year. Uncle Sam never paid him a cent, however, and it was not until thirty years had passed that the Government allowed him $6,000 for the improvements he had made—but not a cent for the land itself!

Passing over many eventful years in the life of Jim Bridger, we find him, in 1866, in the capacity of guide for Col. Henry B. Carrington's expedition, sent into that country— now the present state of Wyoming—for the purpose of building forts and protecting the emigrants, bound for the Montana gold fields and points on the Pacific Coast. Carrington left Fort Kearney, Nebraska, May 19, 1866, under orders to enter the Powder River and Big Horn sections and build three forts. This was invading the very cream of what were then the best hunting grounds of the Sioux tribe— their last and best game section.

The Carrington Expedition was decidedly obnoxious to Chief Red Cloud, the great war chief of the Sioux. He declared, in a conference held at Fort Laramie, in June, 1866, that while he would not object to the government retaining Fort Reno along the Bozeman Trail, under no circumstances whatsoever would he allow the soldiers to penetrate further north into his hunting country, but that he "would kill every soldier or white man who went north of Crazy Woman's Fork."

At this conference Jim Bridger was an attentive spectator

and listener. He sat on a low seat, with his elbows on his knees, chin buried in his hands, listening to every fiery word which dropped from the lips of Red Cloud, who bitterly declared that *"the Great Father had sent soldiers to steal the road, whether the Indian said yes or no."* And when Red Cloud, with head erect and eye flashing fire, stalked haughtily out of the council, refusing to shake hands with any of the assembled government representatives, Bridger shook his head and declared that "Hell'll soon be a-poppin'."

Bridger was right! No sooner had Carrington reached the point north of Fort Reno (where he determined to erect the second fort) than "hell was poppin'" for sure! During the erection of this fort (named Fort Phil Kearny), skirmishes with the Indians were almost a daily occurrence. In fact, during the two short years of its existence, Fort Phil Kearny witnessed *more than FIFTY distinct skirmishes and fights with the Sioux* in the immediate vicinity of the post! The terrible "Fetterman fight" of December 21, 1866, when 81 soldiers, with officers, were drawn into a trap and slaughtered to a man, was only one object lesson drawn by the wily Red Cloud, who was at that time probably the greatest Indian general of any tribe.

During most of these troubles Bridger was acting as post scout for Carrington, who had, meantime, sent a detachment further north, about 100 miles, to erect the third fort, which was to serve as protection along the Bozeman Trail. This post was known as Fort C. F. Smith, and was built on the Big Horn River.

During the time of bitterest trial at Fort Phil Kearny, Jim Bridger was a source of the greatest comfort to the women and children at the post, to all of whom he was a faithful friend and adviser. His devotion and willingness to cheer them was greatly prized, and he was the one man in whom all placed implicit trust. No man was so keenly alive to the dangers all about them; none so well understood Indian wiles and warfare, and none so instinctively seemed to know the invisible as well as the visible operations of the savages.

In August, 1868, the dangers along the Bozeman Trail had become such that the Government determined to evacuate the country! That was exactly what Red Cloud was playing for. In vain had the Government attempted to get him to listen to the appeals that a wagon road be opened into the Montana country. His only ultimatum was that the Government abandon all the forts, and take every soldier out of the country! And Uncle Sam at length was compelled to listen to the great chief. The country was abandoned, the forts evacuated (Fort Phil Kearny was burned to the ground by the Sioux) and that ended the matter for the time being.

Much more could be said of Bridger's great value to the Government. No important military expeditions were planned without employing him as chief guide whenever possible. He was greatly respected and revered by all the old time army officers, who paid the old frontiersman marked deference. Even the Indians regarded him with awe and wonder, and feared the magic power which he seemed to hold over them. And through it all, he remained the same simple-hearted, unpretentious plain prairie-man who hated sham and braggadocio and detested anything which smacked of self-praise.

One of the greatest injustices ever done Jim Bridger, and his fame and notoriety, was that shown some years ago in a moving picture entitled "The Covered Wagon." In this miserable fiasco Bridger was represented as a whisky-soaked, sodden, bleary-eyed old sot, who could not make a move of any consequence, nor remember past events, unless filled to the brim with liquor. While Bridger doubtless liked his "toddy" in common with most of the mountain-men of his day, it is an undeniable fact that he was anything but a confirmed drunkard. It stands to reason that had he been such, the United States Government never would have valued his services as a guide in their most noted expeditions, nor would

Bridger have been respected and revered by all classes of men on the frontier—as he most certainly was.

That "Covered Wagon" picture was libel of the most underhanded sort, and placed that grand old pioneer in a position which called forth the most indignant protests from those, at least, who are familiar with Bridger's history, his past life and his valuable services to the United States Government.

Some twenty-five years ago, Dr. Gilbert E. Bailey of Los Angeles, head of the Chair of Geology of the University of Southern California, knew Bridger intimately, having passed a winter with him in the latter 1860 period, while a member of the surveying party who were putting the Union Pacific Railroad through. The writer of this article was intimately acquainted with Dr. Bailey at the time he was connected with the University, and had many talks with him about Jim Bridger. He distinctly recalls the noted frontiersman, who was acting as guide for the party, and whose quiet deportment and simple manners made a lasting impression on young Bailey.

Still another friend of the writer, Major A. B. Ostrander (now deceased) met and became acquainted with Bridger at old Fort Phil Kearny in 1866. At that time Ostrander was a youth of 19, who had left the headquarters of Gen. Philip St. George Cooke in Omaha, (where he had been acting as confidential clerk to Gen. Cooke), to join his regiment, the 18th U. S. Infantry at Fort Phil Kearny. He describes Bridger as a man who would command a second glance from anyone; admired and respected by all his superiors, and of the strictest honesty and integrity, and far from being the drunken sot which "The Covered Wagon" film foisted on the American public.

There were other old-timers who knew Bridger well enough to recall that he was not a drunken bum, but a gentleman, even though a "diamond in the rough," but who could fully and intelligently describe any section of the West which he had once seen, and could make a map showing the streams, mountains and other features absolutely correct, so there would be no trouble following it and understanding it.

Bridger never made claims of knowledge of any section of country over which he had not traveled. Gen. Grenville Dodge, builder of the Union Pacific Railroad, who employed Bridger as guide, said of him:

"Bridger was a good judge of human nature. His comments upon people whom he had met and been with, were always intelligent and seldom critical. He always spoke of their good parts, and was universally respected by the mountain-men, and looked upon as a leader also by all the Indians. He was careful to never give his word without fulfilling it. He understood thoroughly the Indian character, their peculiarities and superstitions. He felt keenly any loss of confidence in his judgment, especially when acting as guide. If Bridger struck a section of country, while acting as guide, over which he had never traveled, and was not familiar with, he would frankly say so; but would often say he could take our party up to the point he wanted to reach. As a guide, *I do not think he had his equal on the Plains.* So remarkable a man should not be lost to history, and to his country, nor his work allowed to be forgotten."

Bridger married into two different Indian tribes. His first wife was a Ute, by whom he had two children, both of whom were educated in St. Louis. His second wife was also a Ute, by whom he had a daughter, who was likewise sent to school in St. Louis. His third wife was from the Snake tribe. Bridger did NOT have but one wife at a time, in spite of the false scenes depicted in "The Covered Wagon" that he had several wives at the same time.

Bridger died in 1881, at the age of 77. He was buried on the Stubbin Watts farm not far south of Westport, Mo.

In 1902 his friend, Gen. Grenville Dodge, learned for the first time where the body of the grand old plainsman lay, and that his grave was neglected and forgotten. Gen. Dodge felt keenly that this celebrated old pioneer should be more prominently remembered, and with other admirers, he interested the Mt. Washington Cemetery Association of Kansas City in his plans, and they donated a prominent and beautiful burial site, where the remains of the noted old pioneer were removed, and on December 11, 1904, a most imposing monument, in the shape of a huge boulder, beautifully carved, was unveiled, bearing the following inscription:

1804—JAMES BRIDGER—1881

CELEBRATED AS A HUNTER, TRAPPER, FUR TRADER AND GUIDE. DISCOVERED GREAT SALT LAKE, 1824; THE SOUTH PASS, 1827; VISITED YELLOWSTONE LAKE AND GEYSERS, 1830; FOUNDED FORT BRIDGER, 1843; OPENED OVERLAND ROUTE BY BRIDGER'S PASS TO GREAT SALT LAKE. WAS GUIDE FOR EXPLORING EXPEDITIONS, ALBERT SIDNEY JOHNSON'S ARMY IN 1857, AND G. M. DODGE IN U. P. SURVEYS AND INDIAN CAMPAIGNS, 1865-66. THIS MONUMENT ERECTED AS A TRIBUTE TO HIS PIONEER WORK, BY MAJOR-GENERAL G. M. DODGE."

General Dodge further speaks of Bridger as follows:

"In person he was over six feet tall, spare, straight as an arrow, agile, rawboned and of powerful frame; eyes gray; hair brown and abundant, even in old age; expression mild and manners agreeable. He was hospitable and generous, and was always trusted and respected. He possessed in a high degree the confidence of the Indians. He was one of the most noted hunters and trappers on the Plains. Naturally shrewd and observing, he carefully studied the habits of all wild animals, especially the beaver, and he became one of the most expert of trappers. As a guide, he was without an equal, and that is the testimony of every one who employed him. He was a born topographer; the whole West was mapped out in his mind, and such was his instinctive sense of locality and direction, that it used to be said of him that he could 'SMELL' his way where he could not see it.'

JAMES BRIDGER
1804   1881
CELEBRATED AS A HUNTER, TRAPPER,
FUR TRADER AND GUIDE. DISCOVERED
GREAT SALT LAKE 1824, THE SOUTH
PASS 1827. VISITED YELLOWSTONE LAKE
AND GEYSERS 1830. FOUNDED FT. BRIDGER
1843. OPENED OVERLAND ROUTE BY
BRIDGER'S PASS TO GREAT SALT LAKE.
WAS GUIDE FOR U.S. EXPLORING
EXPEDITIONS, ALBERT SIDNEY JOHNSTON'S
ARMY IN 1857, AND G.M. DODGE IN U.P.
SURVEYS AND INDIAN CAMPAIGNS 1865-66.
THIS MONUMENT IS ERECTED AS A
TRIBUTE TO HIS PIONEER WORK BY
MAJ. GEN. G.M. DODGE.

Monument erected to the noted plainsman James
Bridger, in Mount Washington Cemetery, Kansas City,
by Gen. Dodge, builder of the Union Pacific Ry.

"He was a complete master of woodcraft and the Plains,
equal to any emergency, full of resources to overcome any
obstacle, and I came to learn how it was that for months such
men could live without food except what the country afforded.
Nothing escaped the vision of these men—the popping of a
stick, the breaking of a twig, the turning of the growing grass
—all brought knowledge to them, and they could instantly
tell who or what had done it. A single horse or Indian could
not cross the trail but that they discovered it, and could tell
how long since they had passed. Their methods of hunting

game were perfect, and we were never out of meat. Herbs, roots, berries, barks of trees, any and everything that was edible, they knew. They could minister to the sick, dress wounds—in fact, in all my experience I never saw Bridger, nor any of the other voyagers of the Plains and mountains, meet any obstacle which they could not overcome."

Such unstinted words of praise from a man who knew Jim Bridger so intimately should be sufficient to prove that this great man—this AMERICAN—should be placed in the proper niche where he belongs, along with such men as Daniel Boone, Simon Kenton, Davy Crockett, Kit Carson, "Uncle Dick" Wooten, Lucien Maxwell, and other renowned frontier characters.

No better "send-off" can the writer give James Bridger than that he was a true type of the man necessary as a trail-blazer to the then unexplored regions of the mighty West. He had many imitators, but no peers. He was the uncrowned king of all the Rocky Mountain scouts, guides, trappers, trailers, mountain-men and plainsmen, between 1830 and 1870.

"YES, I KNEW JIM BRIDGER,"

Private A. B. Ostrander's Recollections of the Famous old Scout

When I was relieved from duty as Clerk at Headquarters Department of the Platte, at Omaha, Nebraska, on October 1, 1866, I was handed an order which read as follows:

"Headquarters Dept., of the Platte
Omaha, Nebr., Oct. 1, 1866.
Special Order No. 63)
Private A. B. Ostrander is hereby relieved from duty as Clerk at these headquarters, at his own request. He will report in person to his Company Commander, Co. B, 2d Battalion, 18th U. S. Infantry, at Fort Reno, D.T.

The Quartermaster's Department will furnish the necessary transportation.

By command of Brigadier-General P. St. George Cooke,

Dept. Commander.

At the same time I was handed a furlough for 30 days, which would about cover the length of time for my trip.

From the wording of this order, augmented by the furlough, it shows that I was not liable to be assigned to any military duty or assignments enroute, consequently the whole trip was in the nature of a sight-seeing tour.

Upon arrival at each government post on the way, I was sure to first visit Post Headquarters, and exhibit my special order. I would get an order from the Adjutant directing the Post Commissary to issue me rations, and then put in all my time looking around the post, always making my stopping-place the post sutler's store.

Upon arrival at Fort Laramie, we were informed that we would have to remain for probably two or three weeks, until an outfit could be organized sufficient to warrant a safe trip over the Bozeman trail. As soon as I was informed of this, after having secured quarters for myself, I immediately proceeded to the post sutler's store, then being run by Colonel Bullock, and made that my headquarters during the three weeks we remained there.

It was also headquarters and rendezvous for the old-time guides, scouts, trappers and mountain men in that vicinity, and old Nick Janis was a sort of leader among them. I managed to get quite intimate and friendly with him before I left there, and he gave me a beautiful pair of gloves, saying, "When you get up to Fort Phil Kearny show 'em to Jim Bridger, and tell him I gave 'em to you."

I was discharged from the army at Fort Reno on the 20th of February, 1867, and left there the next day for Fort Phil Kearny, where I arrived two days later. We got in about 2 o'clock in the afternoon, and after getting permission to occupy a bunk in the wagon-master's quarters, I immediately made a bee-line for the sutler's store, as usual.

But little was going on at that hour. Over in one corner, where the counter joined up against the wall, with his chair tilted back against the wall and his left arm resting on the counter, sat a man. His hat was pulled down before his face, and I could not see his features; but as men dropped in, I noticed that every one of them would glance over at the figure, and if his hat happened to move up so they could see his eyes, each one would address him with a "How" or "Howdy." He would answer by a grunt, or bow his head in acknowledgment.

Finally one man remarked to him, "Hello, Jim, how's the roomatix?" From this I judged that the man was old Jim Bridger. Finally he got up to stretch himself a little and I got a better view of him. His old battered hat had originally been of some light color, but now looked like smoke. His sack coat was of a dark gray material, and his brown corduroy breeches were reinforced on the seat and inside the thighs with buckskin, evidently to protect those parts while on horseback. Finally he sat down again and pulled his hat down so that it covered his eyes, and apparently went into a snooze.

Shortly a man came in whom I recognized. It was Jack (I found out afterwards his full name was Jack Stead), who had been one of the scouts for our outfit on the way up from Laramie, the previous fall. He went over and saluted the old man, and then walked over to the counter.

I went over and touched him on the shoulder, saying, "Hello, Jack." He was surprised to see me, and asked a few questions, which I answered. Finally I asked, "Isn't that old Jim Bridger over there," pointing toward the old man.

"Of course it is," he replied, "everybody knows Jim."

"Well," I said, "won't you tell him I've got something that Nick Janis told me to show him."

"Why don't you tell him yourself?" he queried.

"I don't know him, and I don't want to seem impertinent," I replied.

"Oh, well, come on over," he said, and I went with him. His introduction was rather a cold-water douche to me. He said, "Say, Jim, here's the kid that killed the big elk coming up with us last fall."

Bridger merely answered, "Howdy." Then I remarked, "Nick Janis told me to see you if I got up here."

"You know Nick?" he queried.

"Yes," I replied, "and he gave me something, and told me to show it to you if I got up here."

He reached out his hand as if to receive it, but I hastily replied, "It's in my valise, down in the bunk-room; I'll bring it around in the morning."

"All right," Bridger remarked, "Nick Janis is a mighty good man—one of the whitest men on the Plains."

After a few more remarks I left old Jim; but next morning I met him in the store, and handed him the gloves, saying "Nick gave them to me."

Bridger took them, turned them over and commenced picking at the bead-work on them. Finally he located a sliver of sinew thread which held the beads, and then, nodding his head said, "Yes, they're all right; made of good stuff. How much did you pay Nick for 'em?"

"I didn't pay him anything; he gave 'em to me," I replied.

Bridger handed the gloves back, shaking his head, and said, "Old Nick ain't givin' such stuff away for nothin'. You must have tickled him somehow."

"Oh," I remarked, "I did give him a little pistol once."

"That so? What kind?"

Then I described it fully. Bridger smiled and said, "Yep, I've seen that kind, but never handled one—was afraid I'd break it. What did Nick do with it?"

"Oh, he broke the gun and peeked through the barrel, pulled out the cylinder and counted the holes; peeked through 'em, and then rolled it across the floor."

Then Bridger threw back his head and roared, "Ho-ho-ho! Nick Janis is a dam' big baby. If somebuddy'd give him a rag baby he'd play with it." Then soberly he added: "but Nick's a square man—none better; only when he gits to yarnin'; then he can tell a bigger lie'n any man this side the Missouri River."

Then he continued, "Well, if you're a friend of Nick's, I guess you're all right."

That afternoon I was offered a job as clerk in Gen. G. B. Dandy's office; he was the District Quartermaster-General.

The office closed every afternoon at 3 o'clock, and from that day till the day I left the fort, the minute the office closed I made a bee-line for the sutler's store, where I met Jim Bridger every day. He was suffering greatly from rheumatism, and couldn't ride, and was often morose and cranky. At such times I kept my mouth shut, but would sit around and look at the different people who came in to trade.

One day I happened to mention Fremont, and said that he had made a lot of wonderful discoveries.

Then old Jim DID blow up!

"Fremont!" he snorted, "Why, he never discovered one dum thing. He never saw a thing out here 'cept what Kit Carson and I showed him, and when I told him 'bout things I'd seen down in the big park, he said I was a liar! After that, I wouldn't tell him any more, and only took him to places where he wanted to go. Then he goes back, and writes a big book tellin' 'bout things HE had discovered—when Kit Carson and myself, and a lot of others, had all been to most every one of them places, long afore he ever saw this country. Fremont was a bigger liar than they say I am."

Bridger sure did hate and belittle Fremont!

I got quite chummy with a boy about my own age, who had come to the fort the August before. He was a great admirer of old Jim, and one day he told me the following story.

"One day I was in the store, and Jim was sitting in his usual place, when three ladies came in. They were Mrs. Carrington, Mrs. Grummond and Mrs. Wands, wives of officers at the Fort Phil Kearny post. Instead of going direct to the counter, they all started over toward Jim. He saw them coming, and with the help of his left arm on the counter, managed to get to his feet. Mrs. Carrington said, 'Oh, Mr. Bridger, please keep your seat; don't try to stand up.' Jim replied, 'Must stand to 'tenshun before the commanding officer!' The ladies laughed, and expressed sympathy for him, and then proceeded to the counter to make their purchases. Jim sat down and mumbled to himself, 'Seems good to meet WHITE LADIES,' showing that he appreciated the call."

One day when Jim was not feeling in very good spirits, and I happened to ask him a question about something I understood he knew all about, he grunted, and said, "Nope, I won't tell you anything 'bout that, for you wouldn't believe me if I did."

I was surprised, and answered, "Why, Mr. Bridger, I believe everything you tell me."

"Nope," he retorted, "Everybody says that old Jim's yarns are all dam' lies. If I heered the bugle sound dinner-call, and should step to the door and holler 'Grub's ready!' there'd be half a dozen fellers sayin' 'Nother one of old Jim's lies'."

I couldn't get another thing out of him for the rest of the day!

Another time several Crow Indians came into the fort with a lot of buffalo robes and other peltries. They had sent word that they wanted to come in and 'make swap.' Permission was given them, and I watched the procession from the time they crossed Lodge Trail Ridge and passed my window, until they went into the corral below. As soon as the offices closed, I hustled over to the sutler's store, and was told that Bridger had gone down to the Indian camp, so I sauntered over there.

I discovered that the Crows had set up a little village of half a dozen tepees, and had buffalo robes and other pelts piled up all around.

Quite a number of men were lounging about, and I noticed Bridger among the buffalo robes, testing their value. I watched him a few minutes, then went over and said:

"Mr. Bridger, I wish I could get one or two of those buffalo robes. Won't you help me buy 'em? I don't know how to 'make swap' with these Indians."

"Sure!" he quickly replied. "You run up to the sutler's and get half a dozen plugs of tobacco; but don't you let any of these bucks see you put them in my pocket."

I hurried over, got the plugs, and when I got back I found Bridger holding up a fine big robe. Under its cover I managed to slip three plugs of tobacco in each of his side pockets. Then I turned to look at the other robes, and saw a very small one, evidently a calf skin, with very long and silky hair. I saw Bridger palaver with a big buck, and then toss the robe to one side. Then I motioned, and Bridger threw that one on top of a larger one, and beckoned to me. "Hold out your arms and hide em away—quick!"

In a few minutes I returned, and found Bridger yet standing around. "Can you get me a couple of those beaver skins?" I asked, pointing to a pile of them against the stockade.

"Run and git a couple more plugs of tobacco," he whispered; then he added, "That's all I'm a-goin to git fer you; other folks'll be wantin' some.' I followed directions and soon saw him throw out two beaver skins. "Take 'em away," he added, and that closed his 'swap' for me.

*　*　*　*　*

I had become acquainted with a French-Canadian, who told me he had trapped for the Hudson's Bay Company for twenty years, and had been down across the line for the past ten years. He had come into the Big Horn country intending to trap, but found it impossible because of Indian troubles. He was getting up a party to go up around Walla Walla in the spring, and suggested that I join it. He said I'd need a good horse, too.

I had often observed a small sorrel horse standing in front of the sutler's store, and learned that it belonged to Lieut. Harrington of the 2d Cavalry. He had gone down to Fort

Laramie some months before, and left the horse with the sutler to be sold. The price was $200—not a cent less.

One day I put the question to Jim Bridger: "What is that horse Billy really worth?"

He seemed surprised, and asked, "Why?" Then I told him. He shook his head and said, "You don't want no hoss here; no place you can get to ride him; 'tain't safe. You got a good job—gettin' good pay. Better stick to it and let hosses alone."

However, I persisted, and he said, "Now I ain't advisin' you to buy no hoss; but that hoss Billy is a good one; sound in wind and limb; not a spot or blemish on him, and he is wuth $200. That's all I'm a-goin' to say!"

* * * * *

Up and until the day I left Fort Phil Kearny, in April, 1867, I spent an hour or so with old Jim Bridger. He appeared to take a liking to me, and talked more freely to me than he did to others. While he was cranky and cross when bothered with rheumatism, he never seemed to object to my presence or inquiries, save that at times, he would shake his head and not answer me. I had sense enough to know that I must be getting tiresome to him, and so I curtailed my questions until such time as he was in better spirits.

* * * * *

On the day I left Fort Phil Kearny, at the last minute, I rode up to the sutler's store where old Jim was standing in the doorway. Taking from his pocket a beaded buckskin pouch, filled with tobacco, he handed it to me saying, "Here, boy, is some tobaccer for you to smoke on the way down."

I could not find words to properly express my thanks to the old scout, but I think he must have felt my appreciation, as I gripped his hand and left him with other friends at Fort Phil Kearny.

That little tobacco pouch he gave me is still one of my most treasured possessions!

(Signed)   A. B. OSTRANDER

(Written and autographed for my old friend, E. A. Brininstool on my 86th birthday Feb. 2, 1931.)

CHAPTER XVII

CALAMITY JANE

The Most Unique, Picturesque and Romantic Figure in Black Hills History

"She was seen in every town, camp and fort in the West, and had wandered over all the trails. So variant were her moods, so many the different incidents of her life, that accordingly there were numerous impressions and ideas of her character. She was a strange mixture of the wild, untamed individual of the plains and the mountain trails, and that of generous, kindly-hearted womanhood. Under her rough exterior there beat a heart so big and friendly as to be without measure. Brave, energetic, unfettered, kind, always on the line of action, with a helping hand ever stretched to aid the poor and unfortunate, the personality of Calamity Jane became indelibly stamped upon the minds of the pioneers."

"WHO WAS 'Calamity Jane'?" This question has been asked me so many times by the younger generation—most of whom seem to have little or no real knowledge of the history of the West—that I am constrained to give some facts about the most-talked-of frontier woman whose name has been linked with border history—and especially the history of Deadwood, South Dakota, and the Black Hills section in general.

"A compound mixture of good and bad," is the way she has been described to me by old frontier friends of mine who knew Calamity Jane in the Black Hills, from her initial appearance there in 1875 to the day of her death in 1903.

"She could swear harder, drink more whiskey and raise hell generally more than any individual I ever met in all my days on the frontier," says another old-timer, "and yet the woman had a kind heart, would give her last dollar to anyone in distress, and was known far and wide for her generous, unselfish and chivalrous nature."

There appears to be very little in print that is really authentic regarding this picturesque and romantic female character of Western history. Her real name was Mary (or Martha) Canary prior to her first marriage. In a statement made public some years ago, the woman gave some facts regarding her life which may, or may not, be true, but which are substantially as follows:

"My maiden name was Martha Cannary. (Note difference in spelling from the generally-accepted version, which is 'Canary.') I was born in Princeton, Mo., May 1, 1852. My father and mother were natives of Ohio. There were two brothers and three sisters, I being the eldest of these children.

"As a child I was always fond of adventure and out-of-door exercise, having an especial fondness for horses, which I began to ride at an early age, and continued to do so until I became an expert horsewoman, being able to handle the most vicious and stubborn animals. In fact, the greater portion of my life, in early times, was spent in this manner.

"In 1865 we emigrated from our home in Missouri by the Overland route, to Virginia City, Montana. We were five months in making this trip. While on the way, the greater portion of my time was spent in hunting, along with the men and hunters in the party—in fact, I was at all times with men when there was excitement and adventure to be had.

"By the time we reached Virginia City, I was considered a remarkable shot and fearless rider for a girl of my age. I remember many occurrences on the journey from Missouri to Montana. Many times, in crossing the mountains, the condition of the trails was so bad that frequently it was necessary to lower the wagons over ledges by hand, with ropes, for the travel was so rough that horses were of no use in getting across the roughest places.

"We also had many exciting times fording the streams, many of which were notorious for quicksands and boggy places, where, unless we were very careful, we would have lost horses and all. Then, we had many difficulties to encounter in the way of streams swelling because of heavy rains. Very often, on such occasions, have I mounted my pony and swam the animal across the stream several times, merely to amuse myself. I have had many narrow escapes from being washed away to certain death on such occasions; but as the pioneers of those days had plenty of courage, we overcame all obstacles, and finally reached Virginia City in safety.

"My mother died at Blackfoot, Montana, in 1866, where we buried her. I left Montana in the spring of 1866 for Utah, arriving in Salt Lake City during the summer. I remained in Utah until 1867, where my father died. I then went to Fort Bridger, Wyoming Territory, where I arrived May 1, 1868. I remained around Fort Bridger during 1868, then went to Piedmont, Wyoming, following up the building of the Union Pacific railroad.

"I joined General Custer as a scout at Fort Russell, Wyoming, in 1870, and started for Arizona for the Indian Campaign.[1] Up to this time I had always worn the costume

---

[1] It is very doubtful indeed if Calamity Jane was ever connected with the Seventh Cavalry as a "scout" or in any other capacity, although it is variously stated that she did succeed in getting in with General Crook's columns as a mule-whacker or teamster until her sex was discovered, when she was invariably ordered to "vamoose." She invariably wore men's clothing. General Custer took no part in any campaigns against Indians in Arizona.

"Calamity Jane," noted Black Hills pioneer character of the early days.
Photo courtesy of H. R. Locke, Deadwood, S. D.

of my sex. When I joined Custer I donned the uniform of the soldier. It was a bit awkward at first, but I soon got to be perfectly at home in men's clothing.

"I was in Arizona up to the winter of 1871, and during that time I had a great many adventures with Indians, for as a scout I had a great many dangerous missions to perform; but while I was in many close places, I always succeeded in getting away safely, for at this time I was considered the most reckless and daring rider, and one of the best shots in the Western country.

"After that campaign I returned to Fort Saunders, Wyoming, remaining there until the spring of 1872, when we were ordered out on the Muscleshell outbreak. In that war Generals Custer, Miles, Terry and Crook were all engaged. This campaign lasted until the fall of 1873. It was during this campaign that I was christened 'Calamity Jane,' the facts being substantially as follows:

"It was on Goose Creek, Wyoming, where the town of Sheridan is now located, where this incident occurred. Captain Egan was in command of the post. We were ordered out to quell an uprising of the Indians, and were out several days. We had numerous skirmishes, in which six soldiers were killed and several severely wounded.

"On returning to the post, we were ambushed about a mile and a half from our destination. When fired upon, Captain Egan was shot. I was riding in advance. Upon hearing the firing, I turned in my saddle and noticed that the captain was reeling as though about to fall from his horse. I wheeled my horse and galloped back in all haste to his side, getting there in time to catch him as he was falling. I lifted him on my horse in front of me, and succeeded in getting him safely back to the fort. When Captain Egan recovered, he laughingly remarked, 'I name you Calamity Jane, the heroine of the Plains.' I have borne the name of Calamity Jane up to the present time. (1895).

"We were afterward ordered to Fort Custer, where we arrived in the spring of 1874.[2] Remained around Fort Custer all summer, and were ordered to Fort Russell that fall. Remained there until the spring of 1875. Were then ordered to the Black Hills to protect miners, as that country was controlled by the Sioux Indians, and the Government had to send soldiers to protect the lives of the miners and settlers in that section. We remained there until the fall of 1875, and wintered at Fort Laramie.

In the spring of 1876 we were ordered north with General Crook to join General Miles, Terry and Custer at Big Horn River. During this march I swam the Platte River at Fort Fetterman, as I was bearing an important dispatch. I had a 90-mile ride to make, and being wet and cold, I contracted a severe illness, and was sent back to Fort Fetterman in an ambulance by General Crook, where I laid in the hospital fourteen days. When able to ride, I started to Fort Laramie, where I met William Hickok, better known as Wild Bill. He and I started for Deadwood, where we arrived about June.

"During the month of June I acted as pony express rider, carrying the United States mail between Deadwood and Custer, a distance of over 50 miles, over one of the roughest trails in the Black Hills country. Many of the riders before me had been held up and robbed of their packages, mail and money.

"It was considered the most dangerous ride in the Hills, but as my reputation as a rider and quick shot was known, I was molested very little, for the Toll Gatherers looked upon me as a good fellow, and they knew I never missed my mark. I made the round trip every two days, which was considered pretty good time in that country. I remained about Deadwood all that summer, visiting all the camps within an area of a hundred miles.

---

[2] Calamity Jane is mistaken regarding Fort Custer. This post was not built until 1877 the year following the battle of the Little Big Horn, in which Custer was killed. There was no Fort Custer in 1874.

"My friend, Wild Bill, remained in Deadwood during the summer, with the exception of occasional visits to the camps. On the second of August, 1876, while sitting at a gambling table in the Bella Union saloon, in Deadwood, he was shot in the back of the head by the notorious Jack McCall, a desperado. I was in Deadwood at the time, and upon hearing of the killing, made my way at once to the scene of the shooting, and found that my friend had been killed by McCall. I at once started to look for the assassin, and found him at Surdy's butcher shop. I grabbed a meat cleaver and made him throw up his hands. Through the excitement of hearing of Bill's death, I had left my weapons on the post of my bed. McCall was taken to a log cabin and locked up, well secured, as everyone thought; but he got away and was afterward caught at Fagan's ranch on Horse Creek, on the old Cheyenne road, and was then taken to Yankton, Dakota, where he was tried, sentenced and hung.[3]

"I remained around Deadwood, locating claims, going from camp to camp, until the spring of 1877. One morning I saddled my horse and rode toward Crook City. I had gone about twelve miles from Deadwood, when at the mouth of Whitewood Creek I met the Overland mail, operating between Deadwood and Cheyenne. The horses were on the dead run, and about two hundred yards from the station. Upon looking closely, I saw that they were pursued by Indians. The horses ran to the barn. As they stopped, I rode up alongside the coach and found the driver, John Slaughter, lying face downward in the boot of the stage. He had been shot by the Indians. When the stage reached the station, the Indians hid in the bushes. I removed all the baggage from the stage, except the

[3] Calamity Jane is sadly mixed in her facts in the foregoing paragraph. McCall was arrested, tried and acquitted the first time. He then went to Laramie City, where he openly boasted of having killed Wild Bill. He was again arrested, tried and sentenced to hang, which sentence was carried out at Yankton, Dak. The statement that Calamity Jane went after McCall with a meat cleaver, is only one other example of the "long bow" she was wont to draw when boasting of her deeds.

mail. I then took the driver's seat, and in all haste drove to Deadwood, carrying the six passengers and the dead driver.[4]

"I left Deadwood in the fall of 1877, and went to Bear Butte Creek with the Seventh Cavalry, and during that fall and winter we built Fort Meade and the town of Sturgis.

"In 1878 I left the command and went to Rapid City, putting in the year prospecting. In 1879 I went to Fort Pierre, and drove trains from Rapid City to Fort Pierre for Frank W. Whittle. I later drove teams from Fort Pierre to Sturgis for Fred Evans. This teaming was done with oxen, as they were better fitted than horses owing to the rough nature of the country.

"In 1881 I went to Wyoming, returning in 1882 to Miles City, Montana, where I took up a ranch on the Yellowstone, raising stock and cattle. I also kept a wayside inn, where the weary traveler could be accommodated with food, drink or trouble, if he looked for it. I left the ranch in 1883, and went to California, going through the state and territories. I reached Ogden the latter part of 1883. I was in San Francisco in 1884. I left San Francisco that summer for Texas, stopping at Fort Yuma, Arizona, the hottest spot in the United States. I stopped at all points of interest until I reached El Paso in the fall.

"While in El Paso I met Mr. Clinton Burke, a native of Texas, whom I married in August, 1885, as I thought I had traveled through life long enough alone, and concluded it was about time to take a partner for the rest of my days. We remained in Texas, leading a quiet home life, until 1889. On October 28, 1887, I became the mother of a girl baby, the very image of its father—that is what he said—but which had the temper of its mother.

"When we left Texas we went to Boulder, Colorado, where we kept a hotel until 1893, after which we traveled through Wyoming, Montana, Idaho, Washington and Oregon, then

---

[4] This story never has been authenticated that I am aware of, and doubtless Calamity is again drawing the "long bow."

back to Montana; then to Deadwood, arriving there October 8, 1895, after an absence of seventeen years. My arrival in Deadwood, after an absence of so many years, created quite an excitement among my many friends of the past, to such an extent that a vast number of citizens who had come to Deadwood during my absence, and who had heard so much of Calamity Jane and her adventures of former years, were anxious to see me.

"Among the many whom I met were several gentlemen from Eastern cities, who advised me to allow myself to be placed before the public in such a manner as to give the people of the Eastern cities an opportunity of seeing the woman scout who was made famous by her daring career in the West and the Black Hills.

"An agent of Kohl & Middleton, the celebrated dime museum men, came to Deadwood, through the solicitations of the gentleman whom I met there, and arrangements were made to place me before the public in this manner.

"My first engagement began in the Palace Museum, Minneapolis, January 10, 1896, under the management of Kohl & Middleton.

"Hoping this little history of my life may interest all readers, I remain, as in the old days,

"Yours,

"MRS. M. BURKE."

(Better known as Calamity Jane)

Thus Calamity Jane gives a haphazard and somewhat rambling account of her meanderings about the United States during the various years, but having little to say as to her ways and means of support.

In none of the books of Western history, written by men of authority, do I find any account of Calamity Jane being employed in the regular army as a scout, and it is doubtful, indeed, if she ever did serve in any such capacity, however "mannish" she may have appeared or acted.

Several writers tell of her associating with troops in various campaigns as a muleskinner or teamster, until her sex was discovered, when she was summarily ordered out of camp. All these reports seem to agree on Jane's ability to drink as much whiskey, chew as rank plug tobacco and swear as blue a streak as any of the rough-and-tough teamsters and mule-whackers with whom she associated.

But there appears to have been another—and better side to the nature of this strange frontier woman. She was known throughout Deadwood and the surrounding gold camps for her unselfishness, kindness of heart and sympathy in respond-ing to the relief of any sick person—man, woman or child. It is stated by many old-timers of Deadwood that they have known of many instances in which Calamity Jane gave her last dollar to relieve the sufferings of unfortunates who were "down and out."

A story is told that the day "Preacher Smith" arrived in Deadwood, he stood on an empty box in front of Jim Purcell's saloon and began a Biblical discourse to the motley crowd which quickly surrounded him. He had been addressing his hearers but a brief time before Calamity Jane happened along. Jane was considerably under "the inflooence," and snatching the preacher's old battered hat from his hand, she turned to the crowd and shouted:

"You sinners dig down into your pokes now! This old fel-low looks as though he were broke, and I want to collect $200 for him—so limber up, you boys!"

She then started through the crowd, and when she returned to the preacher's "pulpit," she was $235 richer. Emptying it all at the feet of the astonished old skypilot, Calamity swag-gered off down the street, looking for some new form of ex-citement.

A friend of the writer, George E. Bartlett, who lived in the Black Hills country in its early days, once related that Calamity Jane nursed him through a most serious illness, and that he undoubtedly would have "cashed in" but for her sympathetic ministrations, for which she would accept no remuneration of any sort.

Another old-timer who knew Calamity Jane, and has written some interesting history about her, is Jesse Brown, a pioneer resident of the Black Hills, and one of its best-known and most respected citizens. There seems to be some difference of opinion between Mr. Brown's account of the birthplace of Calamity Jane and that given in her own biography. Mr. Brown states that she was born near Burlington, Iowa, in 1851, while Calamity asserts she first saw the light of day at Princeton, Mo., May 1, 1852. Mr. Brown's account further says that her father was a Baptist minister. Continuing his reminiscences of Calamity, Mr. Brown says:

"It is stated that Jane, in her younger days, was well cared for and trained, but that she was self-willed and full of the joy of life. We first find her running away from home as the mistress of an army lieutenant on one of the expeditions to Wyoming. She later gave birth to a son at Sidney, Nebraska, whom the officer took and sent back east to his parents to raise as a foundling orphan from the Plains. The boy was given a good education, and no doubt never knew the truth as to his parentage.

"We again find her in the company of her mother and stepfather, named Hart, a retired regular army officer, crossing the Plains to Salt Lake City, Utah, where they lived for a time. From Salt Lake, Jane ran away to Rawlins, Wyoming. Her stepfather followed her to this place and found that she was at a hotel there, but was informed that she was attending school regularly. This appeared strange to him, as he had been unable to get her to attend school in Utah. However, being assured that the girl was 'going straight,' he returned to his home.

"Soon after this, Jane skipped out to Fort Steele, becoming an inmate of a bawdy house, and quite a pal with teamsters

Main Street in Deadwood, 1876. In 1879 a fire wiped out all these buildings. Photo courtesy of H. R. Locke, Deadwood, S. D.

and soldiers. She became expert in tying the diamond hitch and in handling teams, and when an expedition was fitted out to the north, she donned men's attire, and with the aid of her fellow-packers obtained a position as a packer with the government train. In this work she prospered for several months, but when at Hat Creek Station, she and her fellows took an overdose of whiskey and went on a wild spree. As a result, the packtrain master discovered her sex and promptly discharged her, and signified his intention of discharging any of the men who were responsible for getting her into the train; but they all kept their secret.

"For a time Calamity Jane was an inmate of a resort in Green River, Wyoming, from which place her brother ran her off at the point of the gun, taking several shots at her by way of good measure. The brother later passed out of notice when the gold rush to the Hills took place. Calamity then wandered from Salt Lake to Blackfoot, Montana, where she presided over a notorious dive known as "Madam Canary's.'

"Jane was married a number of times—her first husband being named Hunt, and her second, White. White sold out his property and became quite wealthy. He decided to quit the wilderness and rigged his wife out in the finest clothing to be had, and repaired to Denver. A few days of the fancy apparel and classy hotels were enough for the wild, untamed spirit of Martha Jane, and she made her escape. Her husband made search for her, and waited some days for her return, but knowing the spirit of the woman, gave up the search and went his way alone.

"From then on, Calamity Jane became a free lance, roving from town to town and dive to dive, with soldiers, packers, mule-skinners and freighters, as occasion offered. She made her headquarters at Cheyenne, Wyoming. Whenever there was a trip across the Plains, an expedition against the Indians or anything to vary the monotony of the small-town life of the

West, Jane was on hand, and usually contrived to get away by dressing in male attire, and being smuggled away by her pals.

"On the occasion of General Crook's expedition, she was many miles away from the starting point, but upon hearing of the trip, she hired a team and buggy from a liveryman of Cheyenne, drove rapidly away, smuggled herself in among the soldiers and decamped with them, leaving the liveryman to recover his team and outfit as best he could after placing it in charge of a man at Fort Laramie, where the expedition set out.

"On another occasion she had joined a military expedition and was having the time of her life. When the command halted along the banks of a stream, and the members were enjoying the delights of a cool dip in the waters of the creek, an officer passing by espied the form of Jane splashing about with her fellow-troopers, and the remainder of the journey found her under guard.

"Calamity Jane's introduction to the Black Hills was in 1875, for there we find her dressed as a soldier in the military expedition under General Crook, who, in August, 1875, ordered the miners to leave the Hills until treaties could be made with the Indians. Again she came to the Hills in 1876 with the band in which Wild Bill and Charley Utter were members. However, she was not the consort of Wild Bill, for he was not the kind of a man who was attracted by a woman of Jane's class. Colorado Charley was perhaps her champion, for it is said that he furnished her with a splendid suit of men's buckskin clothing, in which she often appeared.

"No doubt the reader by this time will have concluded that Jane was nothing more than a common prostitute—drunken, disorderly and wholly devoid of any element or conception of morality. And the question will arise as to how it comes that out of the hundreds, yes, thousands of her fellow-women of the underworld who threw youth, beauty and life itself into the fiery altar of the Moloch of passion and immorality, the name of Calamity Jane alone should endure in the annals of time. The answer will be had from the other view of this double-sided woman.

"In 1878 there came a terrible scourge of smallpox among the miners and other residents of Deadwood. Hundreds were prostrated upon their rude beds, and most people were afraid to go near them. Women were few to be had, and they, too, were in fear of their lives. In the hour of terror and death, there came to the front a willing volunteer—the mule-skinning, bull-whacking, rough-and-ready woman from the depths, Calamity Jane! Day and night she went among the sick and dying, and for weeks ministered to their wants, or smoothed the pillow for the dying youth whose mother or sweetheart, perhaps, was waiting and watching for the one who was never to return. It made no difference to her that she knew them not, or that no gold would come to repay her for the labor, the sacrifice or the danger. They were fellow beings in distress—and that was enough for Calamity Jane.

"Another time, while waiting on table in Pierre, she heard of a family in destitute circumstances, sick with black diphtheria. Neighbors would not go to their aid. Jane had saved up $20 in gold, and proceeding to a grocery she purchased $15 worth of food and medicines and nursed the family until the sickness was over.

"In 1878 the young sister of C. H. Robinson, later sexton of Mount Moriah Cemetery at Deadwood, was sick with typhoid fever. Calamity had known the family for years in Kansas, and she promptly came to their aid, and for two weeks nursed the child until death claimed her as his own.

"Calamity Jane never hesitated to spend her last dollar to aid an unfortunate, and was never backward in asking for money from others to help someone in distress. Her idea of helping others caused her arrest in Deadwood in the early days. It seems that some rough specimen was having what was then known as a 'hell of a time' in one of the resorts of the town in which Jane was an inmate. When he awoke from his drunken slumbers the next day, he found that he was minus some $30, and at once made complaint to the justice of the peace that he had been 'rolled.' Recalling that Jane was there, he charged her with the robbery. She was brought to the bar of the court. When informed of the charge she stated that 'she found the fool drunk under one of the tables.' Searching his pockets she found the money, and realizing that if she did not take it some of the other girls would, she took the cash. The judge then asked her what she had done with it. The reply was that she had given it to the hospital to pay the charges for a young girl who was lying sick there, without friends or money. The judge promptly turned her free and scored the sporty gentleman who was so unwise as to carry money with him to a dive and expect to carry it away with him!

"Many other like tales might be added. Calamity was an expert packer, an able teamster and a crack rifle shot. She loved the great out-of-doors and the excitement of the trail. She was the pal of the men of the fighting line. It is said by E. H. Warren, of Spearfish, that once while speaking to a pioneer a woman came up to the pair, looked them over, and finally demanded a dollar of the pioneer who, without asking her a question, handed it over to her. After the woman was gone, the pioneer said: 'That was Calamity Jane, and as long as I have two dollars in my pocket she can have one of them, for she saved my life once. We were on a trip, when Indians opened fire on us and shot my horse from under me. Jane stopped her horse, grabbed me by the arm and swung me on behind her and we escaped.'

"Another time, Calamity and 'Antelope Frank' were out riding, when Indians appeared and opened fire upon them. They turned and fled in the direction of the soldiers, but the scout's horse stepped in a hole, fell and broke its neck, leaving him on foot. Frank told her to ride on to safety, and that he would take care of himself, but she said, 'Damned if I will! I will stay right here with you and we will see how many of those red devils we can get.' And she did! The pair got into a buffalo wallow and opened fire upon the advancing Indians with their rifles and sent them away in retreat, with the loss of five of their number, Jane having done her share in the execution.

"As time went by and the wild days of the frontier gave way to the more sedate times of later development, Jane wandered from town to town, making a living by selling books, photos and receiving charity from the pioneers. She had a daughter whom she placed for a time in a Sisters' Convent when the girl was fourteen years of age.

"Once a kind-hearted woman of wealth from Buffalo, N. Y., sought to lift her out of the slough. She took Jane back to her home in the distant east. The lure of the Hills was too strong, however, and Jane soon bade farewell to the stiff and conventional life of that section and hastened back to the big-hearted westerners.

"In physical appearance Jane was a medium-sized woman, with dark-brown hair and eyes. In her youth she was of splendid form, clear complexion and uncommonly good-looking. In her older age the rough life of the Plains and trails coarsened her appearance. She could swear like a trooper, drink like a sailor, and rough it with the roughest. Yet, when sober, she could do the part of a real lady. At all times she evinced a great interest in children, in whose presence she was watchful of her own conduct.

"She was seen in every town, camp and fort in the west, and had wandered over all the trails. So variant were her moods, so many the different incidents of her life, that accordingly there were numerous impressions and ideas of her character. She was a strange mixture of the wild, untamed individual of the Plains and the mountain trails, and that of generous, kindly-hearted womanhood. Under her rough exterior there beat a heart so big and friendly as to be without measure. Brave, energetic, unfettered, kind, always on the line of action, with a helping hand ever stretched to aid the poor and unfortunate, the personality of Calamity Jane became indelibly stamped upon the minds of the pioneers.

"The close of the last century found the rover near to the end of her trail, and in the summer of 1903 she came back to her haunts among the Hills and told her friends that she was sick and going to 'cash in.' One day she came to a hotel in Terry, and being sick, asked for a lodging; but the manager turned her away, thinking her a mere drunk. Soon after, he learned her identity and took her in; but dissipation had done its work, and pneumonia made her an easy victim on August 2, 1903.

"The friends of Calamity took her to the undertaking rooms of C. H. Robinson, at Deadwood. There, while lying upon the cooling board, numbers of curious women came to look upon her, and many clipped locks of hair from her head to the extent of defacing the remains. 'Smoky Tom,' one of her early consorts, upon coming to the room and noticing the work of the vandal hands of the women (who would have scorned Jane on the streets) protested against the mutilation, and a wire screen was placed over Jane's head.

"The pioneers gathered for the funeral, and Rev. C. B. Clark, of the Methodist Church, conducted the funeral services, assisted by other prominent people of the city. Interment was made in Mount Moriah Cemetery, across the way from the grave of Wild Bill. And fate decreed that C. H. Robinson, whose little sister Calamity Jane had so faithfully watched over in the futile struggle with death, should at last lay her form in the couch of dreamless sleep."

*   *   *   *   *

Among men of prominence who were acquainted with the character of Calamity Jane in the old Black Hills days, was my friend, Dr. Gilbert E. Bailey, now deceased, who was for many years at the head of the Chair of Geology in the University of Southern California. Dr. Bailey was at one time State Geologist for Wyoming and had traveled extensively all through the West in his younger days, being a member of the original surveying party of the Union Pacific Railroad. Dr. Bailey was a warm, personal friend of the writer. He died in the Southern California metropolis. Under date of September 1, 1923, he wrote me:

"My friends in the Black Hills often send me interesting papers, and I enclose one, giving accounts of Calamity Jane's death and funeral, as printed in the Black Hills *Pioneer-Times* at that time.

"I was well acquainted with the woman, both in Deadwood and at my camp, which she visited several times. I think you could write a good sketch of her life for the benefit of the old-timers.

"She was a woman adventurer with the bark on, as most knew her; but at heart she was very generous and kind-hearted, especially to the sick and those down on their luck.

"If she had been born a man, her life would have attracted very little comment, if any. Being born a woman does not necessarily kill the desire to go and see; but it takes a brave heart to endure the result of following one's desires."

*   *   *   *   *

The newspaper alluded to by Dr. Bailey is a copy of the Deadwood Weekly *Pioneer-Times* of August 3, 1903, and contains the following account of the last days of Calamity Jane in her beloved Black Hills:

"Mrs. Mary E. Burke ('Calamity Jane'), female scout, frontier woman, and one of the most picturesque characters of the early West, died at the Calloway Hotel in Terry yesterday afternoon about 5 o'clock, aged 52 years.

"At her request her funeral will be held under the auspices of the early Black Hills settlers, and the remains will be buried in Mount Moriah Cemetery, at Deadwood, beside those of

William Hickok (Wild Bill) her former consort, who was murdered in Deadwood in 1876.*

"Mrs. Burke arrived in Terry a week ago Friday from Spearfish. She was sick at the time, and to friends she announced that she 'was going to cash in.'

"Calamity Jane's maiden name was Mary E. Canary. Several of the older settlers of Deadwood knew her as a little girl in Montana, where her mother was a washerwoman at Blackfoot for a long time.

"The sobriquet 'Calamity Jane' is said to have been applied to her by Bill Nye during the early '70's, when he was editing the Laramie Boomerang.**

"She became a rover early in life, and traveled over the country with a number of important expeditions, both military and citizen. She had a rough exterior, but was possessed of a kindly heart and a generous disposition, and many anecdotes are related of her womanly ministrations among the sick and distressed miners, particularly in Deadwood Gulch, at a time when there were but few women in the region, and but for her attentions some of her beneficiaries must have perished.

"She was known to have married a number of times. Her last husband was Clinton Burke, with whom she came to Deadwood in 1895, from Montana. She and Burke separated shortly afterward.

"When she visited Deadwood eight years ago, she had with her a daughter, then fourteen or fifteen years of age, who was placed in school at Sturgis for a short time. Afterwards Mrs. Burke went into a museum in the East, but remained for a short time only, returning to Montana.

---

*It is a peculiar coincidence that the death of Calamity Jane should have occurred at almost the same hour of the same day of the same month, 27 years later, as that of Wild Bill Hickok, one of her former friends, and near whom she was buried.

**This is extremely doubtful. There seems to be a difference of opinion as to just how Calamity Jane acquired her nickname. It is also said to have been given her by a sergeant of the Fourteenth Infantry. There seems to be nothing to authenticate any of these stories.

"She was then taken up by a lady of Buffalo, N. Y., and induced to accompany her to Buffalo, promising her a good home. This proved too tame for Jane, and she again came West. Since then she has spent her time in journeying from place to place, and finally came back to the Black Hills several months ago."

*   *   *   *   *

And the curtain falls on the drama of life for Calamity Jane in the following paragraph under date of August 5, 1903, from the Deadwood *Pioneer-Times:*

"The remains of Mary E. Burke, the Calamity Jane of border history, were laid at rest yesterday afternoon. The funeral services were held in the First Methodist Church, and the church was packed with the old settlers and friends of Calamity. The funeral sermon was delivered by Dr. C. B. Clark, and Mrs. M. M. Wheeler and Miss Elsie Sornwall, with Miss Helen Fowler at the organ, furnished the music."